MACRO MARKETING
Second Edition

Wiley/Hamilton Series in Marketing

DAVID A. AAKER, ADVISORY EDITOR

MACRO MARKETING

Second Edition

REED MOYER
University of California (Berkeley)

MICHAEL D. HUTT
Miami University

JOHN WILEY & SONS
New York   Chichester   Brisbane   Toronto
A Wiley/Hamilton Publication

This book was set in 9 point Vega Lite
by Advanced Typesetting Services
and printed and bound by Kingsport
Press. It was copyedited by
Bernice Lifton and the text
and cover were designed by
Christy Butterfield. Chuck Pendergast
supervised production.

Library of Congress Cataloging in Publication Data:

Moyer, Reed.
    Macro marketing.

    "A Wiley/Hamilton publication."
    1. Marketing. I. Hutt, Michael D., joint
author. II. Title.
HF5415.M678   1978   380.1   77-26816

ISBN 0-471-02699-9
Printed in the United States of America
10 9 8 7 6 5 4 3 2

About the Authors

Reed Moyer is a Professor of Marketing in the Graduate School of Business at Michigan State University. He has also taught at the University of California, Berkeley and the University of Florida. Dr. Moyer has instructed a wide range of courses in marketing, international business, and economics at the undergraduate and graduate levels.

Professor Moyer earned his Ph.D. in Economics at the University of California, Berkeley. He is a past member of the Board of Directors of the American Marketing Association and currently serves on the editorial boards of the Journal of Marketing and the Journal of International Business Studies. Dr. Moyer is a frequent contributor to professional journals.

Professor Moyer's consulting work has included the natural gas, petroleum, and coal industries. He has also served as a consultant to the Federal Trade Commission, The Department of Justice (Antitrust Division), the Council on Wage and Price Stability and the General Accounting Office.

Michael D. Hutt is a member of the marketing faculty at Miami University's School of Business in Oxford, Ohio. He has also taught at the University of Vermont, Michigan State University and Ohio University. Dr. Hutt has instructed graduate and undergraduate courses in marketing management, consumer behavior, marketing research, marketing theory and contemporary issues in marketing.

Professor Hutt earned his Ph.D. in marketing from Michigan State University. He holds memberships in the American Marketing Association, the Association for Consumer Research, Beta Gamma Sigma, and Pi Gamma Mu. He has contributed articles to professional journals and has presented papers at meetings of both the American Marketing Association and the Association for Consumer Research. He is co-author of a monograph, *The Universal Product Code: Price Removal and Consumer Behavior in Supermarkets.*

To Sue and
To Rita and Mary Ann

Preface

Increased consumer concern over marketing activities calls for an evaluation of marketing performance. This book makes that evaluation. It requires a different perspective from that found in the usual marketing textbooks, which are firm-oriented and take a micro approach. The reader is usually shown how to improve the firm's marketing performance. He learns about pricing and pricing strategies, the uses of promotion, ways to gain control of distribution channels, techniques of assessing market opportunities, and the value of market planning. Although social implications of the firm's behavior may receive some attention, the books generally provide a managerial orientation.

This volume has a broader perspective. It focuses on larger societal issues related to marketing. Whereas the typical managerial marketing textbook is firm- or *micro*-oriented, this book is *macro*-oriented. That is, it analyzes marketing in a larger framework than the firm. It studies marketing within the context of the entire economic system, with special emphasis on its aggregate performance.

How well does marketing perform its functions? How effectively does it respond to its challenges? Is it true that marketing creates "false" wants, manipulates people's minds, bamboozles innocent consumers, and wastes precious resources on frivolous and often faulty products? We need to evaluate these and other charges to sift truth from unverified assertion. The issues discussed and the questions raised in this volume will challenge the marketing student. They are topical, they lie at the heart of the discipline, and they have important social implications. In an era marked by unfettered passions, an illumination of the issues by dispassionate discussion will contribute to their better understanding.

The many issues falling within the macro marketing domain are organized for the reader at the outset of Chapter 1. We present a model that captures the dimensions of micro and macro marketing as well as the distinction between the two areas. This model provides the basic organizational structure for the revised edition which is divided into three parts. Part One lays the foundation for a macro marketing perspective and centers on marketing's aggregate performance with separate chapters devoted to marketing efficiency and advertising performance. The focus here is on measures of marketing performance that have commanded considerable interest among both scholars and the typical consumer. Part Two highlights the ethical and legal dimensions of the marketing mix. A separate chapter is devoted to the prominent macro issues that touch each of the mix components: product, promotion, price and distribution. Again, the discussion stresses the micro-macro distinction and the broader challenges facing the marketing manager. Part Three deals with the societal monitors of the marketing process including the evolution and current influences of consumerism as well as the role of government.

In addition to a totally new structure, the revised edition is updated and selectively broadened with new material. To illustrate, expanded treatment is given to product liability and safety. New topical areas include advertising's effect on children, ecological dimensions of channels of distribution, and the contemporary debates involving vertically integrated marketing systems and the Universal Product Code.

This new edition serves several markets. Its greatest value is its use as a text supplement to managerially-oriented texts either at the introductory or intermediate level. Books such as E. J. McCarthy's *Basic Marketing: A Managerial Approach* and Philip Kotler's *Marketing Management: Analysis, Planning and Control* explain marketing from a viewpoint that will aid existing or future marketing managers; and they present useful ways of analyzing marketing problems and managing inputs to achieve marketing objectives. However, books of this type are predominantly firm-oriented, whereas students are clamoring for greater emphasis on the broader social, ethical, and economic issues that are discussed here.

The organization of the new edition closely parallels the structure of these managerially-oriented texts. Thus, an instructor can easily incorporate macro issues into the course as the subject matter dictates. For example, a micro analysis of new product planning can be linked with a macro discussion of product liability and the Consumer Product Safety Act. An instructor who assigns both a managerially-oriented text and this text will give his students a balanced micro-macro mix that will enrich the course and command greater student interest and involvement.

A number of exercises that center on contemporary macro issues are included in the revised edition. These exercises spotlight the issues discussed in each chapter and provide additional points for either class discussions or more in-depth individual research papers. Questions at the end of each chapter offer points for class and small section discussions.

In addition to its supplementary use in marketing management courses, many found the first edition valuable as a base for graduate courses and seminars in social issues and public policy.

Contents

1

System Performance

ONE
Marketing's Role in Society

Increased consumer concern over marketing activities calls for an evaluation of marketing performance. Let's begin this evaluation by examining the following questions:

1. What is macro marketing and why should we study it?
2. Do developing economies have a marketing system?
3. What are the functions of marketing? (Is the answer different if we examine the Russian economy?)
4. What is the modern marketing concept?

ONE
Marketing's Role in Society

Marketing permeates our way of life. Whether a country is rich or poor, technologically advanced or developing, marketing activities play a fundamental role in the formation, development, and growth of its economy. In fact, one author depicts marketing as the "creation and delivery of a standard of living to society."[1]

The standard of living (in economic terms) delivered by the American marketing system is unparalleled in history, yet the system has long been the target of social critics. To illustrate, consumers at the turn of the century were angry over the large spread between the price received by the farmer and the price paid to the storekeeper. Middlemen were viewed as an unnecessary and costly obstacle standing between producers and consumers.

Criticism also centered on the deceptions and exaggerations of advertising. Similar complaints about these and other marketing activities are even more pronounced today.

Public debate of issues affecting the consumer has increased steadily in recent years. Since consumer satisfaction lies at the heart of the marketing concept, these issues cannot be ignored, but must be objectively and rationally evaluated. Thus, specific marketing activities such as advertising can be viewed from two perspectives: (1) managerial (micro) and (2) societal (macro). What are the distinguishing characteristics of these two perspectives?

THE MICRO-MACRO DISTINCTION

There are two distinctions in the functions and research areas falling within these components.[2] First is the obvious distinction between micro and macro. The former deals with small, individual units, the latter with aggregations. The second distinction lies in the welfare focus of the activities performed at each level. Generally, micro marketing activities are oriented toward the *enterprise's* welfare,[3] whereas the focus in macro marketing centers on *society's* welfare.

To grasp the dimensions of micro marketing, consider a product such as a stereo component system that you have recently seen, or even purchased, in a retail store. Let's trace that stereo back to the manufacturing level and envision the range of activities involved in moving the product from the idea stage to your local retailer's shelf. The manufacturer first identifies a need and then attempts to measure the nature and size of the need (market) through marketing research.

---

[1] Malcolm P. McNair, "Marketing and the Social Challenge of Our Times," in *A New Measure of Responsibility for Marketing,* Keith Cox and Ben M. Enis ed. (Chicago: American Marketing Association, 1968), pp. 1–8; see also Paul Mazur, "Does Distribution Cost Enough?" *Fortune,* November 1947, p. 138.

[2] The greater emphasis in the figures on the macro component does not necessarily reflect a value judgment on the relative importance of the two concepts in an economic system; nor does it necessarily indicate the relative depth of the concepts' subject matter. Rather it results from the authors' decision to highlight the macro component.

[3] "Enterprise" here is usually synonymous with the firm, although it need not be that restrictive. Thus, this conception would include marketing activities of cooperatives, government agencies and other not-for-profit organizations. We avoid the question here of whose welfare within the enterprise is being optimized—the stockholders', managers' or employees'.

Figure 1-1   Central Components of Micro Marketing

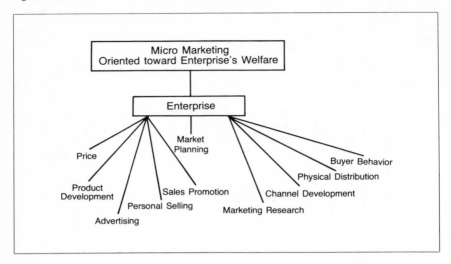

Next, the research findings are infused into the development of the stereo and it is priced, promoted, and transported through a rather complex network to your local retailer. A number of specific marketing management decisions are made in the process. As you select among the offerings of competing stereo producers, you will decide whether or not the right marketing management decisions were made. The central components of micro marketing are highlighted in figure 1-1.

In contrast, the subject areas included under the macro component of marketing concern themselves with broader societal dimensions. Here are specific examples that make the micro-macro distinction clearer. A company decides to increase its advertising to achieve a specified goal—to increase market share or profits, for instance. This is a *micro*-level decision; it is made by the firm and its outcome directly affects the firm. However, the impact on society of *all* advertising expenditures is a *macro* issue. So is an issue like efficiency. Micro analysis might deal with attempts of individual firms to reduce distribution costs, or it might study the effect on the enterprise of abandoning a retail location. At the macro level, emphasis shifts to the efficiency performace of the entire distributive sector or to the social and economic impact of the "wastes" from retail store mortality.

As figure 1-2 indicates, macro marketing issues go beyond the above examples. They include such topics as the effectiveness of marketing in securing the needs of given sectors, for instance, ghetto residents; the whole range of public policy issues relating to regulations and legislation designed to promote product safety, provide market information, and regulate competition; and the broadest issue of all—marketing's roles in our complex socioeconomic system.

Note that many of the functions and researchable subjects in the micro and macro domains are identical. For example, both micro and macro marketing concern themselves with pricing, promotion, and product development, but the focus is different in each case. The firm seeks to manipulate marketing variables to optimize its operation. Thus a marketing manager may develop a mathematical

Figure 1-2   Central Components of Macro Marketing

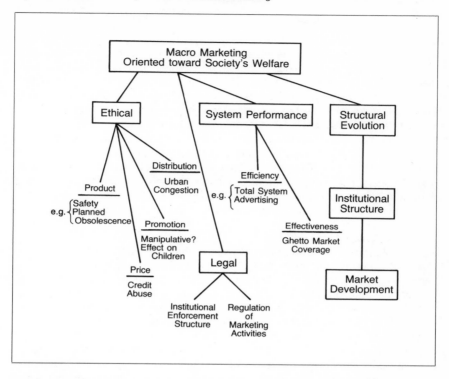

model to maximize the returns from a given advertising expenditure. The macro focus, however, may center on the measurement of total advertising expenditures over time as a function of the Gross National Product (G.N.P.), or on the alleged wastes of duplicative advertising.

Careful!

A word of caution. The distinction between the enterprise's and society's welfare does not lead necessarily to the conclusion that the enterprise's marketing activities are perforce detrimental to the welfare of society at large. On the contrary, the interests of both the enterprise and society may be well served by the former's actions. But their interests may also clash. The high social and economic costs generated by urban goods movement offer an example. Vehicles crisscross paths in transporting small shipments within the urban center. A particular square mile in Brooklyn is visited daily by 4,200 trucks with average consignments of 160 pounds each.[4] Each firm provides a given level of service to its market with relatively little social harm; however, when this behavior is aggregated, urban congestion, pollution, and high operating costs result. Macro analysis can point up the nature and extent of similar conflicts and possibly lead to satisfactory remedial action.

---

[4]Robert T. Wood, "The Structure and Economics of Intra-Urban Goods Movement," in *Urban Commodity Flows,* Highway Research Board Special Report 120, 1971.

Value of Micro-Macro Distinction

Of what value is the micro-macro distinction? It is useful on several counts. First, a total system perspective is needed to grasp the net social benefits and other consequences of marketing activities. For example, an aggregate level of analysis is required in measuring the impact one society's marketing system may have on that of another society. Global shortages of protein and other basic materials make such a research approach particularly timely. Second, the distinction recognizes that the combined behavior of several firms may be creating many problems, and a joint effort may be needed in solving them. Thus, the domain of interest to marketers must include macro issues. Failure to play a meaningful role in resolving these issues may concede solution and control to others. Third, the micro-macro distinction may highlight possible research gaps worthy of more careful consideration. To illustrate, timely estimates of marketing productivity would be particularly useful in monitoring system performance and in isolating current and emerging problems. In contrast with micro dimensions, only limited research attention has been invested in probing many of the macro issues.

A Look Ahead

Figure 1-2 provides an overview of the issues that are examined in this volume. The book is divided into three parts. Part One centers on marketing's aggregate performance. The effective evaluation of marketing requires an understanding, first, of what functions it performs and how its activities have developed over time. Therefore, in the remainder of chapter 1 we examine marketing's role in simple economic systems and show how its role broadens as economies develop. This introduction provides a brief description of the *structural evolution* of marketing. In chapter 2 the discussion turns to the *efficiency* of the marketing system. Here we grapple with a question posed frequently in the media: Does marketing cost too much? In turn, chapter 3 deals with related questions of efficiency: Is advertising wasteful? Does it damage competition?

Part Two focuses on the *ethical* and *legal* dimensions of the marketing mix. A separate chapter is devoted to the prominent macro issues that surround each of the mix components: product, promotion, price, distribution.

Some of the questions that we will examine are outlined in figure 1-3. Note that the issues range from product safety to the ecological problems created by the distribution of goods. Is advertising deceptive? Does it manipulate us? Does the marketing system place the poor at a disadvantage? Would consumers benefit if large petroleum marketers were broken into smaller units? Attention is given to these and other contemporary issues.

Part Three moves beyond these problems and discusses the societal monitors of the marketing process. Here we examine the evolution and current influence of consumerism as well as the impact of governmental regulation on marketing. Our objective is to give you a firm grasp of the macro issues confronting marketers. Let's get started.

MARKETING AND DEVELOPMENT

To evaluate micro marketing activities and put them into a broader societal framework, we need to examine marketing's role in simple economic systems and

Product
- Who must accept responsibility for a faulty or, worse yet, a hazardous product?
- Is the package a source of information or a source of confusion for consumers?

Promotion
- Can advertising persuade us to purchase products that we don't really want?
- What effect does advertising have on children?

Price
- Why do some pricing laws protect consumers while others protect business?
- Do the poor really pay more?

Distribution
- What are the ecological dimensions of channels of distribution?
- What are the central issues in the debate that surrounds the petroleum industry?

see how it grows as economies grow. Much of the remainder of this book analyzes the effectiveness of marketing in a modern society. Since marketing is carried out through the performance of various functions—pricing, advertising, and so on—we look at the functions and ask whether they are universal or associated only with certain kinds of economic systems. In evaluating our modern system, we think the reader will find it useful to learn how it evolved and to recognize alternative ways of organizing the distribution of goods. So we now turn our attention to these questions.

What are the foundations of a marketing system? Adam Smith's well-suited phrase concerning people's inherent tendency to "truck, barter and exchange" has settled, for many, the question of whether trade is an inevitable human process.[5] Recent studies of primitive societies, however, dispute this contention. Anthropologists further question whether the exchange system is the inevitable method of distributing goods.

---

[5]Much of the material in this section is drawn from Reed Moyer's *Marketing in Economic Development* (International Business Occasional Paper #1, Institute for International Business Management Studies, Michigan State University, 1965), with permission.

There are several ways to arrange for the distribution of goods both in primitive and advanced economies.[6] We are familiar with a market exchange system characterized by a multidimensional flow of goods and services whose values are expressed in terms of the things traded (that is, barter) or in terms of another commodity (money). But there are other ways to get the job done. In some primitive societies, workers like tailors and smiths may exchange their products for the food grown by farmers. Each performs the activity he is best suited to, supplying his output to all, knowing that in return he will be supplied the goods and services that he is unable to produce. Under this system of reciprocity, no money changes hands and no formal channels of distribution exist, but the arrangement provides for the production and exchange of vital goods and services.

In other primitive societies, a village chief or some other authority figure in the community may be responsible for allocating the local economy's output. Neither this system of redistribution nor that of reciprocity performs what we think of as traditional marketing activities, yet the essential tasks of production and distribution are accomplished.

The various segments of a total economic system never advance in lock-step. Backward regions are found even in highly developed systems. Likewise, within primitive economies, exchange systems of reciprocity and redistribution may coexist in the same community, each applying to different commodities and different groups of inhabitants. In the emerging sectors of the economy, the market exchange system may be used. Even in the United States one finds all three systems at work. The majority of transactions, of course, use the market exchange principle. Public expenditures for education, welfare, and national defense exemplify the principle of redistribution. Gift exchanges are based largely on the principle of reciprocity.

One of the key distinctions between developed and primitive market systems is in the role of price-making. The limited role of prices in primitive markets sharply contrasts with their dominant position in developed economies, where they serve as signals regulating resource allocation. In both types of economies—developed and underdeveloped—supply and demand forces determine prices in free markets. But in a primitive economic system, the result of price formation is analogous to its effect in antique auction markets. Market forces determine antique auction prices, but their effect ends with the auction. There is no feedback to the rest of the economy to regulate the allocation of resources among various productive activities. Economies characterized by the use of isolated markets also lack this kind of feedback.

To develop, an economy must move away from primitive distribution systems and toward a network of integrative markets. Only by substituting market exchange systems for those embedded in tribal ritualism can the incentives that impel growth be fully provided. Paradoxically, the more an economy depends on price as an allocator of resources, the less relative importance it attaches to the marketplace per se. Labor, land, and capital increasingly enter the market but not in physical marketplaces. The market for aluminum ingots, for example, may

---

[6]Karl Polanyi, Conrad M. Arensberg, and Harry W. Pearson, *Trade and Markets in the Early Empires* (Glencoe, Ill.: The Free Press, 1957), p. 222.

include the entire country, although few of the ingots will move through physical market sites.

We referred to Adam Smith's observation about people's inherent tendency to "truck, barter and exchange." But whether or not trading arises spontaneously is open to question. A trade obviously involves decisions by two or more individuals to exchange goods to their mutual advantage. The incentive could come from the pleasure derived from the act of trading itself. We see evidence of that motivation even today in what for some is the ritual of grocery shopping. In fact, there is ample evidence that the opportunities for social intercourse stimulate interest in trading. But the benefit derived from the social aspect of trading apparently is a by-product of the process and not its root cause. In its earliest stages, trading activity appears to stem from the pressures of population growth and land shortages and, occasionally, from the need to earn income to meet pressing obligations.

THE FUNCTIONS OF MARKETING

We noted that in primitive economic systems little of what we think of as marketing activities are performed, although the essential job of distributing goods and services gets done. As an economy grows, increasing numbers of marketing functions are performed that aid the developmental process. Since this book analyzes these functions and compares their micro and macro dimensions, it is important to understand them. What are some of these functions?

First, marketing performs an important organizational and informational service. When properly operating, it creates "a network through which information can flow among the many firm units performing interrelated activities necessary to produce the final consumer product."[7] Farm planting decisions, for example, cannot be made in a vacuum. Information is needed concerning the requirements of other segments in the production-distribution channel such as the requirements of food processors, retailers, and final consumers. The tasks of organizing the information network and providing the physical facilities to handle the product system's output fall to the distributive sector. Its activities may be varied, ranging from gauging consumer demand and standardizing product quality to organizing physical distribution systems.

Of great importance is the function of equalizing and distributing goods from surplus to deficit areas under shifting demand and supply conditions. Any distribution system—primitive or advanced—faces certain common problems. Goods do not flow in equal amounts in a steady stream from producers to consumers, nor do consumers purchase at a constant rate an amount equal to the output of individual producers. The job of matching and equalizing diverse supplies and demands belongs to the distributive sector. Implicit in the matching concept is the connective function of distribution. Any exchange system requires a linkage of geographically separated entities. The spatial connections may be as simple as the distribution of farm commodities in primitive village markets, or as

---

[7]Norman Collins, "Marketing and Economic Development: The Experience of Southern Italy," in a Report on the General Assembly of the Mediterranean Social Sciences Research Council, Cairo, U.A.R., December 1–5, 1962, p. 153.

complex as some of the distributive networks for nationally marketed goods in highly developed countries.

To appreciate the need for equalizing and distributing goods from surplus to deficit areas, consider the problem of matching the demand for frozen orange juice with the supply of the basic raw material, oranges. The supply is created during a short harvesting season yet the demand for the final product exists throughout the year. A host of marketing activities needs to be performed to insure that this burst of supply matches the stretched-out demand for the product.

One way of accomplishing this task is through the performance by middlemen of what Bert Westerfield calls the "capitalistic" function.[8] The distributor deals in time markets. The uneven character of demand and supply conditions and the need to link surplus with deficit areas separated both spatially and temporally add a speculative dimension to the job. Buying with temporally distant markets in view, the distributor assumes risks supportable only on a base of capital.

To carry out these functions, distributors must perform certain activities. They must store goods and provide special facilities for commodities with unique characteristics, for example, perishable foodstuffs; they must provide a communications network; they must transport goods; they must provide credit facilities.

As a by-product of its activities, marketing may perform two important functions that aid the developmental process. These are the creation of pools of both entrepreneurial talent and capital. Studies of the origins of industrialists in developing countries find that a large share of them move into industry directly from trading occupations. The skills are freely transferable from trading into industry. Profits accrued in trade are also transferable into industry, providing the capital necessary to fuel the engine of development. The creation of these entrepreneurial and capital pools probably has its greatest impact during the period prior to commercial revolution, which Charles Kindleberger views as "a vital and almost necessary step on the way to industrial revolution."[9] The willingness of merchants to assume the risks inherent in trading stands them in good stead when faced with opportunities to enter the industrial field. Also, their contacts with consumers permit them to recognize the prevailing opportunities better than most other members of the economy.

While their talents as entrepreneurs and their position as sources of capital are important when the economy moves from the beginning stages of industrialization to the higher levels that we associate with modern Western society, their biggest developmental thrust occurs at the early stages of industrialization. At later stages the industrial sector is capable of generating pools both of entrepreneurs and of capital. The trading or distributive sector may then play more of a passive, accommodating role than it does in the preindustrial and early industrial stages.

---

[8]Bert Westerfield, *Middlemen in English Business* (New Haven: Yale University Press, 1915), p. 369.
[9]Charles P. Kindleberger, *Economic Development* (New York: McGraw-Hill, 1958), p. 93.

The broadening of markets as economies grow permits economies of scale, that is, the reduced costs that flow from the use of larger production and distribution units. Trade links together local producers and local markets; local markets join to form regional markets; region connects to region, creating national markets. But the economies of scale extend beyond those enjoyed by the primary and secondary industries whose goods the distributive sector is responsible for marketing. Just as industrial producers gain scale economies from the extension of their markets, so too do distributors. Increasing the extent of marketing operations produces economies in several ways: in the processing of orders, in conducting the contactual functions, and in the physical handling of commodities. Organized exchanges develop, and these create scale economies in the communication of market information. Routinization replaces the individual treatment of market transactions.

Critics often charge marketing with being wasteful. We will study this charge in succeeding chapters. Still, the use of marketing intermediaries can economize resources in the sale of goods to consumers. Under a primitive, decentralized system, producers of various goods may exchange their surpluses directly with each other. Thus, in a system composed of six producers who are also consumers, there will be fifteen transactions if each producer trades at least once with all of the other producers. Generalizing, there will be $[n(n-1)]/2$ exchanges, where n is the number of producers. Trading goods through a central market, however, requires only six exchanges, one by each producer with the market intermediary. The ratio of advantage from using a central exchange is $(n-1)/2$.[10]

The same principle applies in a more complex world in which producers and consumers are two distinct groups of people. Figures 1-4 and 1-5 picture the transactions that occur among them with and without the use of retailing intermediaries. In the first case, there are eighteen possible transactions among the three producers and six consumers if each consumer makes one purchase from each producer. Introducing a retailer into the system reduces the number of

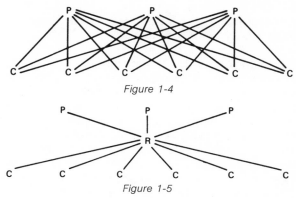

Figure 1-4

Figure 1-5

[10]For an example of this analysis, see Wroe Alderson, "Factors Governing the Development of Marketing Channels," in *Marketing Channels,* ed. Richard M. Clewett (Homewood Ill.: Richard D. Irwin, 1954), pp. 7–8.

transactions to nine, three among producers and the retailer and six among the retailer and the consumers. This is a highly simplified example, but it is useful in demonstrating the economizing principle that is invoived. The principle also applies to the use of other marketing intermediaries, for example, the interposition of wholesalers between producers and retailers.

As economies grow larger, the scope of marketing expands. Also, institutions necessary to perform various marketing activities emerge, grow, and are modified by changing economic and social conditions. For example, local farmers no longer produce just for their own families or for local markets. Refrigerated boxcars thus have been developed to move produce from California to New York and specialized food brokers emerge to distribute the produce.

Agricultural production dominates the economies of countries in early stages of growth. Thus marketing institutions needed to distribute agricultural commodities play a large role in the distribution system. Also, the functions are performed to facilitate agricultural activities. For instance, communications will be more concerned with the dissemination of farm price and supply information than with the use of high-powered advertising techniques to sell consumer goods. With economic growth comes a shift of emphasis away from agriculture and toward industrial goods production, thence toward the production of consumer goods and services. These changes create demands for new channels of distribution and different relative emphases on selling and advertising. Similarly, the trend toward urbanization that accompanies economic growth modifies channels of distribution, storage locations and arrangements, communications media used, and the transportation network that serves the changing markets.

Most of the discussion to this point deals with marketing's role in early stages of an economy's development. As the economy matures, marketing functions arise that facilitate getting goods from producer to consumer. These functions include buying, selling, storage, financing, risk-bearing, communication, standardization and grading, and transportation. It is a mistake, however, to conceive of marketing in a modern society as being limited to these functions on the one hand or necessarily including all of them on the other. Thus, services may be marketed without using functions associated with physical production, for example, storage, grading, and transportation.

Are Marketing Functions Universal?

This discussion of marketing's adaptation to the changing requirements of a growing economy implies that the functions, institutions, and changes in both of them are universals—that is, they apply to any economic system. One might ask: How about a socialist or command system like Russia's? Aren't marketing activities irrelevant in a socialist economy? And is marketing relevant to the distribution of goods and services produced by nonprofit organizations within a free enterprise system? If we are going to evaluate macro marketing dimensions, as we do in the balance of the book, it will be useful to know whether marketing's domain is restricted to the profit-oriented sector of a free enterprise system or whether it extends to nonprofit sectors and to socialist systems as well.

A moment's reflection will indicate that socialist systems cannot avoid marketing. The functions continue irrespective of the manner in which decisions on output and resource allocation are made. A socialist economy can no more dispense with marketing activities than it can do away with production activities. Goods must still flow from producers to users, and this requires channels of distribution and such facilitating functions as storage, transportation, and financing.

The main differences in marketing emphasis between command and free market systems lie in the areas of selling, communication, and product development. In a command system, central authorities determine the kinds and amounts of goods to be produced. Objective judgment substitutes for market pressures in allocating resources to various activities. In a free market system, consumers signal their reactions to prices and product offerings to producers who respond accordingly. Centralization of price, product offering, and production decisions in a command economy reduce the apparent need for advertising and selling. Consumers are expected to accept what producers offer them. This dispenses with the need for competitive advertising and the pressure of selling.

What happens when discretionary income increases enough so that consumers no longer accept what planners provide for them? We have seen this development in the Soviet Union in recent years. The result has been a modification of the rigid, centrally directed system. A number of consumer goods plants now have greater freedom to respond to market demands. Judged by the achievement of profits, these freed enterprises now exercise greater authority than before over pricing, product development, and the eventual disposition of their output. The Russians use profits to evaluate performance rather than as a reward for risking capital as a free enterprise system does. Nonetheless, this new orientation demands that marketing receive greater emphasis to help in achieving profit goals.

The Yugoslavian model makes even greater use of the trappings of marketing. This system lies somewhere between a planned, socialistic state and a free market system. The state limits private ownership of capital. It establishes broad output priorities, which it controls through restraints on financing, but it leaves microplant-level decisions on output, pricing, product characteristics, and the like to the plant managers. They, in turn, answer to Workers' Councils composed of representatives from each enterprise. The system encourages the achievement of profits that either flow to the workers as bonuses, are plowed back into the enterprise, or are invested in local endeavors that are deemed worthwhile (for instance, new schools and housing). This system lays almost as much stress on effective marketing as we find in a system of completely free enterprise. Marketing research may be less sophisticated and less prevalent and advertising less pervasive than in the United States, but these conditions reflect more Yugoslavia's stage of development than its commitment to marketing.[11]

Two things stand out, then, in this assessment of various economic systems. First is the pervasiveness of marketing's functions and institutions. Buying and selling, transporting, storage, financing, grading and standardization, and communicating must be performed in each system. Retailers, wholesalers, and

---

[11]While prices are centrally fixed, marketing reseach and advertising are playing an expanded role in the Polish economy. See J. Hart Walters, Jr., "Marketing in Poland in the 1970s: Significant Progress," *Journal of Marketing*, 39 (October 1975), pp. 47–51.

other intermediaries must exist. The emphasis on various functions may differ from one system to another, but they still go on. The most notable distinction comes in the lesser use of advertising in a command system because of the reduced emphasis on competition and demand creation. Second, the Yugoslavian experience demonstrates the tendency of managers to stress marketing activities when they act in their enterprises' interests, despite operating in a socialistic environment. Critics of marketing decry the apparent waste that results from giving individual enterprises greater freedom. The Yugoslavians evidently feel that the gains outweigh whatever wastes may occur.

THE MODERN MARKETING CONCEPT

While marketing functions are universal and pervasive, limiting the conception of marketing in a modern society to these functions falls short of reality. The modern marketing concept places marketing at the center of the entire business. In this approach, marketing is more than a collection of functions; it is viewed as a corporate philosophy. The firm begins with the market and works back to production. The initial step involves assessing consumers' needs and then fashioning products and services to satisfy them. Thus, marketing begins before the sale. However, it continues after the sale as activities which deliver satisfactory performance of purchased products and which provide feedback to improve marketing performance. Hence, a systems orientation prevails. Marketing, therefore, is concerned with pretransactional, transactional, and posttransactional phases of a product's or service's delivery to a customer.

The foregoing analysis of marketing's broadened conception in a modern economy stresses the pretransactional assessment of market needs. But the process consists of more than this. An economy such as that of the United States long ago passed from a condition of scarcity to one of product abundance. We created and mastered mass production techniques that provided an outpouring of low-cost goods in increasing amounts. But the advent of mass production required a concomitant development of mass distribution techniques and facilities. The task of matching mass production with mass distribution fell to marketers. Since this is a dynamic process, the job of adjusting marketing functions and institutions to the growth of aggregate output goes on continually.

Another result of the shift from an economy of scarcity to one of abundance is the need for marketers to stimulate demand for new products and services. Once production satisfies basic needs, growth relies progressively upon the demand-stimulating activity of marketing. The successful marketer assesses the latent needs of society, creates products and services to match these needs, and persuades consumers to purchase them. The expansion of demand not only benefits the firm that generates it, but it also provides for growth in the economy as well.

In addition to changes in the concept of its function in the business environment, modern marketing adjusts to technological developments and new business concepts. Development of the computer, television, refrigeration and the quick-freeze process, the automobile and truck, containerization, palletization, self-service, and a host of other products and concepts has markedly affected marketing activities. The spread of education and the growing influence of government in business affairs, which have accompanied growth in the United States, have also influenced the way in which marketing is performed. Thus, marketing functions and institutions adapt and modify themselves in myriad ways to meet the needs of the economic system.

The Broadened Concept of Marketing

Throughout this discussion, marketing is assumed to be an activity conducted by business firms seeking a profit. Recently, some marketing scholars have questioned whether this is not an unnecessarily restrictive conception of marketing.[12] Philip Kotler and Sidney Levy have suggested broadening the concept of marketing to include nonbusiness enterprises as well. This wider concept recognizes that nonbusiness and business enterprises are similar in many important respects. Such nonprofit institutions as hospitals, labor unions, museums, political parties, and churches share with business enterprises a common raison d'être: "serving and satisfying human needs."[13] The fact that one institution seeks profits and the other abjures them is immaterial. Each conducts marketing activities.

What are these activities? Every organization produces a "product"; each serves consumers; and each furthers its goals by using certain marketing tools. We are familiar with the products of business organizations. But nonbusiness enterprises have "products" too: ideas (Planned Parenthood: birth control; Alcoholics Anonymous: abstention from consumption of alcohol), health care, union benefits, political candidates. Similarly, each form of organization serves consumers. To varying degrees, nonbusiness organizations may also borrow the business firm's marketing tools. Whenever a nonbusiness organization adjusts its activities to meet its consumers' needs, it is engaging in *product improvement*. Even though it shuns profits, the nonbusiness organization must *price* its "products" to cover its costs. Moreover, the functions of distribution (delivering health care to patients) and customer communication (making known the availability of United Fund services) can be as important to the effective functioning of nonprofit organizations as it is to firms seeking profits. Kotler and Levy argue not only that nonbusiness organizations already perform marketing functions that are similar to those carried out by business firms but also that broader recognition of the similarity along with greater use of marketing techniques may improve the performace of the nonprofit sector.

Others perceive an increased role for marketing to play in advancing social issues.[14] Some social and cultural causes and activities which it is believed marketing can benefit are fund raising, health care delivery, population control, the recycling of solid wastes, urban renewal, and cultural uplift.[15] Broadening the concept of marketing to include social issues and nonbusiness activities represents a substantial shift in focus. This extension of marketing has had its critics, and a healthy debate has ensued.[16] But in an era when attention centers

---

[12]See Philip Kotler and Sidney J. Levy, "Broadening the Concept of Marketing," *Journal of Marketing,* 33 (January 1969), pp. 10–15.

[13]Ibid., p. 15.

[14]William Lazer, "Marketings's Changing Social Relationships," *Journal of Marketing,* 33 (January 1969), pp. 3–9.

increasingly on social concerns, attempts to enlarge the scope of marketing to include them are understandable. Whether this extension takes root remains to be seen.

SUMMARY

What is marketing? While a number of alternate definitions have evolved over time, no one can deny the importance of marketing to the growth and development of our economy. Marketing can be viewed from two perspectives: (1) micro and (2) macro. Micro marketing activities are oriented toward the enterprise's welfare, whereas the focus in macro marketing centers on society's welfare.

To develop an understanding of the macro component, we must first identify the role of marketing in various stages of economic development. In the early stages, marketing performs an important organizational and informational function that serves to match and equalize diverse supplies and demands. Also, marketing contributes to the development process by creating pools of both entrepreneurial talent and capital.

As an economy grows, marketing functions arise that facilitate getting goods from producer to consumer. These functions include buying, selling, storage, financing, risk-bearing, communication, standardization and grading, and transportation. The universal nature of these activities can best be seen by studying other economic systems.

How efficiently do we perform these functions? In the next chapter we look at the available evidence.

Discussion Questions

1. Both micro and macro marketing center on the marketing mix: product, promotion, price, and distribution. But the focus is different in each case. Explain.

2. Distinguish among the use of market exchange systems, reciprocity, and redistribution as ways to distribute goods. Who controls each of the three methods?

---

[15]Philip Kotler and Gerald Zaltman, "Social Marketing: An Approach to Planned Social Change," *Journal of Marketing,* 35 (July 1971), pp. 3–12; and the following articles in the same issue: William A. Mindak and H. Malcolm Bybee, "Marketing's Application to Fund Raising," pp. 13–18; Gerald Zaltman and Ilan Vertinsky, "Health Service Marketing: A Suggested Model," pp. 19–27; John U. Farley and Harold J. Leavitt, "Marketing and Population Problems," pp. 28–33; and William G. Zikmund and William J. Stanton, "Recycling Solid Wastes: A Channels-of-Distribution Problem," pp. 34–39.

[16]David J. Luck, "Broadening the Concept of Marketing—Too Far," *Journal of Marketing,* 33 (July 1969), pp. 53–55; see also Shelby D. Hunt, "The Nature and Scope of Marketing," *Journal of Marketing,* 40 (July 1976), pp. 17–28; Robert Bartels, "The Identity Crisis in Marketing," *Journal of Marketing,* 38 (October 1974), p. 76; and in the same issue, David J. Luck, "Social Marketing: Confusion Compounded," pp. 2–7.

3. Prices exist in a market exchange system but cannot occur in systems of either reciprocity or redistribution. Agree or disagree?

4. Although the United States operates principally under a market exchange system, the commune movement relies, ideally, on reciprocity. To what extent might the trend toward commune living develop in the United States? What effect might substantial growth of this social pattern have on the viability of the market exchange system? Can commune inhabitants divorce themselves completely from the market exchange system? Explain.

5. Distinguish between physical markets and the market mechanism.

6. Does the economizing principle portrayed in Figures 1-4 and 1-5 in this chapter settle the argument about the alleged wastes associated with retailing? Explain.

7. Set up a matrix with marketing's various functions (buying and selling, storage, financing, and so on) in the column headings and a "planned" system and "free market" system in the side headings. Indicate in each cell of the matrix whether the function is "very important," "fairly important," or "unimportant" to the effective functioning of the economic system.

Suggested Exercises: Class or Small Group Assignments

1. A recent survey indicates that consumers feel that grocery prices can be reduced by eliminating the middleman. For example, some shoppers feel that the price of produce items could be reduced if farmers were permitted to sell these items direct to consumers in shopping center parking lots. Others think that lower prices would result if groups of consumers would consolidate their purchasing power and buy direct from manufacturers. Evaluate these recommendations using the functions of marketing as a guide. Would these proposals eliminate one or more of the marketing functions? Explain.

2. Think of a new product that you have recently seen. First, outline the micro marketing decisions that had to be made in developing and distributing this item. Second, list the macro marketing dimensions associated with it.

TWO
Marketing Efficiency

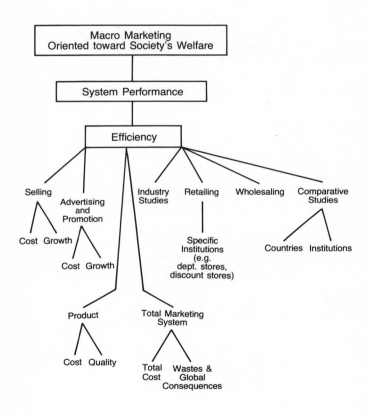

Let's tackle some of the questions that surface frequently in the media: How much does marketing really cost? How efficiently or inefficiently are the marketing functions performed in the United States economy?

Before these questions can be answered, we must first develop an understanding of what marketing productivity is and why it is difficult to measure. Then we can examine the cost and efficiency of marketing from the several perspectives illustrated above. Particular emphasis is given in this chapter to the performance of the total marketing system, the productivity of selected industries, and some international comparisons of marketing productivity.

TWO
Marketing Efficiency

A number of years ago, an influential book asked in its title: *Does Distribution Cost Too Much?*[1] Any assessment of marketing must evaluate its performance from several standpoints. An important evaluation concerns the cost of performing the many activities involved in marketing. More important is an appraisal of the relationships between marketing inputs and marketing outputs. A brief look at the debate over high food prices points up both the complexities of the issue and the need for an objective analysis of marketing efficiency.

A consumer, aware of a price increase on a frequently purchased item such as soup, may blame the retailer for the price hike. In turn, the retailer may point to a wholesaler or the manufacturer. Who is repsonsible? Is the increase justified? A number of factors likely contributed to the price increase. Consider, for example, developments in transportation. Recently, trucking costs have risen as a result of fuel price increases *and*, more subtly, reduced highway speed limits. Higher labor costs; increased cost of other materials, supplies, and equipment; and higher costs of capital contribute to elevated shipping costs. In 1974, the estimated cost of shipping farm products by truck and rail was $7.2 billion, an increase of 18% over the 1973 level.[2] As food prices at the farm level off, and in some cases decline, retail food prices continue to climb because of cost increases of this sort.

Of course, transportation is only one of the marketing functions, and food is but one of the many industries in America. We need to study efficiency across the spectrum of marketing functions and in a wider context than a single industry. Such a study raises a number of questions. What is marketing productivity? What should be measured, and how does one make the measurements? What does available evidence indicate about marketing productivity over time? What are the forces leading to higher or lower marketing costs? Let's begin to answer some of these important macro questions.

HOW TO MEASURE PRODUCTIVITY

Efficiency studies pose two problems: what to measure and how to measure it. Marketing productivity concerns itself with more than the resources used in the distribution sector. One significant measure is the ratio of output (however computed) to inputs used in achieving the output. Productivity improves when marginal physical output increases relatively more than inputs increase, or decreases less than the reduction in inputs. It is the *relation* between the two that has meaning here. To illustrate, the productivity of a warehouse operation might be measured by looking at the relationship between labor input (man-hours worked) and output (volume of goods moved through the warehouse). Productivity would obviously increase if: (1) a fixed number of man-hours led to an increase in volume moved; (2) an increase in man-hours led to a proportionately greater increase in volume moved; or (3) a reduction in man-hours led to a proportionately smaller reduction in volume moved.

---

[1]Paul W. Stewart and J. Frederic Dewhurst, *Does Distribution Cost Too Much*? (New York: The Twentieth Century Fund, 1939). [Phrased this way, the question is bound to elicit an answer similar to the one in the following exchange: Q.: "How's your wife?" A.: "Compared with what?"]

[2]Terry L. Crawford and Andrew Weiser, "The Bill for Marketing Food Products," *Marketing and Transportation Situation*, August 1975, p. 22.

The foregoing measures physical productivity, or what the economists refer to as technical efficiency. Economic efficiency is another way to characterize productivity. This concept stresses the achievement of the highest dollar value of output for a given dollar value of input. We witness economic efficiency when we observe the low prices (and costs) of a large, efficient grocery store compared with its small and inefficient competitor. Joel Dean argues that marketers should rely on economic efficiency in assessing the social usefulness of the individual firm. He claims that ". . . increasing the marketing efficiency of individual firms is the only way to improve the marketing efficiency of the entire system."[3] The efficiency of each firm would be measured by its profitability.

This concept runs head-on into what Furuhashi and McCarthy call the micro-macro conflict.[4] What is optimum for the firm may be less than optimum for society. Take the case of a firm that carves out a protected (monopolylike) position through effective advertising. The result probably would be abnormally high profits. This would reflect an economically efficient condition according to Dean's criterion, but does society benefit? Does this really represent an efficient allocation of resources? The effective advertising may permit prices that exceed those prevailing in a freely competitive market, to the detriment of the consumer. Economists have shown, by analysis that need not detain us, that these elevated prices result in a misallocation of resources for the economy at large.

Problems in Measuring Marketing Output

Measuring the output of marketing is difficult. The problem stems partly from the intangible nature of marketing activities. Productivity in manufacturing is concerned with measuring either the physical volume or dollar value of the output of physical entities. The output of a steel mill will be a given tonnage of, say, cold rolled bars or plates. Expressed in dollars the output will equal the *value added* by production, that is, the difference between the total value of output at the mill door less the cost of material and labor inputs.

In marketing, some measurements are similar to those used in calculating productivity in manufacturing. Man-hours worked may measure the labor input in a department store or a warehousing operation. The value or volume of goods moved through the warehouse and the value added by the department store (difference between cost of goods to the store and its net receipts, that is, gross margins) may accurately reflect output. Deriving ratios of outputs to inputs in these cases, as measures of productivity, should create little problem.

But there *are* problems. The first one arises from the changing character of marketing output. If the real value added by retail stores increases over time (adjusted for changes in price and total volume levels), does this really represent increasing distribution efficiency? If the quantity of labor inputs rises more than the increased value added, efficiency presumably declines. But doesn't this conclusion presuppose that a given gross retail margin covers a fixed, measurable quantity of marketing services? The stores' marketing output is reflected not in

---

[3]Joel Dean, "Marketing Productivity and Profitability," *Productivity Measurement Review*, 1960, p. 47.

[4]Y. Hugh Furuhashi and E. Jerome McCarthy, *Social Issues of Marketing in the American Economy* (Columbus, Ohio: Grid, 1971), p. 8.

their gross margins (value added) but in the *functions* that they perform. What if a store that formerly sold only for cash now provides credit? The addition of this function will add to the store's costs. In this example the functions performed may have increased which, in turn, results in greater value added. In this light, efficiency may or may not have decreased. There is really no effective way to determine which is the case without finding a way to quantify the functions performed. In most cases, this cannot be done. Hence, any productivity study in marketing must be viewed with caution.

The changing mix of functions performed (adding credit, in the example above) is only one factor confounding attempts to measure productivity. These changes may result either from switches in consumers' tastes or from transfers of marketing functions from one entity to another in the producer-marketing intermediary-consumer chain. Such a transfer occurred, for example, when the introduction of self-service substituted the labor of the customer for that of the store operator.

A second problem results from the intangible character of many marketing activities and the complex interrelationships among marketing inputs. For example, advertising may be ineffective if product development falters. Again, the fruits of advertising and selling expenditures are optimized when the two are mixed in appropriate proportions. One can measure the output of marketing in relation to its *total* inputs, but separating the effects of each input element becomes difficult, often impossible.

A third problem arises out of the interrelationships between marketing and production. Marketing research expenditures may increase factory efficiency by improving production planning but they do so by raising marketing costs. Which element in the system—marketing or production—deserves credit for the improved efficiency in this case? And what is the *net* gain? Macro marketing cost studies ignore questions of this sort because they are incapable of handling them satisfactorily.

While these measurement problems cannot be avoided, some important attempts have been made to gauge the efficiency of marketing. Certainly the level of productivity of the American marketing system touches our everyday lives. Gordon Bloom states it bluntly: ". . . All of our ambitious national goals—to eliminate unemployment and pollution and the malaise of our cities—all will be rendered unattainable unless we can improve our productivity and scale down the tempo of inflation."[5]

RESULTS OF MACRO MARKETING COST STUDIES

Marketing productivity translates itself into marketing costs. Hence, a review of marketing cost studies provides insight into marketing productivity performance.

Macro marketing cost studies fall into three categories. First are those that calculate the total value (or gross margins) added by distribution activities. Here the analyst looks at the total contribution of distribution to the economic system and perhaps compares it with the outputs of the manufacturing and agricultural

---

[5]Gordon F. Bloom, *Productivity in the Food Industry* (Cambridge, Mass.: MIT Press, 1972), p. 19.

TABLE 2–1   DISTRIBUTION'S SHARE OF THE CONSUMER'S DOLLAR FOR SELECTED YEARS

Year	Distribution's Share (%)	Investigator(s)
1929	51.1	Stewart, Dewhurst;[a] Cox[b]
	49.2	Converse, Huegy, Mitchell[c]
1934	50.5	Converse, Huegy, Mitchell[c]
1954	45.3	Cox[b]
1958	46.3	Cox[b]

SOURCES. [a]Paul W. Stewart and J. Frederick Dewhurst, *Does Distribution Cost Too Much?* [b]Reavis Cox, *Distribution in a High Level Economy,* p. 148. [c]P. D. Converse, H. W. Huegy, and R. V. Mitchell, *The Elements of Marketing,* 5th ed.

sectors. Productivity ratios are ignored. However, the contribution of this line of analysis is to provide us with a historical perspective of the role of distribution in our economic system. The second class of studies derives measures of productivity over time for retail and wholesale institutions. Likewise, estimates are made of marketing productivity for the economy as a whole. This research determines the increase in distribution productivity, calculated as the ratio of output to some form of labor input. Specific industries (for example, food) are isolated for careful analysis in the third set of macro cost studies.

Gross Margin Studies

The first comprehensive study of the cost of distribution to society was the Twentieth Century Fund's *Does Distribution Cost Too Much?*[6] which analyzed distribution costs for 1929. In that year, out of a total value of finished goods sold to final consumers of $65.6 billion, $38.5 billion, or 59%, represented distribution costs. A later study noted an arithmetic error in the calculations, and the correction reduced the figure to 51.1%.[7] The results of distribution studies conducted in the last several decades are summarized in table 2-1.

Converse and his colleagues,[8] and Reavis Cox[9] have done important work in this area. These researchers used gross margins as a measure of the cost of distribution.

Table 2-1 indicates that distribution's share of the consumers's dollar has remained fairly constant in recent decades. Data indicating the percent of na-

---

[6]Paul W. Stewart and J. Frederic Dewhurst, *Does Distribution Cost Too Much?*
[7]Reported in Reavis Cox, *Distribution in a High Level Economy* (Englewood Cliffs, N.J.: Prentice-Hall, 1965), p. 148.
[8]P. D. Converse, H. W. Huegy, and R. V. Mitchell, *The Elements of Marketing*, 5th ed. (Englewood Cliffs, N.J.: Prentice-Hall, 1952).
[9]Cox, *Distribution in a High Level Economy*, p. 158.
[10]Ibid., p. 153, and *Statistical Abstracts of the United States—1975*, p. 387.

tional income originating in trade industries support this conclusion. In 1929, 15.2% of United States national income originated in trade industries; this compares with 14.5% in 1974.[10]

Is the cost of marketing higher than you expected? On the average, nearly fifty cents out of every consumer dollar goes to cover marketing costs. Transportation, storage, promotion, packaging, and other marketing functions contribute to the total. Thus, the fifty cents represents the cost of providing you with a specific brand of a product, at your preferred store, when you want it. The elimination of marketing activities would not necessarily reduce the cost of products, but would certainly reduce convenience and variety. Frequent drives to a nearby farm or an out-of-state factory would prove expensive, time-consuming, and inconvenient.

An important phenomenon is hidden in the comprehensive studies of distribution costs considered thus far: the diversity of marketing activities in various industries. A number of factors affect the total distribution bill for each industry as well as the costs of each component. Some of the determinants include the weight and bulk of the commodity, its value, whether it is a consumer or an industrial good, the importance of direct selling in the total sales effort, the complexity of the product, service required for the product, structure of the producing industry, and frequency of purchase. The diversity of conditions facing different industries means that one cannot legitimately condemn (or praise) an industry for achieving a given level of distribution costs without analyzing the industry's underlying structural forces as well as the characteristics of its products.

A Longer Perspective   Considered so far have been measures of distribution costs covering recent decades. Harold Barger traces the data for the United States back to 1869.[11] His summary statistics calculate two things: the proportion of the working force in distribution (retailing and wholesaling institutions) and the value added by distribution of all goods that were marketed through retail institutions.

Table 2-2 summarizes the first of these two time series. It indicates a continuous growth in the relative share of total employment represented by workers in retailing and wholesaling. The correspondence between the growth in

TABLE 2-2   PERCENT OF LABOR FORCE ENGAGED IN DISTRIBUTION, 1870–1950

	1870	1880	1890	1900	1910	1920	1930	1940	1950
Percent of labor force engaged in distribution	6.1	6.7	7.7	8.6	9.3	9.9	12.9	14.4	16.4

SOURCE. Harold Barger, *Distribution's Place in the American Economy Since 1869,* p. 8, reprinted by permission of the National Bureau of Economic Research.

---

[11]Harold Barger, *Distribution's Place in the American Economy* (Princeton, N.J.: Princeton University Press, 1955).

these figures and growth of the economy, as measured by deflated Gross National Product, is striking. A regression of per capita G.N.P. (in constant 1929 dollars) on the percentage of the labor force engaged in distribution for the 80-year period found a 1.13 percentage point increase for each $100 increase in constant dollars per capita G.N.P.[12] A parallel study of growth in the United Kingdom for 1861-1951 uncovered a similar pattern. There, an increase of £10 in real net national income per capita was associated with a 1.63 percentage point increase in the share of the labor force engaged, in this case, in commerce and finance.[13] Translating the value of the pound into dollars at an appropriate exchange rate reveals a more rapid growth of the labor force in distribution in the United Kingdom than in the United States. This would indicate relatively greater productivity growth in the United States. Later in this chapter data are given to support this conjecture.

Useful as Barger's figures are, they are subject to criticism on several counts.[14] First, he studies only employees engaged in retailing and wholesaling institutions and fails to enumerate those working in advertising, warehousing, industrial selling, and so on, who are also performing marketing activities. Moreover, his data include the total number of workers employed but not total man-hours, which would give a more accurate measure of employment activity in distribution. The average number of hours worked per week has declined faster in distribution industries than it has in manufacturing over the past century.[15] Finally, there is some question about the overall significance of any figures of this sort. The same objection applies to data on the percentage of the consumer's dollar represented by value added in marketing. Taken alone it reveals little about efficiency in this sector; rather, it indicates where a country is allocating its resources. There may be misallocations involved, but the raw data—either percentage of labor force in distribution or value added by marketing—do not reveal them.

Despite the above objections, one ought to look at Barger's data on gross margins added by distribution agencies to take advantage of his long perspective on the figures.[16] The period covered is practically the same as with the labor force data—1869 to 1948. Again he includes only retailers and wholesalers.

Table 2-3 summarizes his results. Although there was a modest increase in margins absorbed by distribution institutions in the early years covered by the

[12]Reed Moyer, "Trade and Economic Progress," *Journal of Business*, July 1967, p. 272. The correlation coefficient is .968.

[13]Ibid., p. 272. Here, r = .798. Using a curvilinear function, r increases to .915, supporting the intuitive belief that the percentage of the labor force in distribution ought to taper off in time.

[14]See, for example, Cox, *Distribution in a High Level Economy*, summarized here.

[15]Ibid., p. 155.

[16]Barger does not distinguish between what he refers to as "gross spread" and value added. His gross spread, or margin, is "the difference between the value of commodities leaving the distribution system and their value when they entered the system." (Barger, *Distribution's Place*, p. 55.) This measure includes as output activities that go beyond value added by distributors (for instance, rent, utilities), hence exceeds value-added measures. This is indicative of the kind of problem facing one who tries to determine total distribution "costs."

TABLE 2-3   GROSS MARGINS, AS PERCENT OF RETAIL VALUE FOR GOODS MARKETED THROUGH RETAILERS, 1869-1948[a]

Gross Margins Added by:	1869	1879	1889	1999	1909	1919	1929	1939	1949
Wholesalers	9.5	9.6	9.6	9.2	8.9	8.5	8.0	7.6	7.7
Retailers	23.2	24.1	25.1	26.2	27.6	28.0	28.6	29.7	29.7
Total	32.7	33.7	34.7	35.4	36.5	36.5	36.6	37.3	37.4

[a]Barger has two series, one for 1869-1929, the other for 1929-1948. Figures for 1929 were almost identical in the two series. This table uses the 1869-1919 data from the first of Barger's series and the complete 1929-1948 series.

SOURCE. Harold Barger, *Distribution's Place in the American Economy Since 1869*, p. 57 and p. 60, reprinted by permission of the National Bureau of Economic Research.

study, the figures have remained fairly uniform during the twentieth century. The stability in the most recent decades covered by the Barger study supports the findings which have already been reported. There is evidence that Barger's figures for retailer margins fail to account adequately for improved productivity resulting from the development of chains, supermarkets, cooperative whole-salers, and voluntary chains in recent decades.[17] With these adjustments, it is likely that the total gross margins have, in fact, fallen since World War I.

Marketing Productivity Studies

We see that the first category of macro marketing cost studies calculates the total employment in distribution or the value (or gross margin) added by distribution activities. These studies indicate the magnitude of marketing activities in the total economic system, as well as their growth. However, they skirt the issue of productivity, which commands the interest of those who want to assess market-ing's social role.

Again Barger provides us with the longest perspective on marketing productivity. He finds that output per man-hour in retail and wholesale distribution increased at a mean annual rate of 1.0% between 1869 and 1949, compared with 2.6% for the commodity-producing sectors.[18] More recent data support the Barger findings. In a study covering 1929 to 1961, Fuchs shows that the annual increase in output per man-hour for wholesale and retail trade trailed that of the goods sector by approximately 1.3%.[19] Table 2-4 summarizes both the Barger and Fuchs data. One should not read much significance into the higher growth rates in productivity in the more recent years. Fuchs's data are in constant dollar

---

[17]Cox, *Distribution in a High Level Economy*, p. 158.

[18]Barger, *Distribution's Place*, p. 39.

[19]Victor R. Fuchs, *Productivity Trends in the Goods and Services Sectors, 1929-61* (New York: National Bureau of Economic Research, 1964), pp. 44-45.

TABLE 2-4 AVERAGE ANNUAL INCREASES IN OUTPUT PER MAN-HOUR—TRADE AND GOODS
SECTORS, 1869–1961 (PERCENT)

Barger	Mean Annual Rate of Change		
	1869–1909	1909–1949	1869–1949
Output per Man-hour: Commodity production	1.9	3.0	2.6
Wholesale and retail trade	1.1	0.9	1.0

Fuchs[a]	Mean Annual Rate of Change		
	1929–1947	1947–1961	1929–1961
Output per Man-hour: Goods production	2.50	3.50	2.95
Wholesale and retail trade	1.69	1.65	1.67

[a]These calculations are derived from raw data in the appendix to Fuchs.

SOURCES. Harold Barger, *Distribution's Place in the American Economy Since 1869,* p. 39;
Victor R. Fuchs, *Productivity Trends in the Goods and Services Sectors, 1929–61,* pp. 44–45.

terms; Barger's are not. Any data-gathering job of the magnitude of these two
studies and covering such long periods of times is bound to lead to different
results that are not easily reconciled. A study by Louis Bucklin may shed additional light on the productivity of marketing in recent years.[20]

Bucklin employs four steps in preparing an index of marketing productivity:

- Identify all the industries that participate in the marketing process in some
  significant way.

- Ascertain the relative contribution of each of these industries to the total
  work of marketing.

- Obtain existing estimates of productivity for each of the marketing
  industries.

- Weight the productivity indices of the marketing industries by their relative
  contribution to determine the aggregate marketing index.[21]

---

[20]Louis P. Bucklin, "A Synthetic Index of Marketing Productivity" (Paper presented at
the Fifty-eighth International Marketing Conference of the American Marketing Association, Chicago, Illinois, April 1975).
[21]Ibid., p. 2.

TABLE 2-5 AVERAGE ANNUAL PERCENTAGE GROWTH IN PRODUCTIVITY AS MEASURED BY REAL OUTPUT PER MAN-HOUR FOR SELECTED INDUSTRY GROUPS, 1948–1966.

	Domestic Business	Marketing	Farming	Mining	Manufacturing
1948–1966	3.50	2.96	5.87	4.19	3.11
1948–1958	3.56	2.44	6.05	4.34	2.80
1959–1966	3.43	3.61	5.19	3.98	3.49

SOURCE. Louis P. Bucklin, "A Synthetic Index of Marketing Productivity," p. 10, reprinted by permission of the American Marketing Association.

The development of what Bucklin describes as the "synthetic index" grew out of the work of Kendrick.[22] Bucklin applies the term "synthetic" because no true index of marketing efficiency could be developed for those industries *partially* concerned with production activities. The industries represented in the index include transportation and warehousing, minerals and manufacturing, retailing, wholesaling, and advertising. In contrast to the studies of Barger and Fuchs, a broader array of marketing activities is considered.

The index was developed by weighting Kendrick's estimates of productivity for each of the industries included in marketing.[23] The specific weight assigned was determined by the industry's relative contribution to marketing. The most illuminating perspective of the results is the comparison of marketing with other sectors of the economy. How did marketing fare? The results are presented in Table 2-5.

Marketing Versus Other Sectors   Marketing productivity per man-hour lagged behind all of the other sectors of the economy between 1948 and 1966. Note the striking difference between marketing and farming productivity for this period. Bucklin notes that ". . . the rapid increase in farm productivity has meant that marketing and manufacturing charges must inevitably become an increasing proportion of the total."[24]

Observe from table 2-5 that marketing productivity increased at a healthier pace during the last eight years of the period studied, 1959-1966. Output per man-hour in marketing advanced at a mean annual rate of 3.61%. This represents a higher productivity gain than the 1-to-2% increase identified by Barger and Fuchs. Why the discrepancy?

---

[22]John W. Kendrick, *Postwar Productivity Trends in the United States, 1948–1966* (New York: Columbia University Press for the National Bureau of Economic Research, 1973).

[23]A specific productivity index for the advertising industry was not included in Kendrick's work. For a discussion of this and other methodological issues, see Bucklin, "A Synthetic Index," pp. 8–9.

[24]Bucklin, "A Synthetic Index," p. 8.

Again we must consider the multitude of problems involved in measuring the output or value of marketing. Preston states that ". . . an increase in customer service or in the variety of merchandise available may indeed result in increases in both the cost and the value of marketing activity; however, price increases due to monopolistic practices or mutually offsetting competitive expenditures may not."[25] While the measurement problems are severe, productivity research provides a measure of how well the marketing functions are being executed in the economy.

The Productivity Lag   How do we account for the lag in productivity in marketing compared with other sectors of the economy such as agriculture? First, the annual productivity growth rate in marketing indicates that some progress has occurred. The development of self-service in food stores undoubtedly increased efficiency, as did scale economies resulting from the growth of chains. The average increase in the size of certain kinds of stores has also led to efficiency gains. Harwell reports that sales per man-hour in supermarket checkout departments vary directly with the average order size.[26] Other studies report scale economies in wholesaling.[27] Such minor technological developments as the cash register (dating back to the nineteenth century), computing scales (introduced circa 1900), palletization and, more recently, computer telecommunication devices and computerized warehousing technology have helped to improve efficiency.

Other forces have deterred the growth of productivity in marketing. Government intervention has often tended to discourage productivity gains in retailing. The small, independent retailer has effectively lobbied for such protective legislation as minimum markup laws, chain store taxes, and the Robinson-Patman Act, which seeks to prevent price discrimination. These measures protect retailers from their competitors and help to perpetuate a system composed of small, fragmented merchants. Other factors than government intervention lead to atomistic competition in retailing, including the perennial urge of individuals to be their own boss and the ease of entry into the industry. These forces contribute to a retail structure that is top-heavy with small merchants whose output per store employee lags behind that of larger stores. Statistical studies of productivity in the distributive trades reveal that sales per employee increase with increasing store size, at least up to a point.[28]

Industry Studies
As indicated earlier, a third class of macro productivity studies exists—those covering single industtries rather than the entire distribution system. Important

[25]Lee E. Preston, *Markets and Marketing: An Orientation* (Glenview, Illinois: Scott, Foresman, 1970), p. 27. Reprinted with permission.

[26]Reported in David Schwartzman, "Productivity Growth in Food Retailing," in *Productivity in Marketing*, ed. James Heskett (Columbus, Ohio: College of Commerce and Administration, The Ohio State University, 1965), p. 34.

[27]*U.S. Census of Business: 1967*, Wholesale Trade-Subject Reports, Vol. II.

[28]Schwartzman, "Productivity Growth", p. 36, and National Commission on Food Marketing, *Organization and Competition in Food Retailing*, Technical Study #7, June 1966, p. 15.

insights into marketing productivity can be secured by isolating specific industries for analysis.

Robert Steiner tracks the flow of goods from the manufacturer to the consumer in two industries: toy's and women's outerwear.[29] A marketing productivity index is computed for each industry by relating the value of the output to the number of employees involved in marketing. This employee total includes marketing personnel at the manufacturing, wholesale, and retail levels. Dramatic differences emerge between the two industries. From 1958 to 1970, marketing productivity increased by 94.1% in the toy industry, compared with a rise of only 27.5% in the women's outerwear industry. Steiner attributes the rapid advance of productivity in the toy industry to strong advertising coupled with mass merchandising. This position will be explored in the next chapter.

Industries Vary   Studies of distribution costs and productivity changes in different trade sectors reveal enormous variety. Calculations such as Barger's, that output per man-hour in distribution has increased 1% annually, hide varying performances in individual trades. Table 2-6 indicates this variety. One finds

TABLE 2–6   AVERAGE ANNUAL PERCENTAGE RATES OF CHANGE, OUTPUT PER MAN, AND RELATED VARIABLES FOR TEN SELECTED RETAIL TRADES, 1939–1963.

Industry	Real Output Per Worker	Real Output	Compensation Per Worker
Apparel stores	0.99	1.87	4.17
Automobile dealers	2.09	4.82	5.19
Drug stores	2.68	4.71	5.29
Eating and drinking places	−0.18	2.30	5.31
Food stores	2.44	3.62	5.32
Furniture and appliances	2.88	5.37	4.88
Gasoline stations	3.25	5.25	5.08
General merchandise	1.40	3.53	4.38
Lumber dealers	1.21	3.07	4.99
Other	2.09	4.11	4.63
Total	1.63	3.67	4.90

SOURCE. Victor R. Fuchs and Jean Alexander Wilburn, *Productivity Differences Within the Service Sector*, pp. 15–16, with permission.

[29]Robert L. Steiner, "Marketing Productivity in Consumer Goods Industries—A Vertical Perspective" (Paper presented at the Fifty-ninth International Marketing Conference of the American Marketing Association, June 1976).

annual changes in real output per worker for various retail trades running from −0.18% for eating and drinking places to 3.25% for gasoline stations. Compensation per worker increased more uniformly for the ten retail trades, suggesting that changes in labor costs per unit of output varied substantially among the trades.

The table also indicates a strong correlation between increases in total output and in real output per employee for the ten retail trades.[30] Preston has noted the same relationship and ponders its possible significance:

We cannot, of course, easily infer the causal mechanism that is involved here. Do activities grow because they become more productive or do they become more productive because they grow; or are both growth and productivity improvement the results of some other, as yet unidentified, phenomenon?

These questions are not solely of intellectual interest; their answers suggest important implications for marketing management. In an economy characterized by rapid technological progress and increasing labor productivity, are less progressive activities doomed to extinction? If so, the critical managerial task is to develop new and more productive marketing technology. On the other hand, if rapid growth in total output is the key to productivity increase, then increasing demand is the principal task, and cost reductions may be expected to follow rather directly . . . . is it possible that the demand for marketing services is so inelastic that the sector will continue to grow, in spite of rising costs, relative to other sectors of the economy? Some portions of marketing activity seem to fit each of these descriptions, and thus the critical challenge for marketing management differs substantially from one area and industry to another.[31]

INTERNATIONAL COMPARISONS OF MARKETING PRODUCTIVITY

As an economic system develops, specialization grows. Farmers and manufacturers who previously had both produced and sold their output now depend on selling intermediaries to dispose of it. Thus, distribution as an identifiable function absorbs increasing quantities of resources and accounts for a larger share of total output. What forces contribute to improvements in the marketing efficiency of a system? Do countries go through a progression that leads to greater or lesser levels of marketing efficiency? A comparative analysis of marketing productivity in different countries may point to some answers.

Figure 2-1 shows the relationship between private consumption expenditures per capita and sales per person in retailing for 18 countries. Note that the line of fit is fairly good (correlation coefficient .76).[32] If sales per person engaged in retailing are a rough indicator of improvement in trade efficiency, then figure 2-1 shows an association, at least, between growth in efficiency and growth of per capita consumption. Whether there is a causal relationship and, if so, the form it

---

[30]Rank correlation coefficient .91, significant at .01 level.
[31]Preston, *Markets and Marketing,* p. 27 and p. 29. Reprinted with permission.
[32]One can make a good case for excluding the three countries with unusually high sales per retail sales employee compared with their private consumption per capita.

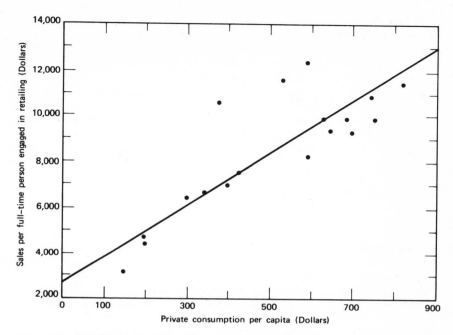

Figure 2-1   Relationship between private consumption per capita and sales per person in retailing, 1955, using official exchange rates.

takes are matters for conjecture. It is likely that the relationship between increased efficiency and its determinants is more indirect than figure 2-1 might indicate. Unfortunately, there are no hard data to allow more positive statements.

Consumption patterns undoubtedly affect trade efficiency levels. Higher per capita personal consumption figures correspond with a transfer of consumer expenditures from food purchases, which account for 60 to 70% of a family's budget in low-income countries (for example, Portugal and Greece) and 30 to 40% in more developed countries, to the purchase of clothing and durable goods.[33] Units of purchase are larger in the latter categories than in the former, thus contributing to improved marketing efficiency. Here, then, the increased personal consumption expenditure per capita (a proxy for personal income) leads to changing consumption patterns that *directly* affect efficiency.

Subtleties in Analyzing Efficiency

There are other, indirect, linkages that account for improved efficiency. Higher incomes permit greater density of buying power in a given geographical region which, in turn, permits the development of supermarkets. Scale economies flowing from this development contribute to higher sales per person engaged in retailing. Related to this chain of events is the linkage between per capita income growth and increased urbanization. Greater population density contributes to the massed

---

[33]See James B. Jeffereys and Derek Knee, *Retailing in Europe* (London: MacMillan, 1962), p. 47 for an elaboration of this point.

purchasing power referred to above, and this force permits larger store size, hence improved efficiency. The Hall, Knapp, and Winsten study of distribution efficiency in Great Britain, Canada, and the United States confirms the existence of a positive correlation between town size and sales per person engaged in retailing.[34] This research suggests a final, and more subtle, connection between higher income and retail store efficiency. Higher incomes increase the mobility of customers who, seeking stores whose names are familiar, shop at chains. Since total sales per chain and sales per employee in chains exceed those of independents, efficiency in retailing is concomitantly increased.

These are a few of the subtleties that both complicate and illuminate the analysis of efficiency in trade. They should permit the reader to understand better the forces contributing to varying levels of efficiency among different countries. They also serve as a warning to avoid explanations that use first-order factors to account for efficiency differences. Appearances deceive. Causality is usually more involved than it appears to be.

United States Versus Soviet Union

A classic example of possible confusion in interpreting distribution cost data arises from a comparison of distribution costs in the United States with those in the Soviet Union. Wholesale and retail markups in the United States are about 37 to 50% of average retail prices. Goldman has estimated the comparable markups in the Soviet Union to be 19 to 29%.[35] Is the Russian distribution system, therefore, more efficient than that of the United States? Goldman finds that sales per employee in retailing in the two countries are similar—$23,790 in Russia for 1958 versus either $29,340 or $20,720 in the United States, depending on the exchange rate used.

How can we account for the apparent anomaly? Lower distribution costs in the Soviet Union result partly from the existence of fewer services and amenities—inadequate lighting, greater prevalence of queuing, limited merchandise variety, and so on. Also, Preston points up the possibility of different costs of the factors of production in the trade sectors in each country, the failure of the Soviets to account properly for the cost of capital in their nonmarket-oriented system, and the different ratios of capital to labor used in each system.[36] Looking only at costs to measure the relative efficiency of the two systems, therefore, can be misleading. This is especially true in assessing input-output relations in a service industry. Costs reflect inputs; the outputs, which reflect services rendered, may vary substantially, making an efficiency comparison ambiguous. If distribution costs in the United States exceed those in the Soviet Union but the bundle of services performed is also greater, which system delivers its "product" more efficiently? Without an accurate measure of the services performed, this question cannot be answered. And, unfortunately, we lack the information necessary to make even a reasonable estimate.

---

[34]Margaret Hall, John Knapp, and Christopher Winsten, *Distribution in Great Britain and North America* (London: Oxford University Press, 1961).

[35]Marshall I. Goldman, "The Cost and Efficiency of Distribution in the Soviet Union," in *Social Issues in Marketing,* ed. Lee E. Preston (Glenview, Illinois: Scott, Foresman, 1968), p. 45.

[36]Preston, *Markets and Marketing,* p. 35.

SUMMARY AND CONCLUSIONS

Answering the question of whether marketing costs too much is not an easy task. First there are important definitional problems. Are we concerned with technical efficiency, economic efficiency, or what Preston calls "innovative" efficiency—"the effectiveness of the marketing unit, firm, or system in making. . .choices among both existing and potential alternatives."[37] One must decide what inputs to measure and how to measure them. Outputs create more of a problem. Marketing is involved with the delivery of a bundle of functions or services. These change over time—some shift from distributor to producer, others shift forward to the consumer. So the output varies not only from changes in the volume of goods moving through the marketing system but also from the changing services performed by marketers in the discharge of their duties.

Fairly assessing marketing efficiency suffers from another problem. What improves efficiency for a firm may not add to macro marketing efficiency. Take the case of a company that increases its advertising budget. If effective, the increase might raise the firm's profits by lowering both per unit production and marketing costs. The higher advertising budget might have a dual impact on marketing costs. It might reduce the per unit costs of advertising by increasing its effectiveness, but it might also reduce the unit selling costs by reinforcing the selling effort and making it more effective. But what impact does this increased marketing efficiency have on rival firms? With rising demand, increased sales of one firm need not detract from another's; however, in stagnant or declining markets, losses in competitors' marketing effectiveness may offset the gains from the increased advertising.

The long-term productivity data in distribution show a fairly constant trend in the share of the consumer's dollar devoted to distribution (in recent decades), and a steady, but slow, growth in labor productivity. The lag in productivity in distribution versus productivity growth in other sectors has led to a steadily rising share of the total labor force engaged in distribution. This appears to be an international phenomenon.

This observation points to an apparent contradiction. How do we reconcile the relatively fixed percentage of the total sales dollar going to distribution with a growing share of labor resources devoted to trade? The answer lies in an affirmation of the theory of marginal productivity. This cornerstone of economic theory holds that factors of production are paid on the basis of their marginal contribution to output. Thus, we would expect a factor such as labor engaged in retail trade, where productivity lags behind productivity in other sectors, to receive correspondingly low wages. This is generally the case. Therefore, although more labor moves into the trade sector as it grows, the lower level of compensation there keeps the share of economic activity in trade relatively constant, when expressed in *dollar* terms.

Whether the United States economy or other essentially free enterprise systems devote excessive resources to marketing remains an unsettled question. Certainly there is room for reduction both in the numbers of distribution entities (retailers, wholesalers, and so on) as well as in the quantity of advertising, selling,

---

[37]Ibid., p. 32.

and other marketing functions. Even marketing's strongest supporters admit to waste in the present arrangement. What remains unclear is how sharply we can contract marketing's functions without tampering with the essence of a free market system. Waste, therefore, may be a by-product of a free enterprise economy. How much of it can we afford? How much of it will an increasingly socially conscious society permit? These appear to be the crucial, unanswered questions.

Discussion Questions

1. Compare and contrast the problem associated with measuring productivity in the distribution and the manufacturing sectors.

2. What is the "micro-macro" conflict? Give several examples of the conflict.

3. Which aspects of marketing are amenable to productivity measurement and which are not?

4. Would a reduction in unit marketing costs necessarily lower total unit costs? Defend your answer.

5. Make two lists of recent (last several decades) innovations in marketing: (a) those that probably resulted in lower marketing costs, and (b) those that probably increased marketing costs.

6. Think of at least one area of marketing that might profit by improved productivity. Suggest one or more ways to increase productivity in that sector and be prepared to defend your proposal. Does your proposal sacrifice customer convenience and satisfaction to achieve greater efficiency?

7. Do efforts to improve retailing efficiency make it harder for small retailers to survive? Explain.

8. How do we account for the lag in productivity in marketing compared with other sectors of the economy such as agriculture?

Suggested Exercise: Class or Small Group Assignment

According to the Department of Agriculture, price spreads—the difference between what a farmer is paid for a product and what a shopper must pay in the supermarket—are at near-record levels. To illustrate, a farmer receives 12¢ for all the ingredients that go into a one-pound frosted layer cake commanding about $1.10 at supermarkets. At the other end of the pipeline, food retailers argue that the store turns less than a penny of profit on the average sales dollar. Who is getting the largest slice of the cake? What factors account for the large price spread?

THREE
Advertising
Performance

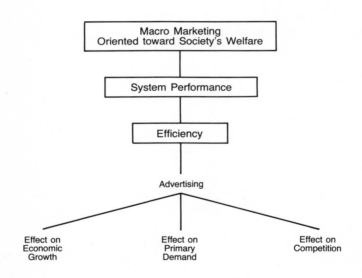

Advertising plays an integral role in the American economic system. This chapter begins with a discussion of the extent and growth of advertising and turns to three important questions:

- To what extent does advertising stimulate economic growth?

- What is the effect of advertising on primary demand?

- To what extent does advertising create or contribute to market power that, some argue, results in high prices and reduced competition?

A reminder! Other charges against advertising—it is deceptive, manipulative, foolish—are treated in a later chapter.

THREE

Advertising Performance

No aspect of marketing receives more criticism than does advertising. Indeed some critics of marketing seem to view advertising and marketing as synonymous.

What are the charges against advertising? First, it drains off valuable resources into nonproductive activity. By increasing costs, it also increases prices. Advertising adversely affects competition by raising entry barriers, making the price for admission into certain industries prohibitive to all but large corporations—and in some instances barring them as well.

These are some of the charges leveled at advertising. How close to the mark are they? This chapter examines these issues and attempts to evaluate them.

EXTENT AND GROWTH OF ADVERTISING

Total advertising expenditures in the United States have grown steadily from $50 million in 1867 to $28.3 billion in 1975.[1] Table 3-1 shows the growth of advertising in dollar amounts and as a percentage of various aggregate economic indicators. Although the totals have risen sharply over the years, advertising expenditures as a share of gross national product remained fairly constant (aside from the World War II aberration) until the last fifteen years, when they declined.

Advertising-Sales Percentages

Enormous disparity exists in the advertising-sales percentages for different industries and companies. In 1972, twenty of the largest advertisers spent 10% or more of their sales revenue on advertising.[2] Over half of these were in the drug and cosmetics industries. On the other hand, some industrial goods producers spend next to nothing on advertising. They tend to substitute expenditures on personal selling for advertising expenditures. Table 3-2 on pages 46–47 indicates the ad-sales percentages for a wide range of industries for 1967. It includes all industries with ad-sales percentages exceeding 2%, plus other representative industries. The table points up the dramatic difference in the emphasis on advertising from one industry to another. The industry at the top of the list spends 32 times the rate of the industry at the bottom.

This comparison is instructive on an important count. Much of the criticism of advertising stems from the repetitive drumbeat of a few leading consumer goods industries such as toilet preparations, proprietary drugs, soap, beer, and automobiles. Consumers who expose themselves to various media can hardly avoid the constant pressure of pleading manufacturers to buy their products. The development of radio and television in the last few decades has accentuated the problem because of the obtrusive character of these media. Their ads are less easily ignored than are those appearing in the print media. But the leading advertisers do not constitute all of industry. Far from it. Many large industrial goods firms advertise so little that many people are unaware of their existence, although they may far exceed the size of well-known consumer goods companies. The advertising they undertake may be limited to business and trade journals. Moreover, even a number of consumer goods products do not lend themselves to advertising because of their nondifferentiated character or because of the fragmented structure of the industry. Sugar and meat products are cases in point. The

---

[1]"200 Years of U.S. Advertising," *Advertising Age,* July 5, 1976, p. 1.

[2]"Top 100 Advertisers Expenditures," *Advertising Age,* August 27, 1973, p. 23.

TABLE 3-1 ADVERTISING EXPENDITURES TOTAL AND AS A PERCENTAGE OF GROSS NATIONAL PRODUCT AND PERSONAL CONSUMPTION EXPENDITURES, 1867-1975.

| Year | Ad Expenditures: (millions of dollars) | Advertising as a Percent of: | |
		G.N.P.	Personal Consumption Expenditure
1867	$ 40		
1890	360		
1900	542		
1915	1,302		
1920	2,935		
1925	3,099		
1930	2,607		
1935	1,690	2.34	3.03
1940	2,088	2.09	2.95
1945	2,875	1.36	2.40
1950	5,710	2.00	2.99
1955	9,194	2.31	3.61
1960	11,932	2.37	3.67
1965	15,255	2.24	3.54
1970	19,550	2.00	3.16
1975	28,270	1.89	2.93

SOURCE. Jules Backman, *Advertising & Competition,* p. 182 (New York: New York University Press, 1967); Reavis Cox, *Distribution in a High Level Economy* (Englewood Cliffs, N.J.: Prentice-Hall, 1965), p. 103; *Statistical Abstract of the United States, 1975; Survey of Current Business,* February 1976; *Advertising Age,* July 5, 1976, p. 1.

total value of the output of firms which, for one reason or another, rely little on advertising is substantial. In 1967, industries for which we have data having ad-sales ratios above 2% accounted for only 10.03% of the weights in the wholesale price index.

ADVERTISING'S EFFECT ON ECONOMIC GROWTH

To what extent does advertising stimulate economic growth? Here is one viewpoint: ". . .advertising, by acquainting the consumer with the values of new products, widens the markets for these products, pushes forward their acceptance by the consumer and encourages the investment and entrepreneurship necessary for innovation. Advertising, in short, holds out the promise of a greater and speedier return than would occur without such methods thus stimulating investment, growth and diversity."[3] Unfortunately, no empirical evidence exists to support this position.[4] It lacks some substance when applied to previously mentioned, little-advertised products, many of which are industrial goods. Even in the consumer goods sector, there is the successful development and expansion of private label brands that lack advertising support. The rebuttal here undoubtedly would be that private brands cannot thrive without the development first of a demand for branded and advertised products. This problem of advertising's effect in creating primary demand for specific products will now be examined.

Effect of Advertising on Primary Demand

Economic growth comes about through increased demand for (and output of) generic products. Jules Backman argues that the absence of advertising would reduce the incentive to create new products through research and development; hence, primary demand for product classes might fall.[5] He points out that big advertisers—for example, firms manufacturing toilet preparations, cleaning and polishing products, and drugs—have witnessed sales increases proportionally greater than increases in consumer spending in general.

From 1935 to 1965, these three consumer product groups accounted for increases in the share of personal consumption expenditures from .67% to 1.00%, from .72% to .98%, and from .85% to 1.07%, respectively. During the same period consumption of these products increased from ten- to twelvefold.[6] Backman claims that advertising has not merely affected market shares of various firms. "Rather it has been a significant force which contributed to an expansion in the demand for these products and to the growth of our economy with the accompanying expansion in job opportunities and in economic well-being."[7]

The most comprehensive study of advertising's effect on the economy is Neil H. Borden's *The Economic Effects of Advertising*.[8] Now over three decades old, it still offers analysis on the performance of advertising that is as timely as it was when originally published.

An important area of Borden's analysis is his study of advertising's impact on primary demand. He traces the growth of several industries during the first four decades of the twentieth century. His conclusions are:

---

[3]David M. Blank, "Some Comments on the Role of Advertising in the American Economy," in *Reflections on Progress in Marketing*, ed. L. George Smith (Chicago: Proceedings of the American Marketing Association, 1964), p. 151. Reprinted with permission.

[4]Francesco M. Nicosia, *Advertising Management and Society* (New York: McGraw-Hill, 1974), pp. 178–204.

[5]Jules Backman, *Advertising & Competition* (New York: New York University Press, 1967), p. 23.

[6]Ibid., p. 24.

[7]Ibid., p. 24.

[8]Neil H. Borden, *The Economic Effects of Advertising* (Chicago: Richard D. Irwin, 1942).

TABLE 3–2 ADVERTISING-SALES PERCENTAGES FOR VARIOUS INDUSTRIES, 1967, AND CONTRIBUTION TO WHOLESALE PRICE INDEX.

Industry	Ad-Sales Percentages	Weights in W.P.I. Dec. 1966[c]
Costume jewelry	10.74	.237
Soap products	10.42	.436
Perfumes and toilet preparations	10.36	.437
Drugs	9.22	.888
Bottled soft drinks	6.19	.493
Chemical and allied products, not allocable	6.18	N.A.
Tobacco products	5.99	.802
Malt liquors and malt	5.89	.529
Miscellaneous food products	5.87	N.A.
Watches and clocks	4.82	.126[a]
Wines and brandy	4.38	.097
Cutlery, hand tools, and hardware	3.76	.593[a]
Toys and sporting goods	3.74	.513
Book publishing	3.50	N.A.
Grain mill products	3.37	.449[a]
Optical, ophthalmic, and medical goods	3.35	N.A.
Confectionery and related products	3.19	.099[a,b]

Cigarettes He sees advertising increasing primary demand for cigarettes by reducing prejudices against their consumption, especially by women.

Dentifrices "This period (1914–31) of increased consumption corresponded with the period of heavy increase in the use of advertising for dentifrices. Hence it seems fair to assume that advertising was an important factor in stimulating the practice of brushing teeth."[9]

Sheeting Borden finds no strong evidence showing the effect of advertising on the primary demand for bed sheeting. He believes, however, that advertising shifted the demand from piece goods to finished sheets and pillowcases.

---

[9]Ibid., p. 296.

TABLE 3–2   (*continued*)

Industry	Ad-Sales Percentages	Weights in W.P.I. Dec. 1966[c]
Canned and frozen foods	2.55	1.023[a]
Distilled liquor	2.49	.246
Photographic equipment and supplies	2.49	.386
Household appliances	2.37	.953[a]
Bakery products	2.34	1.188
Tires and tubes	2.03	.533[a]
Footwear—except rubber	1.58	
Household furniture	1.13	
Motor vehicles	1.12	
Women's, children's, and infants' clothing	0.75	
Cotton woven fabrics	0.61	
Meat products	0.55	
Petroleum refining	0.51	
Sugar	0.37	
Total		10.028

[a]December 1962.
[b]Candy bars; solid chocolate.
[c]It might be possible to show Consumer Price index weights here, but it was impossible to get data on the industry categories used for the ad-sales ratios.

SOURCES. Internal Revenue Service, *Source Book of Statistics and Income,* 1967; U.S. Department of Labor, *Wholesale Prices and Price Indexes,* January 1967; Jules Backman, *Advertising & Competition* (New York: New York University Press, 1967), p. 208.

Refrigerators   Heavy advertising accompanied the vastly increased use of refrigerators during the 1920s and 1930s. Borden thinks that advertising and selling affect the elasticity of demand for some new products like refrigerators by gaining initial acceptance for them which, in turn, leads to emulative buying.

Sugar   Borden observed a minimum amount of advertising of sugar, yet demand grew steadily, presumably from the effect of other factors.

His overall conclusion concerning advertising's effect on primary demand is cautious. Its "chief effect on primary demand has been either to speed up the expansion of a demand that naturally would have come without advertising, or to check or retard an adverse trend."[10]

Was Advertising the Cause?   Reviewing Borden's work, one is hard-pressed to find solid support for his conclusions. The growth of refrigerator sales, accompanied by increased advertising expenditures, was also accompanied by sharply lower prices. Which factor—advertising or lower prices—provided the impetus for higher sales? Or did the product's manifest advantages over the icebox plus word-of-mouth account for sales growth? How much of the growth in dentifrices resulted from advertising and how much from consumer education about oral hygiene? There is another cause and effect problem—the possibility that increased sales of a product stimulate more advertising than vice versa. Increased usage may have encouraged more dentifrice firms to enter the industry and more to turn to advertising. In fact, between 1914 and 1921 the number of dentifrice firms advertising in leading magazines rose from three to ten.[11] Borden supports none of his conclusions with statistical analyses and even if he had, he probably would have encountered the cause and effect dilemmas just noted.

However, there are statistical analyses available that show advertising playing a limited role in stimulating primary demand. These studies seek to uncover a relationship between a dependent variable such as automobile sales and several independent variables, for example, price and income. Researchers have conducted a number of these studies in the last several decades for nondurable and durable goods, industrial goods, and agricultural products. For durables and nondurables, where advertising might have contributed to growth, the studies show that other independent variables account principally for the change in the dependent variables. For example, using such variables as retail price, household income, scrappage rate, change from previous year's income, studies "explain" most of the variation in automobile sales, leaving little room for advertising as a determining variable.[12] Other statistical studies of such products as television sets, beer, gasoline, and refrigerators reveal a similar pattern. The choice of independent variables may be different, but their explanatory power is very high *in the absence* of advertising as a determining variable.

A word of caution is important here. Since this kind of statistical analysis has been widely used only in recent years, most demand studies cover years when products have already matured. Television demand studies are an exception. Confined to middle and later stages in product life cycles, these studies fail to ascertain the demand determinants in the products' early years, when advertising might have exerted a prominent influence.

---

[10]Ibid., p. 434.

[11]Ibid., p. 434.

[12]Among studies of automobile demand are those of Roos and von Szeliski, Suits and Chow, and Atkinson. The Commerce Department has also conducted demand studies for durables. For a brief review of some of this research, see Milton H. Spencer and Louis Siegelman, *Managerial Economics* (Homewood, Ill.: Richard D. Irwin, 1959), pp. 161–187.

Advertising and Output

The question arises: What would happen to *total* output in the absence of advertising? The previous discussion would indicate that limiting advertising might affect demand for specific product classes (hence would diminish economic growth in those sectors). But what would be the *overall* effect on the economy?

In the short run, a ban on advertising should have no appreciable impact. The carry-over effect of advertising should provide a continuing impetus to business. Buying habits should remain essentially unchanged.

The long-run impact, however, requires some scrutiny. Take the case of an individual firm and assume for the moment that it is able to advertise. Assume further that the company creates a new product, advertises it, and the product sells satisfactorily. Increased sales generate greater employment as the firm hires new workers to produce the added output. Unless the new sales divert expenditures from the purchase of existing products, the increased output spells an addition to gross national product.

This conclusion presupposes that resources are available for employment. They usually are. They take two forms. First is the pool of unemployed resources that exists because the economy generally operates below capacity. This condition applies both to capital and labor. Even if resources are fully utilized, there is a second source. This is the "expansion" of resources that flows from increased productivity. Higher productivity means that fewer resources produce the same output, or the same resources produce more output. The process of productivity improvement frees resources for new ventures. If both fail—if neither unemployed factors of production nor the capability for higher output from increased productivity is available—then the firm expands its output at the expense of others in the system. This condition results in no net expansion of total output in the system.

Now assume that the firm introduces and advertises the product, but it does not sell well. What is happening here? Consumers, for one reason or another, either prefer other products to the new one or they elect to save income instead of spend it. If consumers buy alternative products, economic growth should continue unabated. However, the decision to save money should slow economic activity unless investors—government or private—put the mobilized savings to use in some productive way.

What happens now if we postulate no advertising? The new product may not get off the ground. Uninformed consumers may neglect to purchase it not because it fails to meet their needs, but because they are unaware of its existence. However, won't consumers continue to spend their income on *other* products? Does aggregate economic activity depend upon the purchase of *new* products? The production of goods and services generates incomes. Presumably individuals will spend those incomes. If this is the case, then aggregate economic activity ought to grow.

Is There a Saturation Level?   But what happens when people have consumed as much of certain goods as they could possibly enjoy or use? Consumption takes several forms. Some products are consumed continuously and almost immediately after purchase. Food is an obvious example of this kind of consumption. Other products are "consumed" over a longer period of time. Durable consumer goods fall into this category. The purchase represents only the beginning of a consumption process that may continue for years.

Each product has some effective saturation level that differs from one to the other. For quarter-inch drills, it may equal, at most, one per household plus one for each professional carpenter. For automobiles, the figure may be one per person —a frightening possibility! In any event, at some point consumers will refuse to purchase more of many products, except as replacements. When this occurs, what will take up the slack? What will consumers purchase that will cause total economic activity to expand? If advertising is necessary for the successful introduction of new products, then a ban on its use may stifle economic growth since new products and services offer the outlet for expanded output.

Impact of a Prohibition   What impact does the prohibition of advertising have on the firm and its employees? The expectation of greater sales will lead the firm developing the new product to hire additional resources. It will employ workers, build plants, and purchase materials. These decisions will generate income—latent demand—in other sectors of the economy. These are all growth-generating activities. But what happens when, or if, the new product fails to sell? Workers are laid off. Purchasing agents scale down orders for materials. Aggregate income declines, both from the loss of income of the firm's employees and from second and higher order effects that reverberate through the economic system. This is what economists refer to as a multiplier effect.

In this analysis, therefore, much depends upon the impact of the advertising prohibition on new-product development. Does the development of new products depend absolutely on the use of advertising? Clearly the answer is no. The discussion above concerned consumer products, yet industrial goods, as previously indicated, account for a great deal of economic activity. Moreover, there are other ways to push the sale of new products—personal selling and promotion of various kinds. Nonetheless, a ban on advertising would seriously hamper efforts to develop national *mass* markets for new products. Such a prohibition may re-create, to some extent, conditions found at an early stage of an economy's growth cycle. Less developed countries today, hobbled by low growth rates and underutilized resources, lack mass markets that permit large-scale, low-cost output. They rely heavily on local, fragmented markets. They are caught in a vicious circle of small markets and small-scale, high-cost plants. This condition prevents the establishment of low prices that will increase real income at home and expand sales abroad and bring about the necessary expansion of aggregate output and employment. Denied the opportunity to develop new products, would an advanced economy revert to an emphasis on local markets and move away from national, mass markets? Proponents of a ban on advertising need to consider the consequences of this possibility.

Galbraith's Suggestion   Is there no remedy to this problem? The affluent society thesis, outlined by John K. Galbraith, may offer an alternative.[13] Galbraith argues for a realignment of priorities to emphasize the public sector at the expense of consumer goods production. The impetus for growth would

---

[13]John Kenneth Galbraith, *The Affluent Society* (Boston: Houghton Mifflin, 1968), p. 148.

emanate from the government. Recasting priorities would involve restructuring the mix of private and public spending. Government-directed production would account for a larger share of total economic activity than it now does. People would consume more in the areas of public recreation, education, and public health, and relatively fewer consumer goods. Higher taxation rates would presumably drain off the increased incomes generated by the government spending. This shift of discretionary income from individuals to the government via taxation would reduce the pressure to generate growth from the private sector and would, therefore, accommodate a policy of limiting advertising.

Is Economic Growth Desirable?

Throughout this discussion one issue is ignored. This is the question of the social desirability of economic growth. The discussion implies that growth is desirable. In most countries of the world—especially in the less developed countries—one encounters little resistance to the goal of economic growth. However, in recent years the United States has witnessed increased concern over the desirability of this goal. The argument usually is tied to concern for the environment. Critics of unimpeded expansion see increased industrial output threatening our survival through the depletion of irreplaceable natural resources and pollution of the environment. Despite increasing concern over unfavorable side effects, the prevailing sentiment in the United States still appears to favor growth as a desirable goal. Whether this attitude will change remains to be seen. In a later chapter we look in more detail at some of the ecology issues as they relate to marketing.

Advertising in the U.S.S.R! The Russian experience seems to confirm the belief that growth can occur with minimal emphasis on advertising and other forms of sales promotion. Starting from a lower base than the United States, the Soviet Union increased its national income 205% between 1953 and 1969, while for the United States, national income was rising at only a slightly higher pace.[14]

Pepskis?

"A drink of cold Pepsi-Cola will create a good mood and will refresh you." This is an advertising slogan that is being used in Pepsi Cola's new market, the Soviet Union. Other campaigns depict the product as a "health-giving tonic." Sales in the Soviet market reached 50 million bottles in 1976.

SOURCE: *Time*, 10 January 31, 1977.

---

[14]United Nations, *Statistical Yearbook*, 1970, and *Statistical Abstract of the United States*, U.S. Census Bureau.

Most of the Soviet economy is centrally directed. The government decrees what goods will be produced and in what quantities. In the past, they emphasized the production of heavy, industrial goods. Recently, however, emphasis has shifted increasingly to the manufacture of consumer goods.

Economic growth in the Soviet Union has occurred in the absence of much advertising. Does this indicate that the United States, too, could sharply scale down advertising without diminishing economic growth? Developments in the Soviet Union raise doubts. The end of the Khrushchev era witnessed a gradual switch away from a command system in the consumer goods sector toward some reliance on a free market system. This shift gained impetus from the rapid buildup in inventories that took place during the Khrushchev regime. Between 1954 and 1961, retail inventories rose from a 71- to a 94-day supply.[15] Several factors contributed to creation of a glut. Often, wholesalers dumped goods onto reluctant retailers. Inventories also piled up because of a divergence between retail prices (set by the authorities) and clearing prices (where demand and supply are in balance). This was a direct outgrowth of the command system, which centralized price-making authority. As discretionary incomes grew, the problem magnified itself. Consumers were increasingly able to decide whether or not to buy the goods that planners made available to them. The burgeoning total of unsold goods indicated that many consumers had decided not to buy.

Liberman Plan   The shift away from the pure command system involved implementation of the so-called Liberman plan. This plan called for decentralization of economic authority and reliance upon a modified profit-oriented system to guide economic activity at the company level. The consumer goods firms covered by the plan still submit to central direction, but they assume greater initiative in guiding their activities. A profit system measures their performance. Emphasis shifts somewhat from the production of goods to their sale. This development and the growing output of consumer goods to match larger amounts of disposable personal income have heightened Soviet interest in advertising as a persuasive tool. Russians are now exposed to various advertising media—radio, television, handbills, and newspapers.[16] The government has created state advertising agencies. Expenditures for promotion are still low compared with other moderately developed countries, and little emphasis is placed on competitive advertising. Nonetheless, the Soviet Union's experience supports the view that advertising plays a key role in any system in supporting economic growth—especially as incomes and consumer goods output increase.

EFFECT ON COMPETITION

The assertion is frequently made that advertising reduces competition. Before we examine this charge in depth, let's consider the nature of a competitive market.

---

[15]V. Bel'chuk, "On the Relationship between Demand and Supply of Consumer Goods in the Period of Communist Construction," *Problems of Economics*, 7 (July 1964), p. 6.

[16]For more details on the developments discussed here, see Reed Moyer, "Marketing in the Iron Curtain Countries," *Journal of Marketing*, 30 (October 1966), pp. 3–9.

How do we judge whether a particular industry is competitive or not? Economists and others interested in preserving competition are concerned about *market structure*, that is:

- The number of firms in the industry
- Whether it is dominated by a few large firms or a lot of small ones
- Whether entry into the industry is easy or difficult

The hoped for end result of a satisfactory market structure is vigorous competition, easy entry, and the moderate profit rates one would expect from tough competition. To measure the effectiveness of the market structure, economists calculate *concentration ratios* which center on the amount of output in an industry coming from the top few firms. The smaller the share of output controlled by the top four firms, for example, the more competitive the industry. Likewise, the easier it is for firms to enter the industry, the more likely it is that concentration ratios will be low. A number of factors create entry barriers, including the need for heavy expenditures on advertising which makes entry difficult for the small firm.

The best measure of the competitiveness of a market structure is profit rate. If the industry is competitive, we should observe moderate profits. In turn, high entry barriers and concentrated market structures provide at least partial monopoly power for the leading firms in the industry. Their higher profit rates reflect that monopoly power. Critics contend that advertising plays an influential role in creating conditions leading to such abnormally high profits. So, we need to turn our attention to the effect of advertising on competition and consider entry barriers, concentration rates and, the end result, profit rates.

Selected portions of the Federal Trade Commission (F.T.C.) complaint against the four largest manufacturers of ready-to-eat (RTE) cereal highlight common charges about the influence of advertising on market structure. The complaint charges that the manufacturers in question have:

1.   . . . erected, maintained and raised barriers to entry to the RTE cereal market.

2.   . . . maintained and now maintain a highly concentrated, noncompetitive market structure.

3.   . . . established and maintained artificially inflated prices.

4.   . . . obtained profits and return on investment substantially in excess of those that they would have obtained in a competitively structured market.[17]

While this particular case is still pending (in late 1977), similar charges are likely to reappear in the future. A clear grasp of the key concepts is needed to analyze the following questions objectively. Does advertising create barriers to entry? Are the industries that commit large sums to advertising also the ones with high concentration (that is, industries in which a few firms hold a large market share)? Are consumer prices higher or lower as a result of advertising? Do firms

---

[17]"Text of Key Section of FTC Complaint against Cereals," *Advertising Age,* January 31, 1972, p. 78.

that advertise heavily tend to reap the highest profits? These questions have generated considerable debate and controversy. An analysis of each follows.

Advertising—A Barrier to Entry?

Advertising faces the charge that it diminishes competition by erecting barriers that small firms cannot surmount.[18] There are several subproblems here. First, certain products need large advertising expenditures to let them compete in national markets. The price, in annual advertising expenditures, for entering the cigarette or dentifrice market is enormous. Second, advertising expenditures benefit from economies of scale, the lower cost advantage accruing to firms with high levels of output, giving bigger firms another advantage. The scale economies arise principally from discounts that media grant to large advertisers. This gives large advertisers more media exposure per dollar expended. Third, the need for large-scale promotion may increase the size of optimum-scale plants so that few firms are necessary to serve a given product market. Fourth, high levels of advertising expenditures are a source of product differentiation, and product differentiation is a barrier to entry. Why? An advertiser seeks to create a strong enough preference for a product that the consumer will consider buying no other. A company's success in holding off the effect of competitors' offerings adversely affects not only existing producers but potential entrants as well, who find entry barred by the consumer's loyalty to the advertiser's product.

The Other Side   There are several rebuttal arguments to the entry barrier charge. Some evidence shows that the discount advantage for large advertisers may be illusory.[19] Also, the use of participation arrangements in television advertising and regional issues of magazines increases access to these media. Jules Backman offers several other arguments.[20] He cites the market opportunities that are available in regional and local markets. Many products enjoy strong positions in local markets in competition with national brands. The regional or local firm's small size may pose no entry barrier problem. Furthermore, the effectiveness of advertising may count for more than its volume. The small firm may compensate for its size with effective advertising. This, coupled with a superior product, may be enough to overcome entry barriers that massive advertising needs are supposed to create.

Backman mentions two other factors that weaken the entry barrier arguments. First, entrants need not be new firms. Diversification moves firms into new product areas. If the companies are large, they can afford high advertising budgets as easily as existing producers. Thus, they are not deterred from moving in by the need for large-scale advertising. Second, potential entry may keep competition nearly as effective as actual entry does. The threat of entry may restrain firms in the industry from engaging in anticompetitive activity.

---

[18]See, for example, William S. Comanor and Thomas A. Wilson, *Advertising and Market Power* (Cambridge, Mass.: Harvard University Press, 1974), pp. 41–63.

[19]Julian L. Simon, *Issues in the Economics of Advertising* (Urbana, Ill.: University of Illinois Press, 1970), p. 22.

[20]See Backman, *Advertising and Competition,* pp. 42–51, for a rebuttal of the entry barrier charge.

Available data seem to support the position that high advertising requirements do not necessarily deter new market entrants. Backman cites the explosion in the number of deodorant brands (459 in 1964), cigarettes, hair spray, and dentifrices that have flooded the market in recent years. Between 1950 and 1963, the number of soap and detergent products available to grocery stores climbed from 65 to 200; paper products increased from 52 to 145; baking mixes and flour from 84 to 200.[21] Backman fails to point out that more brands do not necessarily spell more producers. Existing firms try to spread-eagle the market by offering new brands with an appeal to different consumer segments. Also, a few brands dominate most markets even when the industry includes many small firms.

There is another aspect to the entry barrier issue. Advertising is alleged to weaken competition by creating brand loyalties strong enough to discourage potential entrants. However, brand loyalty studies find fairly sharp shifts in loyalty over time for certain classes of products.[22] A study by Lester G. Telser uncovered moderate shifts in market shares for leading firms in industries with high ad budgets. He compared market shares in 1948 and 1959 for (1) foods; (2) soaps, waxes, and polishes; and (3) toiletries and cosmetics. For the three groups, average market shares for the leading brands in 1948 declined from 42.6% to 34.1%, 38.9% to 29.9%, and 35.5% to 25.4%, respectively.[23]

Expansion in the consumption of private label brands also weakens the entry barrier argument. A survey of sales by retailers of nine product categories revealed that private label and unadvertised brands accounted for from 34.7% to 54.7% of total sales in each category.[24] The rise of private label merchandising attests to the growing opportunity in some product lines for manufacturing firms to thrive without resort to advertising. Of course, private branding is not restricted to small firms. Many major firms that use highly advertised brands in some markets rely on private labeling to serve others. Small firms that must fall back on private labeling to serve markets barred to them by high advertising barriers may achieve satisfactory profits, but they weaken their chances to earn abnormally high profits which differentiation through advertising may accomplish for them. Also, small firms may not be able to enter the market at sufficiently high volumes to achieve the economies of scale necessary to compete in this private-label segment with existing firms.

Is Entry Easier or More Difficult?   Phillip Nelson argues that advertising reduces barriers to entry by expanding the consumer's knowledge of alternative products.[25] With no advertising, consumers might sample at random along the brands in a given product class before becoming loyal to a particular

[21]Ibid., p. 68.

[22]For example, see Ross M. Cunningham, "Brand Loyalty—What, Where, How Much?" *Harvard Business Review*, January-February, 1956, pp. 116–128.

[23]Lester G. Telser, "Advertising and Competition," *Journal of Political Economy*, December 1964, p. 550.

[24]*Special Studies in Food Marketing*, Technical Study # 10, National Commission of Food Marketing, June 1966, p. 20.

[25]Phillip Nelson, "The Economic Consequences of Advertising," *Journal of Business*, 48 (April 1975), pp. 213–241.

brand. However, evidence indicates that consumers turn to other sources of information in the absence of advertising. These sources include the recommendations of friends or of consumer magazines. Clues may also be found by observing the number of consumers using a brand or, more subtly, the amount of retail shelf space allocated to a particular brand. Nelson contends that new brands cannot enter the market under these conditions because these sources of information are based on *past* or *present* sales. What happens to the entry barriers when advertising is introduced into the picture? The proportion of sales that entrants can obtain is increased because advertising is a function of *expected* sales, not of past sales. Thus, Nelson surmises that advertising makes entry easier rather than more difficult.

Product Differentiation and Entry Barriers   Joe S. Bain has conducted the most searching inquiry of the barriers to entry.[26] It may be instructive to summarize his findings. He determined the impact of product differentiation on the creation of entry barriers. This goes beyond the effect of advertising alone since differentiation stems from all factors that impel buyers to select one brand rather than another. These include differences in quality and product features, buyer ignorance of product attributes, and locational advantages, as well as various sales promotional activities, including advertising.

Several findings emerge from Bain's detailed study of 20 consumer and industrial goods markets:[27]

First, product differentiation is of at least the same general order of importance as an impediment to entry as are economies of large-scale production and distribution. . . .the product-differentiation barrier to entry differs widely among industries ranging from "slight," through "moderate," to "great."

Second, great entry barriers are more frequently attributable to product differentiation than to scale economies in production and distribution. Only two of our twenty industries qualified as having such barriers on the basis of these scale economies alone—automobiles and typewriters.[28] But these two and roughly four more qualified as having great product-differentiation barriers. Extreme barriers to entry . . .seem to be linked to a substantial degree with product differentiation in favor of large established firms.

Third, the sources of high barriers to entry attributable to product differentiation are varied and complex, but several things stand out as important. Although the simple force of heavy advertising plays a significant role in most cases, the strategic underlying considerations in strong product differentiation seem frequently to include (1) durability and com-

---

[26]Joe S. Bain, *Barriers to New Competition* (Cambridge, Mass.: Harvard University Press, 1962).

[27]Ibid., pp. 142–143. Reprinted by permission of the publishers.

[28]Industries studied by Bain were flour milling, shoes, canned fruits and vegetables, cement, distilled liquors, farm machines (except tractors), tractors, petroleum refining, steel, metal containers, meat packing, rubber tires, gypsum products, rayon, soap, cigarettes, automobiles, fountain pens, copper, and typewriters.

plexity of the product . . .generally associated with poor consumer knowledge or ability to appraise products, and thus with dependence on "product reputation". . .; (2) integration of retail dealer-service organizations by manufacturers, either through ownership or exclusive-dealing arrangements. . .; (3) importance of "conspicuous consumption" motives on the part of purchasers, attributed mainly to the manner or surroundings in which the goods are used by the buyer.

These conclusions might "suggest that advertising *per se* is not necessarily the main or most important key to the product-differentiation problem as it affects intra-industry competition and the condition of entry."

Overall, the evidence points to advertising's creating less than a complete barrier to entry—less perhaps than is commonly assumed. Whether it effectively impedes entry depends partly on the industry studied. Almost half of the products that Bain analyzed were industrial goods. Part of Backman's argument rested on the ability of existing firms to invade new product fields. But the odds are stacked against the successful entry of a small, consumer goods firm into product areas where advertising looms large in importance—especially in national markets. This condition may have pronounced anticompetitive effects on prices and profits in the affected industries and may adversely affect concentration ratios.

Advertising and Concentration

Why should concentration ratios be of concern? Economists point to the possible linkages between structural conditions in an industry and industry performance. An important structural factor is the number of firms accounting for a specified share of industry output. Other things being equal, a large number of firms in an industry (low concentration ratios) ought to encourage vigorous price competition and lead to normal profits. A few large firms dominating an industry might limit price competition and contribute to monopolistic profits. Thus, one needs to see whether an association exists between high advertising levels and high concentration ratios.

The results of studies on this subject are a mixed bag. An analysis by Telser found a statistically insignificant correlation between the ad-sales ratios and share of total sales won by the top four firms in 42 consumer goods industries.[29] His study covered the years 1947, 1954, and 1958. A Census Bureau study showed that 13 of 50 industries had the same Big Four (four leading firms in the industry) in both 1947 and 1958. Only one of these 13 had an ad-sales ratio greater than 3%.[30] One would expect more continuity among the top firms in an industry if advertising effectively created market power. And in those 13 industries, one would expect high and not low levels of advertising if there was a linkage between market dominance and advertising levels.

Both of these studies suffer from limitations. The latter does not necessarily deal with concentration; rather it centers attention on the makeup of the four leading firms in each industry. Changes in the composition of industry leaders could occur without a reduction in concentration ratios. In fact, concentration

---

[29]Telser, "*Advertising and Competition,*" pp. 537–562.
[30]Backman, *Advertising and Competition,* p. 113.

Coffee: A Concentrated Market?

The Maxwell House Division of General Foods, the nation's largest seller of regular coffee, accounts for about 45 percent of such sales in the eastern market. A complaint by the FTC alleges that General Foods has used its market position, size, and economic power to limit the growth of smaller regular coffee producers and to discourage entry of other producers. The firm has allegedly (1) sold regular coffee below cost or at unusually low prices; and (2) used extensive trade and consumer advertising to forestall entry or lessen competition. According to the complaint, the conduct violates Section 5 of the Federal Trade Commission Act because it increases entry barriers, preserves highly concentrated market structures, and limits competition.

SOURCE: "Legal Developments in Marketing," *Journal of Marketing,* 41 (January 1977), p. 97.

could increase. The Telser study has several limitations, which its author acknowledges. Not least of the problems is the ambiguity arising from using government data that group several product lines into "industries." Advertising propensities may differ widely for the various products included.

What Does Research Tell Us? Studies which link high advertising levels with high concentration rates include the following:

- A study of 36 industry or product classes which made heavy use of television advertising found that four-firm concentration ratios had increased for 25 of the industries in 1963 when compared with 1947 and 1954.[31]

- In 13 of the 21 industries that made large expenditures on television advertising, the market share of the leading four firms in the industry increased in the 1963-1967 time period.[32]

- In 12 of 17 industries with high advertising rates, concentration increased between 1947 (or 1954) and 1963. A little over one-half of the industries

---

[31] John M. Blair, Statement at Hearings of Subcommittee on Antitrust and Monopoly, Senate Committee on Judiciary in *Concentration and Divisional Reporting*, Part 5, 89th Congress, 2nd sess., 1966, pp. 1888–1910.

[32] John M. Blair, *Economic Concentration Structure, Behavior and Public Policy* (New York: Harcourt, Brace, Jovanovich, 1972), reported in James M. Ferguson, *Advertising and Competition; Theory, Measurement, Fact* (Cambridge, Mass.: Ballinger Publishing, 1974), pp. 97–98.

with moderately differentiated products and around one-third of those with undifferentiated products witnessed increases during the same period.[33]

- Backman, analyzing the effect of advertising rates on industry dominance by a few large firms, notes the shifting of market shares among the leaders—presumably evidence that advertising cannot necessarily prevent loss of markets. Yet in beer—one of the industries cited by Backman—the four-firm concentration level increased from 21% to 34% between 1947 and 1963.[34]

- Other research shows a "marked relationship" between advertising-sales ratios of 14 four-digit industries (that is, industries narrowly defined by the Department of Commerce) and concentration rates in the 1954-1963 period.[35] This appears to contradict Telser's findings and may carry more weight than his research by more satisfactorily dealing with data limitations.

- Another study reveals that the number of firms declined in industries whose ad-sales ratios *increased* between 1948 and 1958.[36]

- Finally, C.J. Sutton reports a positive association between advertising intensity and concentration in a sample of British consumer-goods industries, but uncovers no significant relationship in a sample of producer-goods industries.[37]

The scales seem to be tipped in favor of a relationship between high advertising and high concentration rates. If such a relationship is to affect performance (profits, specifically) it will do so partly from its impact on prices. Therefore, let us examine the charge that advertising leads to monopolistic prices and excess profits.

Advertising and Consumer Prices

Backman summarizes the charges against advertising as follows:

1. Advertising encourages product differentiation in order to develop selling points.

---

[33]Willard F. Mueller, Statement at Hearings of the Senate Select Committee on Small Business, *The Status of Small Business in the American Economy*, Part 2, 90th Congress, 1st sess., pp. 447–495.

[34]Lee E. Preston, "Advertising Effects and Public Policy," mimeo. (Paper presented to American Marketing Association Conference, Denver, Colorado, August 1968), p. 20.

[35]H.M. Mann, J.A. Henning, and J.W. Mecham, Jr., "Advertising and Concentration: An Empirical Investigation," *The Journal of Industrial Economics*, 16 (November 1967), p. 38.

[36]Senate Subcommittee Hearings, *Concentration and Divisional Reporting*, pp. 2153–2163.

[37]C.J. Sutton, "Advertising, Concentration and Competition," *The Economic Journal*, 84 (March 1974), pp. 56–69.

2. The differentiated product then pre-empts a share of the market by building up customer loyalty.

3. This makes demand less elastic, that is, less responsive to changes in price.

4. As a result, the firm is able to charge higher prices.[38]

Backman's rebuttal stresses the failure of this line of argument to consider the potentially favorable effects of scale economies resulting from advertising-induced higher sales and promotion. These economies may more than compensate for the advertising expenses incurred. Furthermore, if ad expenses were eliminated, firms would substitute other means of marketing their products, for example, enlarging the personal selling effort. Backman further contends that factors other than costs determine prices—such factors as the degree of competition in the industry and the stage in the product's life cycle. But the level of demand, which is influenced both by these elements and by the firm's advertising expenditure levels, will affect price via its effect on costs. In other words, costs, in the final analysis, affect prices but it may be a second-order effect that depends upon demand factors. Which position should we accept? Let's look at the available evidence.

Eyeglasses   Lee Benham capitalizes on a unique setting in testing this question.[39] He compares the prices paid for eye examinations and eyeglasses in states that prohibit the advertising of these services and products with prices in states that allow advertising. The total price averaged $4.43 *less* in states allowing advertising. An important implication of this study is that the use of advertising permits the more efficient larger-volume, lower-markup retailer to become a major outlet for these services.

Toys   Strongly supporting the position that advertising reduces consumer prices is Robert Steiner's study of historical trends in the American toy industry.[40] Traditionally, the toy industry invested little in advertising, but a dramatic shift in strategy occurred in 1955. Three elements triggered what Steiner refers to as a "marketing revolution" in the toy business: heavy television advertising to children, retail newspaper cut-price advertising to parents, and mass merchandising through discount stores. (A discussion of the effects of television advertising on children is presented in chapter 5.) Expenditures for television advertising by the toy industry hit a peak in 1970, and leveled off in the range of $75 million to $80 million annually in the early 1970s. What impact did this large-scale advertising program have on toy prices?

The focus here is on the effects of advertising on the markup between the factory and the consumer—the distribution margin. This margin is simply the

---

[38]Backman, *Advertising and Competition*, p. 117.

[39]Lee Benham, "The Effect of Advertising on the Price of Eyeglasses," *Journal of Law and Economics*, 15 (October 1972), pp. 337–352.

[40]Robert L. Steiner, "Does Advertising Lower Consumer Prices?" *Journal of Marketing*, 37 (October 1973), pp. 19–26; see also Steiner, "Economic Theory and the Idea of Marketing Productivity," working paper (Marketing Science Institute, Cambridge, Mass., December 1974).

Lower Dental Fees with Advertising?

The Federal Trade Commission (F.T.C.) has filed a complaint against the American Dental Association (A.D.A.) charging that its ethics code that bans advertising has resulted in price fixing. The F.T.C. alleges that consumers are deprived of information that would help them select a dentist and get the best price. The A.D.A. counters that unrestricted advertising would not benefit the consumer and might lead to lower quality dental care.

SOURCE: *Wall Street Journal,* January 17, 1977.

difference between the average consumer price and the average manufacturer's selling price, expressed as a percentage of the consumer price. Steiner reports that the distribution margin declined by one-third, from 49% in the mid-1950s to 33% in the early 1970s. Also, by 1970, strongly advertised toys enjoyed a distribution margin nearly 25 percentage points less than nonadvertised products. Why? Steiner argues that advertising facilitates (1) the more rapid turnover of advertised products and (2) increased consumer awareness of products and price levels. Likewise, strong competition from advertised brands forces down the prices of unadvertised products of the same type.[41]

The "Cost" of Information   Supporting the contrary view that the use of advertising raises prices is the fact that advertised products tend to cost more than nonadvertised products.[42] This may result from the emphasis on high quality by producers of advertised products to protect their image.

H. Demetz feels that the debate over the impact of advertising often strays off the mark by excluding the real costs incurred by consumers in acquiring information.[43] "With advertising, a significant portion of the communicating cost is contained in the product's price, but without advertising the cost of communicating may be hidden in the expenditures by consumers to acquire information about the product."[44]

Conflicting evidence exists concerning advertising's effect on prices. To learn the impact of advertising on competition, then, one might do better to measure performance directly rather than to study price behavior. The ultimate test of performance is profit. How do heavy advertisers' profits measure up to profits of those who advertise less?

---

[41]Steiner, "Does Advertising Lower Consumer Prices?" p. 21.

[42]For several references to this phenomenon, see Telser, *"Advertising and Competition,"* p. 543.

[43]Reported in Francesco M. Nicosia, *Advertising, Management & Society, A Business Point of View* (New York: McGraw-Hill, 1974), pp. 214–220.

[44]Ibid., pp. 218–219.

Advertising and Profitability

One study reports that industries which advertise heavily tend to have higher profit rates than low advertisers.[45] This study of 41 industries reveals that those with an advertising : sales ratio above 3% earned a 9.4% average return on invested capital; those spending less than 3% earned a 7.2% return. An analysis of the 111 largest advertisers in 1965 discloses that their average return on invested capital was slightly above that of the Fortune 500 largest industrial companies—13.6 versus 13.0%.[46] Other similar studies of large manufacturing companies produce similar results—modestly higher average profit rates for major advertisers.

But there are conflicting views. Roger Sherman and Robert Tollison argue that industry advertising has no independent effect on profit rates. They contend that cost variability rather than advertising is the determinant of profit rates.[47] Likewise, others argue that the relationship between advertising intensity and profit rates disappears when the latter is properly measured.

Since advertising has long-term effects on sales, the expenditures should be treated as an *investment* rather than a *current expense*.[48] The failure to include past advertising as an asset (investment) tends to overstate the profit rate on assets of firms that advertise heavily. One researcher contends that the positive relationship between advertising intensity and rates of return previously indicated is entirely due to this measurement problem.[49]

Advertising: Only One Form of Product Differentiation

We have emphasized the research dealing with advertising's alleged anticompetitive effect. It is not clear, however, that this is the appropriate way to approach the problem. Product differentiation (among other things) distinguishes the economist's model of perfect competition from models of imperfect competition (for example, monopolistic competition). Deviations from perfect competition open up opportunities for monopoly profits. Yet, product differentiation—a key contributor to imperfect competition—results from more than advertising. Product characteristics—including patented features, trademarks, locational factors, and personal selling effort—may account in varying degrees for a product's unique differentiation. Market conditions and management decisions may dictate what mix of differentiation-producing factors the firm will use. The cosmetics industry spends approximately 15% of its sales dollar on advertising; yet, Avon Products, Inc., a very successful cosmetics firm, stresses personal selling and spends only 2.7% of its revenue on advertising.[50] Table 3-3 throws added light on the situation. The

---

[45]William S. Comanor and Thomas S. Wilson, "Advertising, Market Structure and Performance," *Review of Economics and Statistics*, 49 (November 1967), pp. 423–440.

[46]Reported in Backman, *Advertising and Competition*, p. 150.

[47]Roger Sherman and Robert Tollison, "Advertising and Profitability," *Review of Economics and Statistics*, 53 (November 1967), pp. 397–407.

[48]Ferguson, *Advertising: Theory, Measurement, and Fact*, p. 161.

[49]Harry Bloch, "Advertising and Profitability: A Reappraisal," *Journal of Political Economy*, 82, reported in Ferguson, *Advertising: Theory, Measurement, and Fact*, p. 167.

[50]Backman, *Advertising and Competition*, p. 18.

[51]"FTC Substantiation Missing in Attack on Cereals: Brozen," *Advertising Age,* March 6, 1972, p. 57.

TABLE 3-3 IMPORTANCE OF SELECTED MARKETING COMPONENTS FOR THE FOUR LARGEST
COMPANIES, BREAKFAST CEREAL AND CRACKER AND COOKIE INDUSTRIES, 1964.

	Percent of Sales	
Marketing Component	Breakfast Cereals	Crackers and Cookies
Personal selling	2.0	7.9
Advertising	14.9	2.2
Sales promotion	2.1	2.0
Marketing research	0.5	0.1
Research and development[a]	2.3	0.4
Physical distribution	5.2	11.7
Total	27.0	24.3

[a]Included with marketing components because the majority of expenditures are for new
product development.

SOURCE. National Commission on Food Marketing, *Studies of Organization & Competition
in Grocery Manufacturing,* Technical Study #6, June 1966, p. 147.

table shows widely disparate emphases on elements of the marketing mix for two
similar industries that stress product differentiation.

Thus, legitimately, we should study the anticompetitive effects of product
differentiation and not just of advertising. But if the advertising studies create
thorny cause-and-effect problems, broadening the analysis to product differentiation magnifies the difficulties manyfold. One is hard-pressed to suggest a workable research design. Even in the analysis of advertising and competition, one is
not certain how much advertising creates monopoly power and how much is a
response to threatened loss of market position.

Commenting on the F.T.C. complaint against the cereal industry, Yale
Brozen argues that "advertising is used as a means of informing the customers of
the appearance of a new product. It is used as a means for entering a market, not
as a means of barring entry."[51] Willard Mueller counters that ". . .for decades no
significant new competitors have hurdled the high advertising-created entry
barriers."[52] In support of this argument, he notes that the three leading cereal
producers spent over two-thirds of their advertising budgets on products introduced before 1959.

What *is* advertising's effect on competition? The debate continues. The
arguments and rebuttals presented in this section indicate both the complexity of
the question and the difficulty of providing simple answers.

---

[52]Willard F. Mueller, "Marketing Competition on Oligopolistic Industries: The Attack
on Advertising," in *Public Policy and Marketing Practices,* ed. Fred C. Allvine
(Chicago: American Marketing Association, 1973), p. 301.

SUGGESTED REMEDIES

If public policy opposed advertising, what forms might the limitation take? An outright ban is an obvious possibility. Let's examine how the elimination of advertising would affect economic growth.

Although critics fail to speak with a single voice, there appears to be no criticism of informational advertising. This would include such things as classified ads, the announcement of sales, and the dissemination of useful information about products, all of which assist customer decision-making. Criticism centers on so-called persuasive advertising which, it is argued, induces people to buy one brand rather than another, may add little information to the purchaser's store of knowlege, and may even distort product information.[53] It is difficult to imagine an outright ban on all advertising of this type but, presumably, critics would settle for a sharp reduction in persuasive advertising. The effect on economic growth, therefore, needs to be examined in light of diminished advertising rather than its complete prohibition. Whether limiting rather than prohibiting advertising would diminish the impact on new product development as discussed above cannot be answered definitively. One way to resolve this question would be to institute a limitation and observe the results. This leads to a final question: Who will bell the cat? If advertising is wasteful and unnecessary for continued economic growth, limiting its use will benefit the economy by efficiently reallocating resources. If, on the other hand, the unimpeded use of advertising is a necessary concomitant of growth, the results of an experimental limitation of its use may be disastrous.

The impact would depend, in part, on the way in which an advertising limitation operated. A complete ban, whatever other effect it had, would give existing products an enormous edge over potential newcomers. The reduction in product differentiation resulting from a prohibition would also limit product variety. If the ban limited new product development, it would reduce the opportunities for improving the standard of living that flow from their introduction. Whether society is better off in a world with television sets, frozen foods, electrically powered appliances, penicillin, and other recent product developments goes beyond the present discussion and is best answered by the reader. Limiting the use of advertising might well take the form of reducing the volume of competitive ads that cancel each other out. It is hard to imagine aggregate economic growth suffering from some reduction of this kind of advertising.[54] The frustrated advertiser's lament that "I'm wasting half of my advertising expenditure, but I don't know which half," supports the view that little harm would result from such a reduction.

Further support of the view that reduced advertising would not harm growth comes from an analysis of advertising-economic growth ratios in other countries. Available data indicate a tendency for total expenditures to increase as aggregate economic activity increases. However, some countries maintain high growth rates with far lower levels of advertising than exist in the United States.[55]

---

[53]Although the literature often distinguishes between informational and persuasive advertising, providing clear definitions of each may be difficult.

[54]We assume here that resources diverted from the advertising industry and the media that handle advertising would be reallocated to other productive activity in the economy.

Other Options

Outlawing the use of specific media for advertising or banning the advertising of specific products from certain existing media is another option. In the case of cigarettes, such a ban has already been effected. In January 1971, cigarette advertising on television and radio was outlawed. Pressure grows also to limit or eliminate highway billboard advertising. Effective January 1972, Canada prohibited all advertising and promotion of cigarettes.

Set Dollar Limits?

Another suggestion would provide for setting dollar limits for specific product lines, firms, and industries.[56] This approach opens up enormous problems of determining appropriate maxima. Moreover, it raises serious enforcement problems. This proposal also suffers a defect common to all measures that limit advertising—how to prevent shifting expenditures to other forms of promotion. Preston questions whether this drawback is important if the anticompetitive "culprit" is advertising.[57]

Tax Ad Expenditures?

The most common suggestion to alleviate the alleged evils of advertising is to tax advertising expenditures. The taxing power could be used in a couple of ways. First the federal government might limit the tax deductibility of a firm's advertising expenditure. For most corporations this proposal could nearly double the effective cost of ad expenditure beyond the prescribed ceiling. A more prevalent suggestion calls for the taxation of advertising. This measure could take several forms, from a flat sales tax on advertising to a levy on the advertising expenditures of highly concentrated industries. Borrowing a suggestion of Donald Turner, former assistant attorney general in charge of the Antitrust Division, a Nader-sponsored study calls for a 100% tax on firms with excessive market power. Firms with a market share exceeding 10% would qualify if four or fewer firms controlled 40% of the market or eight or fewer had a 60% market share. The tax would apply to advertising expenditures in excess of prescribed ad-sales ratios to be determined by the Federal Trade Commission.

Some Drawbacks

The outlawing of television advertising of cigarettes allows a study of the effect of such a limitation. An immediate repercussion was noted—the shifting of expenditures to other forms of promotion and to other media. Advertising of cigarettes in magazines increased sharply in the months immediately following the television and radio prohibition.[58] Special promotions also stand to absorb much of money freed by the ban. Still, despite a 25% reduction in advertising expenditures in all media, cigarette sales did not level off, but instead increased after the ban.[59]

---

[55]For supporting data, see S. Watson Dunn, ed., *International Handbook of Advertising* (New York: McGraw-Hill, 1964), pp. 726–777.

[56]Preston, "Advertising Effects," p. 24.

[57]Ibid., p. 25.

[58]John D. Morris, "Cigarette Ads Found Doubled in 14 Magazines," *New York Times,* May 17, 1971, p. 19.

[59]Frederick E. Webster, Jr., *Social Aspects of Marketing* (Englewood Cliffs, N.J.: Prentice-Hall, 1974), p. 88.

Spending freed advertising funds on other forms of promotion or on increased personal selling is only one of the drawbacks to a ban or tax on advertising. Another is the possible harmful effects on competition. Some feel that limiting advertising might benefit the large firm which might be better able than a small company to substitute effective personal selling for advertising.[60] For the small firm, competing with a large rival possessing a superior sales force and distribution system, the best hope for survival may be an effective advertising program. Limiting advertising would weaken its hand and reduce, not strengthen, competition. Also, as noted earlier in the chapter, curtailing advertising would increase entry barriers by strengthening established brands against the incursion of many new brands, whose success depends a great deal on introductory advertising.

A CONCLUDING NOTE

Advertising, the most visible element of marketing, has been praised and condemned for a long time. In this chapter we examined the extent and growth of advertising in the United States and considered its impact on economic growth. Since current attitudes center on the possible adverse effects of advertising on competition, four components of this broad issue were explored: (1) advertising and entry barriers; (2) advertising and industry concentration; (3) advertising and consumer prices; and (4) advertising and profitability.

Important questions remain. Is advertising wasteful? Does it manipulate? What are the public attitudes toward advertising? What is the impact of advertising on selected segments of the population, for example, children? These and other important questions are treated in Part II.

Discussion Questions

1. Think of a product that has been successfully introduced in the past several years. If advertising had been banned, would the product have sold as well as it has? Support your position.

2. Do you favor banning or limiting advertising expenditures? If so, would your ban or limitation apply to new products as well? What effect would a ban have on competition?

3. Draft—in lay terms—a bill that would outlaw or limit advertising. Be as specific as possible.

4. Can one distinguish between informational and persuasive advertising? Explain.

5. Some argue that advertising raises consumer prices while others contend that advertising actually lowers prices. What is your position? Explain.

6. Would limiting advertising affect the standard of living? How about total employment? If so, try to trace the mechanisms bringing about changes. Analyze both the short- and long-run effects, if any.

---

[60]Raymond A. Bauer and Stephen A. Greyser, *Advertising in America: The Consumer View* (Boston: Division of Research, Graduate School of Business Administration, Harvard University, 1968), p. 375; and Preston, ''Advertising Effects.''

7. Some observers claim that the United States is more accurately described as a mixed economy rather than a pure free enterprise economy. Do you see evidence of this condition? Where? Would you expect a mixed economy to rely less on marketing than a completely free system of enterprise does? Explain.

8. Advertising is often criticized as a waste of a capitalistic system. How do we then account for advertising's increasing use in Russia?

Suggested Exercises: Class or Small Group Assignments

1. Should lawyers be allowed to advertise? This question has spawned considerable debate. Some lawyers contend that fee information through advertising is essential because the fear of fees is one of the things that prevents people from consulting attorneys. Advertising would also stimulate competition and encourage the profession to provide more responsive services. Others counter that advertising by lawyers would lead to the debasement of the profession. The public would be exploited by the false promises and misrepresentation of the incompetent practitioner. Develop a position—pro or con—in this debate. Be prepared to defend your case. Can you extend your position to other professionals such as dentists?

2. What is your judgment about the F.T.C. case against the cereal industry (discussed in this chapter)? Develop a position on this question. If you feel that the government should take action against the industry, what type of action do you recommend?

2

The Marketing Mix:
Ethical and Legal
Dimensions

Both micro and macro marketing deal with the marketing mix. The focus is different in each case. The manager seeks to manipulate these marketing variables to optimize some objective function. The macro focus, however, centers on ethical and legal dimensions. In Part II we scrutinize the debate that encircles each component of the marketing mix. The figure below highlights selected issues in the debate.

Critics charge that products are often unsafe, deceptively promoted, exorbitantly priced, and ineffectively distributed. Often such criticism is accompanied by calls for increased governmental regulation at the federal, state, and local levels. Proponents counter that society benefits from an unrestricted free market system. They argue that the consumer, rather than government, should rule in the marketplace.

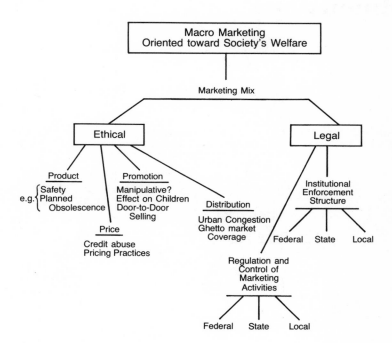

Chapter Overview

FOUR
Product: The Ethical and Legal Dimensions

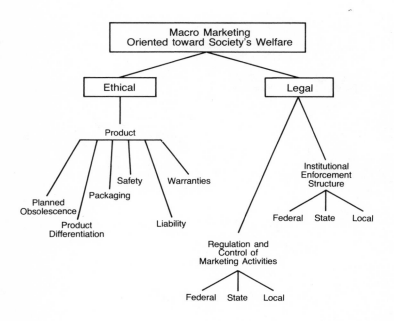

This chapter focuses on the ethical and legal dimensions of product policy. The issues highlighted in the figure above serve to structure the discussion. The chapter begins with treatment of a timely subject—the ecological dimensions of product. Planned obsolescence and the depletion of resources are examined. Next, product information—the package—is considered from a consumer decision-making perspective. Finally, the domain of the marketer's responsibility is examined with regard to product safety, liability, and warranties.

FOUR

Product: The Ethical and Legal Dimensions

Perhaps the most conspicuous aspect of marketing is the product itself. Several questions surround the product policy decisions of marketers. Are the nation's scarce resources being wasted in the production and marketing of frivolous products? Does product differentiation coax the consumer into believing that a preferred brand is now obsolete? Is the package a source of information or a source of confusion? Who must accept responsibility for a faulty or, worse yet, a hazardous product?

These questions outline the broad domain and complex nature of the product management function. In this chapter, attention centers on the macro marketing implications of product policy. The marketer's responsibility in this area begins prior to manufacture and extends beyond the sale of the product.

PRODUCT: ECOLOGICAL CONSIDERATIONS

There are few issues in the 1970s that have captured more attention in the United States than problems related to ecology. In the early 1960s Rachel Carson and a few other prophetic voices sounded the warning. They contended that humanity, through the indiscriminate use of chemicals, was upsetting nature's delicate balance, threatening irreparable harm to certain species of plants and animals. But few listened. However, a combination of factors—the perceptible worsening of the environmental problems and a heightened concern for the quality of life—has moved ecological considerations up to the front burner. Industry now finds its actions increasingly scrutinized and judged by its performance in this area.

With fewer people and less industrialization, the world could afford the luxury of wasting resources. But the level of waste, the rapid depletion of resources (for example, oil, natural gas) and the increasing interdependence effect (oil spills, nuclear fallout, and widespread global repercussions) make it necessary to address the problem. That leads to a discussion of (1) general ecological considerations, (2) the depletion of resources, and (3) planned product obsolescence (a waste that we can't afford?).

Attention centers on air and water pollution. The fouling of the environment is a by-product both of the consumption of certain products and of various production processes. Gasoline burned in automobile engines pollutes the atmosphere. The disposal of detergents contributes to the eutrophication of lakes and slow-moving streams. Litter from disposable containers fouls the countryside. The environmentally harmful side effects of various production processes are legion: air pollution from stack gases and particulates being spewed from industrial smokestacks; water pollution from the indiscriminate outpouring of waste products from chemical and steel manufacturing processes; the despoiling of the countryside and polluting of adjacent bodies of water by strip coal mining. The intense concern for ecological problems by interested citizens, action groups, and various governmental agencies lays an obligation on industry to deal effectively with them. Not only will products have to meet the test of the marketplace but they will also have to satisfy ecological criteria if they are to pass muster.

No Easy Answers
Early experience with attempts to improve the environment shows that corrective action will not be easy. The detergent case illustrates the complexity of the

problem. Phosphorus in detergents promotes the eutrophication of bodies of water. This has led some federal government agencies and administrators to discourage the use of phosphates in cleaning compounds and some local and state governments to propose banning their use. Detergent manufacturers have reacted to these moves by lobbying against the restraints on the one hand and introducing substitute products on the other. But evidence points to possible harm from the caustic properties of the substitute products. Some government officials cite the danger to children of inhaling or eating the caustic compounds. Others feel that proper labeling and packaging could minimize this threat. Also, some in government urge a "go slow" policy with respect to discouraging the use of detergents, citing the fact that other products, some chemicals for example, also contain phosphorus and contribute to the eutrophication problem. Banning detergents, therefore, will not necessarily cure the problem. Moreover, not all bodies of water are equally affected by introducing detergents into them. For example, fast-moving streams may be relatively unharmed.

Confusion

The uncertainty over how to deal effectively with the problem of detergents has led to some confusion in policy statements coming from Washington. Hard-line approaches in one government agency may be contradicted by a softer stance in another agency. The effect on the consumer may have been accurately described by a newspaper headline on the subject: "Detergents: What's a Mother to Do?"[1]

Confusion over appropriate government policy concerning environmental questions is not limited to detergents. The bewilderment stems from several sources.[2] First is the technical confusion noted in the detergents' case. We are simply uncertain what the facts are and what constitutes a legitimate hazard. Second, the existence of competing and overlapping governmental jurisdictions muddies the waters. Agencies at the city, county, state, and federal levels are dealing with environmental matters, and their approaches and standards do not always coincide. Confounding that problem is the fact that governmental standards present a moving target. Today's standards may give way to tougher requirements tomorrow. Finally, the interrelatedness of the pollution evil creates problems of its own. Example: coal-fired electric generating plants use precipitators to reduce the emission of soot and fly ash from their smokestacks. These devices operate by using the sulphur in coal to attract an electrical charge that precipitates the solids in the stack gases. Using coal with low sulphur content can reduce the emission of noxious sulphur dioxide but it renders precipitators ineffective. Furthermore, low-sulphur coal is in short supply and is higher priced than ordinary steam coal. The use of nuclear power plants resolves the air pollution dilemma but creates thermal pollution problems from the discharge of condensing water into streams and lakes adjacent to the plants.

Coordination of environmental matters through the Environmental Protection Agency may reduce confusion at the federal level, but the problem of coordinating activities at other governmental levels still would exist. Developing

---

[1]*Wall Street Journal*, October 22, 1971, p. 8. This article is a good review of the conflicting public policy stands.

[2]"Companies Complain that Pollution Laws Conflict, Change Often," *Wall Street Journal*, December 23, 1970, p. 1.

THE COSTS OF A CLEANER ENVIRONMENT

What are the "incremental costs" of meeting the federal air and water quality standards? Estimates by the Environmental Protection Agency are presented below:

INCREMENTAL COSTS OF POLLUTION ABATEMENT, (1973–1982)

	$ Billions
Air pollution	
Auto	74
Stationary sources	59
Water pollution	
Government	24
Industry	27
Solid waste	5
Surface mining	5
Total	194

SOURCE: Council on Environmental Quality, Fifth Annual Report, December, 1974, Superintendent of Documents, Washington, D.C., and reported in Stahrl Edwards, "Trade-Offs in Assessing Environmental Impacts," *California Management Review,* January 1976, p. 348.

products and production processes under the handicaps of enforcement confusion, gaps in our technical knowledge of the subject, and shifting standards will create a particularly challenging environment for business firms in the coming years.

Depletion of Resources

The challenge to business becomes more apparent when we examine the rate of depletion of several vital natural resources. If the rate of use continues to grow as it has in the past, one expert, at least, has warned that the following *irreplaceable* resources will be depleted by the turn of the century: petroleum, natural gas, copper, mercury, gold, silver, lead, and tungsten.[3] While the precision of the forecast may be debated, few refute the global implications of the depletion problem. New technology (solar energy, synthetic materials development) may alter the time horizon or offer partial solutions, but a comprehensive perspective of resource utilization is needed.

Nicholas Georgescu-Roegen emphasizes that ". . .all economic processes must be modeled in their entirety, from extraction to fabrication to distribution to

[3]Forecast by D.H. Meadows, reported in Frederick E. Webster, Jr., *Social Aspects of Marketing* (Englewood Cliffs, N.J.: Prentice-Hall, 1974), p. 59.

"Mr. Semple, who wants to stimulate the economy, help the cities, and clean up the environment, I'd like you to meet Mr. Hobart, who wants to let the economy, the cities, and the environment take care of themselves. I'm sure you two will have a lot to talk about."

Drawing by Stan Hunt; © 1976 The New Yorker Magazine, Inc. Reprinted by permission.

consumption to waste to recycling.''[4] This approach examines the ecological implications of a product throughout its entire life cycle. Applying this method to the life cycle of the automobile, Stephen Berry contends that the largest energy savings are found in the basic method of metal extraction and fabrication.

---

[4]Quoted in Hazel Henderson, ''Ecologists Versus Economists,'' *Harvard Business Review*, 51 (July-August 1973), pp. 153–156.

Likewise, this method highlights the ever-present energy utilization trade-offs—for instance, extending the life of the automobile results in substantially greater energy savings than does recycling it.[5] From a marketing perspective, emphasis is given to the distribution and consumption components of the life cycle while the waste and recycling dimensions of the process are often overlooked.

Planned Product Obsolescence

Recent years have seen the growing charge that continuing product changes by manufacturers are an attempt not to improve the consumer's welfare but to create sales through forced obsolescence of existing models. The charge is related to the criticism of product differentiation, only here the differentiation over time is seen not so much as a move to meet or beat competitors' offerings as an attempt to extend the product life cycle by continually making existing models obsolete. The automobile industry feels the full brunt of the charge of planned obsolescence, but other manufacturers—especially of durables and fashion goods—also come under attack.

Few argue against product developments that genuinely improve the quality and functional ability of products.[6] One need only recall earlier versions of automobiles, television sets, radios, airplanes, and a host of other modern products to recognize the value of product development. The critics thus do not necessarily rail against all product change; rather, they attack what they see as planned obsolescence. But how can we make a distinction? To do so might require probing the manufacturer's mind to see what motivates the product changes. Presumably producers hope that enough consumers will view their new product offerings as sufficiently attractive to warrant purchasing it. If a model is changed to induce sales, and buyers are unimpressed, the producer suffers.

So-called planned obsolescence is not necessarily confined to manufacturers. Most inventors and developers of new processes usually create obsolescence of something previously developed. The development of the transistor rendered vacuum tubes obsolete for some uses, and one could argue that the outcome was "planned." Some of the most vocal critics of planned obsolescence are economists who regularly consign editions of their best-selling economics texts to obsolescence by publishing revised editions that closely resemble the original.

Are Frills Wasteful? What is the cost of creating product obsolescence? It often results in a squandering of resources. The new edition of the economics text requires, for all practical purposes, the scrapping of previous editions, with its attendant waste. For some products—automobiles, for example—a second-hand market prolongs the useful life of obsolete models until they reach the end of their functional life. For other products—some books, clothes, furniture—the used markets may offer only partially effective means of prolonging product life and, hence, conserving resources.

---

[5]Quoted in ibid., p. 156.

[6]Increased concern for the quality of life raises the number of those who look with disfavor on a growing list of "improvements" which society formerly assumed to be civilized advancements.

Those who condemn planned obsolescence see a waste not only in the creation of obsolete models but also in the use of resources designed to differentiate the products. Whatever form the waste takes, however, it results in the depletion of precious, nonrenewable resources. Thus the needs (whims?) of the current generation are satisfied at the expense of generations unborn. Furthermore, it is argued, in addition to being an *absolute* waste of resources, planned obsolescence results in a misallocation of resources. This is essentially the Galbraithian "affluent society" thesis—the issue of tail fins versus public parks.

The waste-of-resources argument is hard for marketers to rebut in view of the demonstrably threatened exhaustion of certain natural resources in the foreseeable future, and the force of arguments concerning pollution and ecological imbalance.

As a matter of public policy and necessity during World War II, the United States resolved the problem of wasting resources on "frills" by decreeing their abandonment. Thus, trousers were cuffless and books were printed without large margins. Presumably, we could institute a similar policy to conserve resources, but the absence of a perceived emergency might make it unworkable. Alternatively, the federal government might impose sanctions on producers who waste resources through the use of "unnecessary" product obsolescence, but here, too, implementation may be next to impossible without putting the economy in a straightjacket. A consumers' revolt against frequent and insignificant model changes probably holds the best hope for reducing planned obsolescence. The success of the Volkswagen in competition with Detroit's constantly changing models augurs well for this alternative solution. Interestingly, the domestic subcompact models have undergone minimal style changes in recent years, reflecting a possible shift in Detroit's philosophy.

Clarence Walton raises an interesting question that closes this discussion. He asks whether we can be sure that the consumer is better off by having a choice of a television set lasting five years and one, at twice the price, lasting fifteen years (which the consumer, rationally, selects), in view of the genuine product improvement that can occur in the interim.[7] He also wonders whether building things to last forever is necessarily good, citing the ugly, solid homes on Riverside Drive in New York City as case examples arguing for impermanence.[8]

PRODUCT DIFFERENTIATION AND BRANDING

Marketing critics deplore the use of brand labeling and product differentiation for several reasons. They see some product differentiation as an attempt—with the aid of advertising—to make minor product differences appear major. Producers of major durables, such as automobiles, often come under attack. Critics point to the use of nonutilitarian product features as ways to confuse the buyer and add unnecessarily to the cost of the product. They view advertising as the agent that magnifies the importance of minor differences and as another contributor to

---

[7]Clarence C. Walton, "Ethical Theory, Societal Expectations and Marketing Practices," in *The Social Responsibilities of Marketing*, ed. William D. Stevens (Proceedings of Winter Conference, American Marketing Association, December 1961), p. 22.
[8]Ibid., p. 22.

higher costs. Branding draws similar criticism. Producers are seen to engage in it to increase market power by establishing customer loyalty for their brands over others.

To some extent, producers view product differentiation and branding through the use of trademarks as similar. Marketing texts extol branding and differentiation as tools in the marketer's profit-maximizing kit. But they also ascribe to these measures features which benefit the consumer and which critics ignore. Among product differentiation's alleged advantages to the consumer are the opportunities it provides for greater variety and choice, for improved product quality, and for better services, including warranties.[9]

Trademarks Not New

Trademarks, as adjuncts to product differentiation, date back to the medieval period. Artisans used marks to distinguish the output of particular guilds as a way to police the quality of their workmanship. Thus, guild members viewed the use of marks as a liability since, with their use, workers could not escape responsibility. Later, when guilds sold goods in nonlocal markets, trademarks developed a new function of assuring the buyer of product quality. The use of trademarks flourished in this way from the fifteenth to the seventeenth centuries, especially in the clothing and cutlery trades.[10]

Factories competing with the guilds also used product differentiation. As markets expanded following the medieval period, individual factory operators sought to compete with guild merchants by offering distinctive (differentiated) products to win consumer favor. Emphasis centered on maintaining quality to combat the quality image of guild-produced goods. Not until much later, under the pressure of competition, did sellers consciously create minor product differences to develop "selling points"—the alleged practice that now attracts criticism.

Russian TVs Won't Move

Branding is not necessarily limited to capitalist societies. Theodore Levitt reports on the Russians' use of trademarks to correct a problem in their television industry.[11] Russian television manufacturers found sales lagging. Several factories produced identical 17-inch sets but the output of one was inferior to the others. Buyers, however, tended to shun purchases of *all* sets of this type, not knowing which were defective. Inventories built up. This condition led to the use of trademarks to identify brands. Started as a convenience to planners, the trademark became a buying aid for the consumer. In this instance, brand recognition promoted economic welfare in two ways: by aiding the buying process and by singling out efficient producers for reward and exposing producers of shoddy goods.

---

[9]O.J. Firestone, *The Economic Implications of Advertising* (London: Methuen, 1967), p. 83.

[10]Neil H. Borden, *The Economic Effects of Advertising* (Chicago: Richard D. Irwin, 1942), pp. 22–23.

[11]Theodore Levitt, "Branding on Trial," *Harvard Business Review,* 44 (March–April 1966), pp. 113–115.

Defenders of branding argue that it has the same beneficial effects in the United States' market-oriented system. Its use assures consumers of quality. But, the critics ask, why pay for the enormous advertising necessary to provide brand-name recognition? Why not emphasize the use of private, nonadvertised brands that afford excellent bargains in many lines of consumer goods? The marketer responds that private branding depends upon the prior successful acceptance of advertised brands that stand as buying reference points.

Differentiation or Homogeneity?

To the charge that product differentiation harms consumers by deceiving them into thinking that nominal product differences are significant, the defender of marketing answers that far from harming them, it can serve them. How? By permitting producers to fashion products that meet consumers' *precise* needs. Differentiation recognizes that needs and desires among consumers vary with respect to colors, sizes, features, and psychological significance of products. The absence of product differentiation is product homogeneity. Is this, the marketer asks, an acceptable alternative?

The critic, however, wants less to dispense with product differentiation than to correct its abuses—the use of deceptive packaging to create the illusion of size, the nonfunctional gadget adorning a new model which distinguishes it from the old, the drumbeat of advertising which tries to distinguish one brand from its essentially identical competitor. As the critic sees it, this behavior both confounds the consumer and adds to the cost of goods he or she purchases without providing corresponding benefits.

Product Differentiation and Industry Concentration

The Federal Trade Commission (F.T.C.) complaint against the cereal industry (discussed in chapter 3) adds another dimension to the controversy surrounding product differentiation. Past actions taken by the F.T.C. centered on unfair methods of competition such as false and misleading advertising and deceptive packaging. While misleading advertising is one of the issues in the complaint, an accompanying charge has more striking implications for marketers. The basic contention is that product differentiation creates and maintains concentrated industry structures that are anticompetitive.[12]

The combination of marketing practices (product differentiation) and a concentrated industry (70% of market held by four or fewer firms) is fundamental to the F.T.C. charge. The focus here is on product differentiation only as it occurs in industries dominated by a few large firms. Two questions are important. Is competition nonexistent in a concentrated industry? Is product differentiation the primary factor in creating and maintaining a concentrated industry? H. Paul Root contends that a successful case against the cereal industry might well make other industries vulnerable to the same charges. Industries that rely on product differentiation and are often labeled "concentrated" include such important consumer goods as cigarettes, refrigerators, detergents, and automobiles.[13]

---

[12]H. Paul Root, "Should Product Differentiation Be Restricted?" *Journal of Marketing*, 36 (July 1972), pp. 3–9.
[13]Ibid., pp. 3–9.

PRODUCT INFORMATION: THE PACKAGE

The package is a source of information for consumer decision-making. Legislation concerning packaging information assumes that the average shopper lacks sufficient data to make intelligent buying decisions. Likewise, the assumption is made that shoppers will use the new information available to them to improve the buying process.

Before beginning our discussion of the package as a source of information for consumer decision-making, let's look briefly at the problem of information overload. Does more and more information benefit or hinder decision-making? Jacob Jacoby and his colleagues explored the effects of increasing information load upon both brand choice and consumer satisfaction. They found that while consumers feel more satisfied and less confused with more information, they may actually make poorer decisions.[14] This research has spawned considerable debate.[15]

"Truth-in-Packaging" Act

What information is now provided to consumers via the package? A part of the so-called Truth-in-Packaging Act (Fair Packaging and Labeling Act), passed in 1966, reads: "Informed consumers are essential to the fair and efficient functioning of a free market economy. Packages and their labels should enable consumers to obtain accurate information as to the quantity of the contents and should facilitate value comparisons."[16] It is the failure of many packages and labels to inform consumers adequately that led to passage of the law. Extensive congressional hearings revealed the depth and character of consumers' displeasure with packaging practices. Congressman Leonard Farbstein cited the most frequently mentioned abuses:

1. The widespread lack of uniformity in the location of the information, such as the quantity statement, that is required by law to appear on the package.

2. The lack of reasonable and efficient standardization of package sizes.

3. The use of such misleading qualifying terms as "jumbo," "giant," "full," and others.

4. The smallness of type and the lack of contrast in colors.

5. The use of packages and containers in designs that make the package appear to be larger than its actual contents justify.

---

[14]Jacob Jacoby, Donald E. Speller, and Carol A. Kohn, "Brand Choice Behavior as a Function of Information Load," *Journal of Marketing Research*, 11 (February 1974), pp. 63–69.

[15]William L. Wilkie, "Analysis of Effects of Information Load," *Journal of Marketing Research*, 11 (November 1974), pp. 462–466; Ibid., John O. Summers, "Less Information Is Better?", pp. 467–468. See also J. Edward Russo, "More Information Is Better: A Reevaluation of Jacoby, Speller, and Kohn," *Journal of Consumer Research*, 1 (December 1974), pp. 68–72.

[16]Public Law 89-755, 89th Congress, p. 1296.

6. The practice of marking a package "cents-off" when all too frequently such offers represent no actual price reductions.[17]

Widely quoted in support of the bill, during debate prior to its passage, was research conducted by Professor Monroe Friedman, a psychologist from Eastern Michigan University. He asked 33 young women college graduates to shop for 20 supermarket items. Each was instructed to seek out the cheapest brand. This stricture resulted in their spending three times longer to shop than usual. The research revealed that 43% of the purchase decisions involved buying other than the cheapest brand. Not one shopper, for example, bought the lowest price detergent. Overall, the women spent 9% more than they would have had they selected the best bargains.[18] The inference that one presumably should draw from the results is that if college-educated women, taking extra time and care, cannot discern values from packages and labels, the average buyer is hopelessly handicapped.

Damage or Enhance Competition? Opposition to the bill centered on the deleterious effects it might have on competition. D. Beryl Manischewitz argued that "standardized packages can lead to standardized products and standardized quality, and thereby limit the range of choice of the purchasing public. Under such conditions, marketing innovation and competition as well cannot help but suffer."[19] It is hard to understand why standardized packages necessarily lead to standardized products. Couldn't one argue that standardization would lead to *more* and not less competition since evidence points to standardized products being subjected to more price competition than differentiated ones? For example, regulations sponsored by the National Bureau of Standards governed package sizes for the dairy industry before passage of truth-in-packaging. They have led to the absence of odd-ounce containers for dairy products. Dairies limit themselves to pints, quarts, gallons, and so on, yet the industry exhibits as much price competition as can be expected from one bound by restrictive state laws. Restricting package sizes also has not inhibited the introduction of new products.

Key Provisions The Fair Packaging and Labeling Act provides that

1. Goods must bear labels identifying the product, and the name and place of business of the manufacturer.

2. The quantity of a package's contents (weight, measure, or count) must be stated on labels in conspicuous type. Ingredients must be listed in order of their proportion.

3. Authority to issue regulations under the act rests with the Food and Drug Administration (F.D.A.) and the F.T.C., which can exempt prod-

---

[17]U.S. Congress, House Committee on Interstate and Foreign Commerce, *Hearings on Fair Packaging and Labeling*, 89th Congress, 2nd sess., 1966, p. 20.
[18]Ibid., p. 20.
[19]Ibid., p. 80.

ucts from coverage of the act if its provisions are impractical or unnecessary for the consumer's protection. These agencies may also issue regulations concerning placement of printed matter relating to "cents-off" on labels and to "nonfunctional slack-fill of packages."

4. If certain products spawn a proliferation of package sizes, the secretary of commerce may seek the establishment of voluntary product size standards from manufacturers.

5. Labels must bear the "common or usual" name of the product.

Both foes and advocates of the law find fault with its final version. Ralph Nader has labeled truth-in-packaging "the most deceptive package of all." His objection stems from the voluntary mechanism for reducing the number of package sizes. Even in the absence of mandatory controls, by mid-1968, a number of industries had agreed to eliminate many package sizes. Cereal packages had been cut from 33 to 16, detergents from 24 to 6, toothpaste from 57 to 5.

Others argue that previously existing F.T.C. rulings prohibited practices that the new law sought to abolish—especially with respect to the use of slack-filled packages and deceptive labeling.[20] The new law, however, moves beyond the prevention of deception, which may be hard to prove, but permits the setting of standards that will improve the buyer's knowledge of what he or she purchases.

Nutrition Labeling

Consumer advocates' demand for more meaningful and useful nutrition information emerged in a congressional review of the effectiveness of the Fair Packaging and Labeling Act. The importance of processed foods in the American diet and the corresponding need for nutrition information also surfaced in a White House Conference on Food, Nutrition, and Health. Acting in accordance with the Federal Food, Drug and Cosmetic Act of 1938, the F.D.A. revised its regulations to reflect the growing concern for nutrition information.[21]

The regulations are designed to insure complete disclosure of information concerning the content of processed foods. These measures, which became fully effective in 1975, apply only to those processed foods for which nutritional claims are made or which are fortified with nutrients. Among other provisions, a regulation requires a standardized format for the listing of vitamin, protein, carbohydrate, and fat content.

Open-Code Dating

Most packaged foods bear a code indicating a date that measures the product's freshness. The average consumer would have to be an amateur cryptographer to decipher the many codes in use. They are designed for use by the distributors and manufacturers. In recent years consumers have sought to change the coding

---

[20]See, for example, "The Truth about Truth in Packaging," *Nation's Business*, October 1966, p. 75.

[21]Warren A. French and Hiram C. Barksdale, "Food Labeling Regulations: Efforts toward Full Disclosure," *Journal of Marketing*, 38 (July 1974), pp. 14–19.

system to improve their knowledge of product freshness. A survey of consumers found that those citing open-code dating as a needed consumer reform outnumbered those favoring unit pricing more than two to one (49% versus 23%).

Jewel Tea Company claims to have been the first retailer to introduce open dating; it did so in July 1970.[22] Although no data exist on the dollar volume of food products sold with open-code dating, increasing numbers of food chains and manufacturers have begun the practice. Most manufacturers, understandably, prefer coded dating. It permits them to control quality without letting consumers sort out newer from older merchandise. Manufacturers complain that earlier dated merchandise may be of acceptable quality, yet consumers choose fresher products when given a choice. This presents the manufacturer with unsold inventory problems. Retailers suffer the same handicap. Shoppers may buy five-day-old eggs and leave ten-day-old ones unsold, even though eggs should remain fresh for 15 days.

Open-code dating creates additional problems. What date should be used? Should it be the date when it was manufactured, the date beyond which one should not eat the product, the date when it should leave the shelf and make way for fresher products, or the date when its nutritional value begins to decline? Frozen foods create another problem. If improperly handled by the customer, they can spoil before the code's expiration date. Is the company liable for loss in this event?

Although the survey cited above found consumers strongly favoring open dating, many fail to use it when it is made available to them.[23] Even if many ignore it, however, consumers should benefit from the pressure on retailers to be alert to the need for product freshness.

Usage of "New" Information

Are consumers using the new sources of information on the package—nutrition labeling and open-code dating? Available evidence is presented in table 4-1. Note that approximately a quarter of the consumers sampled were aware of nutrition labeling while only 16% understood the label. For open dating, 65% noticed the date but only 36% knew what the date signified. Clearly, many consumers are not using these new information sources.[24]

Analysts who have studied marketing practices of low-income buyers see a drawback to the conception of truth-in-packaging. The criticism applies equally well to the nutrition labeling requirement and the call for expanded use of open-code dating. These laws assume the shoppers have certain characteristics:

- They shop around for good buys.

- They are able to judge, and therefore secure, the best values.

---

[22]"Chains Woo with Open Dating," *Business Week,* January 16, 1971, p. 48.
[23]Ibid., p. 51.
[24]For a complete discussion of past research, see George S. Day, "Assessing the Effects of Information Disclosure Requirements," *Journal of Marketing,* 40 (April 1976), pp. 42–52.

TABLE 4-1   Evidence of Effects of Selected Information Disclosure Requirements.

	Disclosure Requirement	
Effect	Nutrition Labeling[a]	Open-Code Dating[b]
1. Awareness of information	26% saw label	65% noticed
2. Comprehension of information	16% understood label	36% knew that the pull date was used
3. Satisfaction	————	Higher degree of satisfaction with freshness
4. Claimed use of information (one or more times)	9% used labels at least once	39% used open-code dating on one or more products during last trip

[a]R. J. Lenahan et al., "Consumer Reaction to Nutritional Labels on Food Products," *Journal of Consumer Affairs,* 7 (Spring 1973).
[b]R. C. Stokes et al., *Food Dating: Shoppers' Reactions and the Impact on Retail Foodstores,* Report No. 984 (U.S. Department of Agriculture, Economic Research Service, January 1973).

SOURCE. Adapted from George S. Day, "Assessing the Effects of Information Disclosure Requirements," *Journal of Marketing,* 40 (April 1976), p. 46, reprinted by permission of the American Marketing Association.

- They are aware of their legal rights and are willing to use legal remedies to protect themselves.[25]

Unfortunately, many low-income buyers—and others as well—lack the three characteristics listed above which enable them to take advantage of the law's passage.

This objection raises a philosophical question concerning the informational bills just mentioned, as well as other proposed consumerism measures. To what extent should the state take action to provide information that will make for more rational buying decisions? Should it act even though the majority of buyers fail to use it? How can one balance the potential gain to those who use (and presumably profit by) it against the alleged disadvantages—for example, stifled competition, bureaucratic red tape, and so on? Few people would disagree that the public deserves protection from deception and should have access to information that will improve buying decisions. Dispute rages over the extent of the information

---

[25]For an analysis of these points, see Eric Schnapper "Consumer Legislation and the Poor," in *Consumerism: Search for the Consumer Interest,* 2nd ed., ed. David A. Aaker and George S. Day (New York: The Free Press, 1974), p. 84.

that shoppers can effectively use, whether the government ought to mandate its dissemination, and whether, if the demand is sufficient, a free market system cannot adequately provide for it. The reader might consider these questions and try to reach a reasoned position.

PRODUCT SAFETY

What is the measure of exposure of United States consumers to unreasonable product hazards? In 1967, Congress created a National Commission on Product Safety to examine such product safety questions.[26] The commission reported that 20 million Americans are injured annually as a result of accidents associated with consumer products. Of the total, over 100,000 persons are permanently disabled while 30,000 lose their lives. The annual cost of product-related injuries in the United States exceeds $5.5 billion. The commission noted that industry attempts at self-regulation of product safety were generally ineffective while federal and state product safety legislation focused only on specific hazards in narrow product categories. A strong recommendation was made for a more comprehensive consumer product safety law.

The Consumer Product Safety Act (1972) addressed the problems cited by the commission and initiated a new era in marketing legislation.[27] The act is intended to (1) protect consumers from unreasonable risks of injury which result from unsafe consumer products; (2) aid consumers in evaluating product safety; and (3) develop uniform product safety standards to minimize conflicting state and local regulations. An independent regulatory agency, the Consumer Product Safety Commission, is also created by the act. A central function of this commission is the acquisition and dissemination of information which links injuries to specific products. Importantly, the commission has the power to prescribe mandatory safety standards for virtually all consumer products that are not already covered by specific safety legislation.

Information on hazardous products is secured from the commission's National Electronic Injury Surveillance System (NEISS), a computer-based network that monitors over 100 hospital emergency rooms across the country. Data gathered by the system are used to produce a Product Hazard Index. Products are ranked according to (1) the age of the injured, (2) the frequency of the type of accident, and (3) the severity of the injury. The ten most hazardous products appear in table 4-2. While these products are likely candidates for early attention by the commission, a high ranking on the index does not mean that an item will be banned or be the subject of a product safety rule. Critics charge that the NEISS figures have a built-in bias against widely used products.[28]

---

[26]National Commission on Product Safety, "Perspective on Product Safety," in Aaker and Day, *Consumerism,* pp. 321–333.

[27]Walter Jensen, Jr., Edward M. Mazze, and Duke Nordlinger Stern, "The Consumer Product Safety Act: A Special Case in Consumerism," *Journal of Marketing,* 37 (October 1973), pp. 68–71.

[28]Paul Busch, "A Review and Critical Evaluation of the Consumer Product Safety Commission: Marketing Management Implications," *Journal of Marketing* 40 (October 1976), pp. 41–49.

TABLE 4–2 THE TEN MOST HAZARDOUS PRODUCTS

Rank	Product Description
1	Bicycles and bicycle equipment
2	Stairs, ramps, landings (indoors and outdoors)
3	Doors, other than glass doors
4	Cleaning agents
5	Tables, nonglass
6	Beds (including springs and frames)
7	Football, activity-related equipment and apparel
8	Swings, slides, seesaws, playground climbing equipment
9	Liquid fuels, kindling
10	Architectural glass

SOURCE. *Consumer Product Safety Commission Annual Report,* Washington, D.C., July 1, 1973–June 30, 1974, p. 11.

The first mandatory safety standards proposed by the Consumer Product Safety Commission affect the swimming pool slide market.[29] The commission initiated the development of a safety standard for the slides after a number of severe injuries had been reported. Consumers and an industry trade association participated in the development process. The commission is proposing specifications for construction along with the provision that permanent warning labels be placed on the swimming pool slides to show graphically the potential injury if the warnings are ignored.

When the Consumer Product Safety Act is added to other, more narrowly focused, consumer protection laws, the growing interest of the government in product safety becomes apparent. Other representative consumer protection laws include:

- Several amendments to the Federal Hazardous Substances Act to ban the sale of toys and other products intended for use by children if they present an electrical, mechanical, or thermal hazard (1966 and 1969).

- An amendment to the Flammable Fabrics Act (1967) to expand consumer protection against flammable fabrics used in draperies, curtains, and rugs.

---

[29]"Proposed Safety Standards and Warning Labels for Swimming Pool Slides," 39, *Federal Register* 42562 (September 15, 1975), see "Legal Developments in Marketing" section, *Journal of Marketing*, 40 (April 1976), pp. 87–88.

- The Poison Prevention Packaging Act of 1970, which provides that the Secretary of Health, Education, and Welfare "may establish . . . by regulation, standards for the special packaging of any household substance if he finds that . . . the degree or nature of the hazard to children in the availability of such substance, by reason of its packaging, is such that special packaging is required to protect children from serious injury or serious illness resulting from handling, using or ingesting such substance."[30]

- A law requiring the secretary of transportation to establish minimum federal safety standards for the transportation of gas and for pipeline facilities (1968). This legislation grew out of Ralph Nader's exposure of the safety hazard of gas pipelines.

When compared with the consumer protection laws of the past, the Consumer Product Safety Act not only possesses more effective administrative and legal sanctions but also broadens the application of safety standards to nearly all consumer products. Thus, the changing legal environment is forcing manufacturers to take greater responsibility for the products that they make and sell.

A number of complex questions emerge when considering the nature and degree of product hazards.

1. Is there a causal relationship between the product and the injury?

2. If a product is banned, what is the effect of this loss of consumer choice?

3. Do consumers assume the risk voluntarily or involuntarily?

4. What are the costs to industry and consumers of a proposed change in a product?[31]

For some products, minor adjustments can be made to improve the safety of the item at little or no cost to producers or consumers, while in other cases the required changes may be costly, technologically infeasible, or ineffective. To illustrate, injuries could be reduced by removing a jagged edge from a toy, but little can be done to improve the safety of a skateboard. Such cases raise a number of challenging liability questions. Product liability suits have grown 2,000% in the last 30 years and now total over 1.0 million per year.[32]

PRODUCT LIABILITY

When is a manufacturer liable for product defects or product failures? Since product liability has entered the domain of the marketing decision maker, let's examine this question carefully. A firm's liability for defects or failure to perform

---

[30]Public Law 91-601, 91st Congress, S.2162, December 30, 1970, p. 1.
[31]Robert T. Gray, "Washington's New Little Giant," *Nation's Business*, September 1973, p. 21, reported in Busch, "The Consumer Product Safety Commission," p. 43.
[32]Ibid., p. 45.

may be based on any of several legal grounds.[33] If an injury grows out of the use of a product, the injured party may sue the seller, alleging that the latter's negligence in the design or production of the product or in inadequate instructions concerning its use led directly to the injury. In the past, an injured claimant faced formidable barriers in seeking recovery on this basis. Proving a manufacturer's negligence often created problems.

But a new development in product liability law—the concept of strict liability—eliminates some of the barriers and makes the seller much more vulnerable than before to legal attack.[34] This concept provides that a manufacturer may be held responsible for injury caused by a defective product even though all possible care has been exercised in its production and sale. The consumer must prove only that the product was defective when it left the seller's hands. Proof of negligence is not required. The strict liability doctrine embodies a belief by the courts that the seller is better able to bear the risk of loss (for example, through insurance coverage) than is the injured consumer.[35] Adverse implications of the strict liability doctrine for the manufacturer are enormous.

Critics of the doctrine argue that the strict liability concept renders the seller almost defenseless in many jurisdictions. The seller must counter with proof that the product was misused, had no defect, or that the injury in no way related to the defect. The wealth of information required by the Consumer Product Safety Act may pose additional problems for manufacturers. The availability of data gathered by the government will likely enhance the injured consumer's case.[36]

Consumer Protection Perspective

Lynn Loudenback and John Goebel argue that this legal trend points up the need for a careful assessment of consumer needs both before and after the sale.[37] Indeed, the marketing concept applies to the product-use period. Others emphasize the importance of a periodic safety audit and a marketing management program that includes a consumer protection perspective in product planning, promotion, and distribution. Warranties influence consumer postpurchase satisfaction and constitute another sensitive area that creates problems as well as opportunities for the marketing manager.

PRODUCT WARRANTIES

A warranty is a written guarantee of a product's integrity and the manufacturer's responsibility for repairing or replacing defective parts. Far from reassuring consumers as to product reliability, product warranties are often sources of concern to

---

[33]For another discussion, see William L. Trombetta and Timothy L. Wilson, "Foreseeability of Misuse and Abnormal Use of Products by the Consumer," *Journal of Marketing*, 39 (July 1975), pp. 48–55.

[34]Lynn J. Loudenback and John W. Goebel, "Marketing in the Age of Strict Liability," *Journal of Marketing*, 38 (January 1974), pp. 62–66.

[35]David L. Rados, "Product Liability: Tougher Ground Rules," *Harvard Business Review*, 47 (July-August 1969), pp. 144–152.

[36]Loudenback and Goebel, "Strict Liability," pp. 62–66.

[37]Ibid., pp. 62–66.

consumers and of conflict among them, retailers, and manufacturers. Retailers usually feel the brunt of consumer complaints about inadequate products and unsatisfactory warranty treatment. Some manufacturers feel that responsibility for warranty service should rest with the retailer as an incentive to provide satisfactory installation or repair of products (especially appliances).[38] Retailers, in turn, feel that the warranty burden should rest with the manufacturer whose promotion may have induced the consumer to buy the product in the first place.

Pointing up the consumer's problem with warranties, a representative of the Consumer's Union argues that there is a "problem of misrepresentation as to what the guarantee is all about. 'Lifetime guarantee,' 'unconditional guarantee,' 'fully guaranteed' and just plain 'guaranteed' are words skillfully used by manufacturers and retailers as part of the sales pitch. If at the point of sale, the consumer makes a genuine effort to cut through the verbiage to see what is being guaranteed, more often than not he is confronted with a legal document which he does not—and cannot be expected to—fully comprehend. Moreover, any written guarantee is extended to him on a take-it-or-leave-it basis. There is . . .no negotiation over the terms of the guarantee."[39] This is a consumer advocate's indictment of warranties. What are the consumers', manufacturers', and retailers' points of view?

Consumers   They complain about:

- Faulty products with parts that break and fail prematurely.

- Unreasonable delays in repairs by retailers or manufacturers.

- The "problem" dealers who are supposed to make repairs under warranties but cannot because they have moved, are out of business, or no longer carry the warranted brand.

- Exorbitant labor charges where the warranty covers parts but requires the buyer to absorb labor charges.

- Manufacturers failing to respond satisfactorily to complaints about product quality.

Manufacturers   They claim that:

- They tend to recall defective goods.

- They are handicapped by a shortage of qualified technicians to repair products.

- Consumers are often the source of the problem through their failure to read instructions.

- Part of the problem is the dealer who carries insufficient repair parts because of handling more than one manufacturer's line of products.

---

[38]See U.S. Congress, Senate, Consumer Subcommittee on Commerce, *Hearings on Consumer Products Guaranty Act*, 91st Congress, 2nd sess.
[39]Ibid., p. 256.

- Competition has forced manufacturers to produce more elaborate products with fancier features, and this product complexity has enlarged the problem.

Retailers They argue that:

- It is difficult to hire and keep good repair personnel.
- There is inadequate quality control at the manufacturer's level.
- Fussy customers—many of whom have not read operating instructions— require unnecessary service calls.
- Customers exacerbate the problem by abusing the warranted products.
- Too much of the financial burden of the warranty rests with the retailer.[40]

Magnuson-Moss Warranty Bill

The Magnuson-Moss Warranty Bill—Federal Trade Commission Improvement Act (1975) is designed to correct some of these alleged inequities.[41] First, the act requires that sellers make guarantees available to buyers prior to purchase, and it empowers the F.T.C. to specify the manner and form in which guarantees may be used in promotional material. Second, the warranty must utilize simple language and disclose who is the warrantor, what products or parts are covered (and excluded) by the warranty, what the warrantor is obliged to do in the event of a product defect (and who pays to have it repaired), how long the warranty applies, and what are the obligations of the buyer. The law also provides consumer remedies for violation of guarantee or service contract obligations.

Enforcement Complex

The implications of such laws are enormous. They open up vastly more business transactions to governmental scrutiny than was true heretofore. The same situation exists with other recent consumer legislation, such as the Consumer Product Safety Act. In previous years most legislation regulating business conduct either affected transactions between firms or, if between firm and customer, it covered actions affecting consumers as a class and not as individuals. An example of the first class of legislation is the Robinson-Patman Act, which prevents price discrimination in transactions between businesses; the Pure Food and Drug Act, protecting all consumers from adulterated food products, characterizes the second type of legislation. Even in these cases, enforcement of legislation is profoundly complex. Consider the millions of transactions that are subject to these laws' provisions. No one pretends that enforcement is complete. The staffs available for enforcement are hopelessly inadequate to monitor the transactions and relationships that might result in violations of the laws. Now imagine the

---

[40]Federal Trade Commission, *Report of the Task Force on Appliance Warranties and Service,* January 1968, reprinted in Aaker and Day *Consumerism,* 1st ed. (1971), pp. 259–275.

[41]Laurence P. Feldman, "New Legislation and the Prospects for Real Warranty Reform," *Journal of Marketing,* 40 (July 1976), pp. 41–47.

complexity of policing laws that give *individual consumers* redress for alleged mishandling of warranties whose number runs into the tens or hundreds of millions each year!

Corporate Response

The pressure for further governmental action to improve warranty protection will probably continue unless voluntary action by manufacturers and distributors blunts the need for corrective measures. The Whirlpool Corporation has introduced innovations that alleviate two of the consumers' problems with warranties.[42] First, it has replaced the typically forbidding warranty, couched in "legalese," with a standard letter to the customer that spells out the warranty's terms simply and succinctly, as shown in figure 4-1. Second, it has buttressed the improved warranty with the installation of a "cool line," which permits giving the customer information about the nearest Whirlpool service source or, alternatively, provides necessary technical information. In the event of a serious breakdown, the company, in rare instances, may respond by dispatching a field service representative to help the customer.

Whirlpool's simplification of the warranty triggered a trend among white goods manufacturers. A majority of major appliance manufacturers have adopted simpler and more comprehensive warranties.[43] The new guarantees tend to have several features in common: They are shorter than the older versions, more simply written—freer of "legalese"—and more prominently featured. Rather than being buried in fine print on the back page of the owner's manual, the guarantee now appears up front, and one's attention is drawn to it

A CONCLUDING NOTE

Product policy poses significant challenges for the marketing manager in contemporary society. The growing recognition of the external costs of production and consumption, coupled with the increasing sensitivity to the depletion of vital natural resources, add a new dimension to product planning. Insights into the complexity of the process can be secured by examining a product's entire economic life cycle. This perspective illustrates the environmental trade-offs that evolve in the formation, production, consumption, and waste or recycling of a product. Clearly, product planning does not end with an item's sale, but must extend to the product-use period.

Discussion Questions

1. Some people argue that a continued expansion of output will create intolerable ecological problems. If so, do marketers perform a social disservice by encouraging more purchases (hence more output)? Defend your position.

---

[42]Stephen E. Upton, "The Use of Product Warranties and Guarantees as a Marketing Tool" (Address to the American Marketing Association, Cleveland, Ohio, December 11, 1969, and reprinted in Aaker and Day *Consumerism,* 1st ed., pp. 277–282.
[43]Opinion of Mr. Sheldon Lee, Marketing Research Department, Whirlpool Corporation, who has studied the hard-goods industry's warranties.

Figure 4-1 Sample Warranty Letter

Whirlpool
CORPORATION

Administrative Center

BENTON HARBOR, MICHIGAN 49022 • AREA CODE 616 925-0651

Dear Customer:

Good performance. That's what this letter is all about.

We know that you expect good performance from your Whirlpool dryer, and we aim to see that you get it. Here's how its performance is protected.

YOUR WARRANTY

> During your first year of ownership, all parts of the appliance (except light bulbs) which we find are defective in materials or workmanship will be repaired or replaced by Whirlpool free of charge, and we will pay any labor charges.
>
> During the second year, we will continue to assume the same responsibility as stated above, except you pay any labor charges.
>
> This protection is yours as the original purchaser for your home use, and requires that all service be performed by a service organization authorized to service Whirlpool products. Naturally, it doesn't cover damage by accident, misuse, fire, flood or acts of God. But it does cover you wherever you live in the United States. . .even if you move.

Now about servicing. Let's face it. Sometimes even the best products need service. So, if that's ever true of your Whirlpool dryer, there is a way to get action fast. Just call your servicing Whirlpool dealer or a Whirlpool Tech-Care agent. He is trained to make whatever's wrong right. We do not pay for service calls that only involve instructing you on how to use your new Whirlpool appliance.

On the other hand, we do offer a unique telephone information and assistance service. If you have any questions about operating, maintaining or servicing any Whirlpool appliance, just dial (800) 253-1301*. Free. From anywhere in the continental United States. We'll give you, day or night, the name and number of the authorized Whirlpool Tech-Care serviceman nearest your home.

We suggest you keep this letter with your sales slip and Operating Instructions. It's nice to know you'll have protection, even though you may never need it.

Sincerely,

WHIRLPOOL CORPORATION

* In Michigan (800) 632-2243
AD

From address by S. E. Upton to the American Marketing Association, Cleveland, Ohio, Dec. 11, 1969. Reprinted in Aaker and Day, *Consumerism,* p. 279, with permission of Macmillan Publishing Co., Inc.

2. Think of a product that is periodically modified. Do these changes represent planned obsolescence? Are the changes wasteful? Deceptive?

3. Check with a local drugstore on the number of toothpaste brands it carries. Are there too many, in your opinion? What criteria do you use in

making this judgment? Do a large number of available brands for a product represent waste? Explain.

4. The package is a source of information for consumer decision-making. Does more and more information benefit or hinder decision-making? Explain.

5. Define the concept of strict liability.

6. How extensive should be the list of products protected by safety legislation? What criteria do you suggest using in establishing such a list?

7. The consumer often feels victimized by the inability to get warranty satisfaction from the retail dealer or manufacturer. Outline the key provisions of the Magnuson-Moss Warranty Bill. Why are such consumer protection measures often difficult to enforce?

Suggested Exercise: Class or Small Group Assignment

The pollution control expenditures of federal, state, and local governments must come either from higher taxes or from curtailment of other government programs. Likewise, consumers will bear the very large outlays for auto emission control. The food processing, pulp and paper, chemical, and primary metals industries will be particularly affected by controls, whereas light industries that deposit few residuals in the environment will face few changes. What impact will such pollution control programs have on the marketing system?

Chapter Overview

FIVE
The Ethical and Legal Dimensions of Promotion

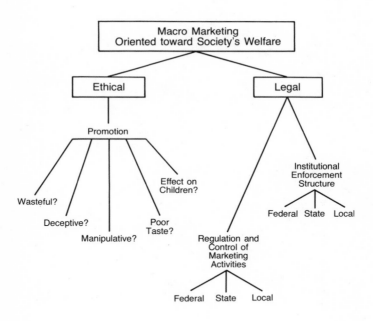

Criticism of advertising takes several forms. The charges often lodged against it are outlined in the figure above. Are they valid? In this chapter, we examine these charges and selected remedies used by the F.T.C. in regulating advertising. Another form of promotion—personal selling—is likewise considered from an ethical and legal perspective.

FIVE

The Ethical and Legal Dimensions of Promotion

Throughout history, promotional practices—advertising and personal selling—have been criticized by the public. What are the charges? Advertising is alleged to be manipulative. It "sweet talks" us into buying things that we do not want or, worse, that are bad for us. It creates desires where none existed before. It prods us to covet material possessions and feel cheated when denied them. As for salespeople, Plato comments that ". . . in well-ordered states they are commonly those who are the weakest in bodily strength and therefore of little use for any other purpose . . ."[1] Despite the abundance of criticism aimed at promotion, advertising and personal selling continue to play a pivotal role in the United States' economic system.

In chapter 3 we considered the aggregate performance of advertising from several perspectives, with emphasis given to its effect on competition. In this chapter, we explore the ethical and legal dimensions of advertising and other selling practices. Advertising is not only of concern to the marketing manager, but is also a topic commanding public interest.

THE CHARGES AGAINST ADVERTISING

Advertising provides a channel of communication to a potential market. Critics contend that the messages passing through this channel are deceptive, distorted, manipulative, redundant, and often in poor taste. When the receiver of the message is a child, the criticism is even more pronounced. Others argue (as we discussed in chapter 3) that heavy advertising generates strong brand loyalty that tends to create barriers to potential competitors, leading to less competition and higher prices.

Is advertising wasteful? Does it perform an informative role or a deceptive one? Can the sheer "power" of advertising manipulate a buyer into making a decision against his or her will? Let's examine these charges.

ADVERTISING IS WASTEFUL

Borden distinguishes two types of waste in advertising. First is the inefficiency in its use and application. The other stems from the duplication resulting from the competitive process. This is the waste that critics point to with disfavor. Advertising is seen as an unnecessary annoyance. In addition to manipulating pliable customers, it uses resources that might be utilized more productively. It is wasteful by being duplicative. Not only does it pound messages into our brain with maddening persistency but it also confuses us by presenting counterclaims for an array of competitive products that are almost identical. Why pay for an activity that warps the consumer's judgment and is of doubtful utility? The share of the retail price represented by advertising for many products is substantial. This is waste on a grand scale. So run the charges.

---

[1]Plato, "The Republic," in *The Works of Plato,* trans. B. Jowett (New York: Tudor Publishing, 1937), p. 64, cited in Robert L. Steiner, "The Prejudice Against Marketing," *Journal of Marketing*, 40 (July 1976), p. 2.

A Counterview

What is the defense? First, Neil Borden points out that waste is not confined to advertising. Producers incur other marketing costs to attract customers. They differentiate their products, extend credit, and provide delivery service to induce the purchase of their products rather than the competitors'.[2] Second, much advertising is informational. In 1970, of the $12 billion spent on newspaper and magazine advertising, more than one-half was invested in local advertisements—classified and retail.[3] A great deal of this kind of promotion represents reporting of sales and specials, and the announcement of merchandise availability rather than attempts to persuade. Third, advertising largely supports the media that carry its messages. Fritz Machlup, a leading economist, estimates that advertising covers 60% of the cost of publishing periodicals, 70% of newspapers, and 100% of radio and television.[4] Without this financial support, consumers of the media would be required to make up the loss of revenue either by being charged more or by being taxed (if radio and television were to become supported by the government, as they are in the United Kingdom). However, from an economic point of view, direct government subsidy of radio and television may be a more efficient way to pay for the operation of these media. But the gain in economic efficiency must be balanced against the possible loss of freedom that could accompany government sponsorship of broadcasting. Critics of the media might respond to this point by arguing that threatened government interference poses no more serious threat to freedom of expression than does the current commercial system, which finds large corporations financing the programming.

Finally, waste is inevitable in a competitive system. Indeed, waste and duplication are the prices an economy pays to maintain a free market system. Those who attack the waste of competition are really attacking the competitive process itself.

The Verdict

The foregoing is a summary of the charges of wasteful advertising and a rebuttal. To evaluate the allegation of waste requires more detailed information than we now have. The Machlup findings represent rough estimates. A better evaluation of the "wastes" of advertising requires more precise calculations. These would cover not only the cost of advertising, net such trade-offs as the financial support of media, but also the nonmedia costs of advertising. These need to be included in the total to get a true evaluation of the resources devoted to advertising. It also requires a determination of the merits of partially financing the media with advertising revenue. Could it be done more effectively some other way? Part of the media's costs now represents costs of soliciting the revenues that are used to help support the media. Perhaps this is a waste that some other form of financial support could avoid. There may be other drawbacks to the use of advertising

---

[2]Neil H. Borden, *The Economic Effects of Advertising* (Chicago: Richard D. Irwin, 1942), p. 297.

[3]Reported in Francesco M. Nicosia, *Advertising, Management, and Society: A Business Point of View* (New York: McGraw-Hill, 1974), p. 212.

[4]Reported in Jules Backman, *Advertising and Competition* (New York: New York University Press, 1967), p. 31.

revenue to support the media—for example, possible editorial interference. Better data would also measure more closely the content and source of advertising to determine more accurately how much is informative and how much is persuasive. Finally, whoever evaluates the alleged waste of advertising must determine whether the maintenance of a competitive system is worth the price and whether competition can flourish with a lower level of advertising.

WHAT IS DECEPTIVE ADVERTISING?

A thorough examination of other charges against advertising must begin with a definition of "deceptive advertising." Interestingly, a definition cannot be identified which satisfies all the interested publics. While the Federal Trade Commission (F.T.C.) has been involved in the regulation of advertising since 1914, David Gardner notes that "it is not clear that the F.T.C. or anyone else has an adequate understanding of deceptive advertising that is based on a sound conceptual model and backed with good research studies."[5] In general, the F.T.C. has held that deception occurs when a material fact is presented falsely, is misleading, or is ambiguous. Since this definition has evolved on a case-by-case basis, a comprehensive classification of deception in advertising does not exist.[6]

Gardner proposes the following definition:

> If an advertisement (or advertising campaign) leaves the consumer with an impression(s) and/or belief(s) that is (a) different from what would normally be expected if the consumer had reasonable knowledge, and (b) factually untrue or potentially misleading, then deception is said to exist.[7]

Three categories of deception are included within this definition:

- *Unconscionable Lie*—a completely false claim.

- *Claim-Fact Discrepancy*—some *qualification* must be placed upon the claim for it to be properly understood and evaluated. *Example*: three out of five doctors recommend X. Qualifications needed: what types of doctors, and how were they surveyed?

- *Claim-Belief Interaction*—an advertisement "that interacts with the accumulated attitudes and beliefs of the consumer in such a manner as to create a deceptive belief or attitude about the product without making either explicit or implied deceptive claims."[8] *Example*: Suppose a detergent marketer discovered that adding a pine scent to some detergents resulted in a significant number of housewives attributing more cleaning power to pine-scented detergents. The simple statement that "Brand X has a pine

---

[5]David M. Gardner, "Deception in Advertising: A Conceptual Approach," *Journal of Marketing*, 39 (January 1975), p. 40.

[6]Ibid.

[7]Ibid., p. 42; see also Ivan L. Preston, "A Comment on 'Defining Misleading Advertising' and 'Deception in Advertising,'" *Journal of Marketing*, 40 (July 1976), pp. 54–57; and the following articles in the same issue: Jacob Jacoby, "A Reply," pp. 57–58, and David M. Gardner, "A Reply," pp. 58–59.

[8]Gardner, "Deception in Advertising," p. 42.

scent'' would be deceptive, even though no claims about increased cleaning power were made.[9]

This classification scheme may raise questions in your mind, especially the third category, claim-belief interaction. The focus here is on how consumers respond to particular advertisements. While many consumers are confident that they can recognize deception in advertising, this understanding must be translated into legal terms. It is this translation that poses problems for advertisers and regulators.

ADVERTISING DISTORTS AND MANIPULATES

"Critics of our society have arisen who feel that advertising has gone far beyond the status of being a neutral device for selling and has become a threat to the free, judging personality of the American citizen. Some claim, for instance, that advertisers can make the American people buy and think anything they wish. It is further asserted that advertisers can subvert the process of individual judgment and reduce the individual to the status of a pawn manipulated by the forces of mass communication."[10]

This quotation summarizes neatly one of the principal charges leveled at advertising—that it molds and manipulates the minds of individuals, inducing them to buy products that they neither need nor desire.

Critics point to the power that large advertisers possess. Many firms have the financial capacity to achieve brand awareness for a new product in a matter of days. Other critics center on the highly sophisticated techniques that are available to large advertisers for developing, testing, and fine-tuning advertising campaigns. Some observers believe that these sophisticated tools increase even further the advertiser's ability to manipulate the consumer. Messages that say "just the right thing" can be developed and efficiently delivered to each segment of the market. Such messages shape and control the mind of the consumer.

The Debate

It is difficult to find concrete evidence to support this charge. Critics point to the repetitive character of much advertising and its increasing total volume as evidence that advertising perverts rational thought processes in a way that will benefit the advertiser. The belief that advertising manipulates minds is a subjective judgment. Interestingly, critics who level this charge tend to fear the consequences on *others*. They are presumably immune to the manipulation.[11]

Defense against the charge takes at least two forms: that attempts at persuasion often fail and that advertising is not unique in its propensity to persuade. The first says that we need not fear the manipulation charge because advertising may not work; the second tells us not to worry because life is filled with embellishment, and advertising is only one among many creators of distortion.

---

[9]Ibid., p. 42.

[10]John Dollard, "Fear of Advertising," in *The Role of Advertising*, ed. C.H. Sandage and Vernon Fryburger (Homewood, Ill.: Richard D. Irwin, 1960), p. 307.

[11]One senses this, for example, in various works of J.K. Galbraith and Vance Packard, which criticize advertising.

Advertising Often Fails   John Dollard uses the first approach to refute the charge of advertising's power to distort and manipulate.[12] The delusional nature of the charge is evidenced, he says, by the economists' assertion that advertising is wasteful. The waste stems from its ineffectiveness. If it is ineffective, how can it, at the same time, be manipulative?

Several pieces of evidence defuse the charge of manipulation. First is the failure of the Army's orientation program, during World War II, to increase soldiers' motivation to fight. Despite the efforts of skilled advertising specialists, the results were indifferent. An evaluation of the program found that "information was increased but basic attitudes were left relatively unaffected."[13]

Attempts by Chinese Communists to brainwash American soldiers and civilians in the 1950s also point up the limits of persuasion. When subjected to threats of death while under complete dominance of their masters, the prisoners apparently succumbed to attempts to indoctrinate them with Communist ideology. However, the effect of the propaganda generally evaporated when control disappeared. Dollard asks, "How can advertising in a free society, not controlling the actual conditions of life produce the robotized personality which is feared?"[14]

Two other facts emphasize the absence of advertising's invincibility as a manipulative force. First is the failure of so many advertising campaigns. History records countless ad programs which, for any number of reasons, were colossal flops. Hence the critics' claim of waste might be appropriate, but not the charge of manipulation. The second fact diminishing advertising's manipulative power is the individual's skepticism and ability to "turn off" advertising messages. Studies of recall often indicate a weak ability to remember even the most basic elements of ad messages. Skepticism arises out of the consumer's continual exposure to competitive claims for products and the wariness which, for the experienced consumer, becomes an automatic response to the huckster's exaggerations.

A factor said to contribute to advertising's weakened grip on consumers is their increased sophistication.[15] Clarence E. Eldridge sees this development reducing brand preference, which partly depends upon effective promotion. Today's better educated and more knowledgeable consumers are less inclined to "buy" advertised claims. A study by the American Association of Advertising Agencies showed that "consumers consciously react" to only 15% of the ads to which they are exposed.[16] Out of that 15%, one-third were considered objectionable.

Poets Distort   Theodore Levitt enlists the second argument—that advertising is not alone in its use of distortion. But first he defends its use. He claims that

---

[12]This section summarizes Dollard's views in "Fear of Advertising," pp. 312–314.

[13]Ibid., p. 312.

[14]Ibid., p. 313.

[15]For this view, see a report of a speech by Clarence E. Eldridge in E. B. Weiss, "Advertising's Crisis of Confidence," in *Consumerism: Search for the Consumer Interest,* 1st ed., ed. David A. Aaker and George S. Day (New York: The Free Press, 1971), p. 124.

[16]Weiss, ibid., p. 125.

"embellishment and distortion are among advertising's legitimate and socially desirable purposes."[17] Wrongdoing "consists only of falsification with larcenous intent."[18]

Who else distorts? The poet, for one. Poetry tries to create illusions and not necessarily accurate descriptions to influence the readers' perceptions. "Keats does not offer a truthful engineering description of his Grecian urn."[19] But what about motives? Doesn't the advertiser exhibit a base motive of earning a profit which is lower than the poet's or artist's purpose? It is true, Levitt says, that the ad writer seeks to earn dollars; but Michelangelo's purpose in painting the Sistine Chapel's ceiling was to "convert man's soul." The goal may be loftier but the result of his "embellishment" has more impact than the advertiser's feeble effort.

Compare the distortions of advertising with religion's embellishments.

If religion must be architectured, packaged, lyricized and musicized to attract and hold its audience. . . it is ridiculous to deny the legitimacy of more modest and similar embellishments to the world of commerce.[20]

Levitt continues: In many of our endeavors, we seek to achieve something beyond reality. We are immersed in reality. We don't need more of it. Advertising goes outside of reality by promising us things that we do not have. The things may not measure up to the claims made for them, but this is true with many aspects of life. Life, Levitt concludes, would be pretty dull without distortion and embellishment.

Do the venal characteristics attributed to advertising date to the beginning of large-scale advertising, or do they precede it? Dollard claims that the advertising agency is a kind of "front man" absorbing the blows formerly directed at the producer-seller. "Scorn of the unctuous tradesman beaming over his woolens may have been transferred to the smiling people of Advertisingland."

He continues:

[In] the world of the primary or face-to-face group man showed all the traits, good and bad, that he shows now when confronted by mass communication. Suggestion was powerfully used in the face-to-face group. Gossip had its effect in controlling behavior. "Facts" were what the community created them to be. The salesman or the huckster distorted his personality to please his customer. Artificial properties were attributed to objects by sales arguments in the direct buying situation. Status pressures influenced buying choices. Word-of-mouth artificially glamourized some objects and artificially damaged others. Shrewd, if unprofessional calculation of unconscious motives influenced the sales transaction. . . .The manias and crazes reported for simple people during the Middle Ages were not produced by advertising but by old-fashioned "word-of-mouth." All of the fallibility of human judgmental operations, and the accessibility of the human mind to influence, which is noticed today in the case of advertising,

---

[17]Theodore Levitt, "Morality (?) of Advertising," *Harvard Business Review*, 48 (July 1970), pp. 84–92.
[18]Ibid., p. 85.
[19]Ibid., p. 85.
[20]Ibid., p. 90.

was known in the simpler world of face-to-face relations. Advertising has not made man venal and lack of it will not make him the individual judgmental machine which social philosophers wish he were.[21]

The Verdict: You Decide
We cannot summarize all of the accusations and defenses concerning the alleged ability of advertising to manipulate minds and distort the truth. The argument has raged for a long time and many people have hurled the charges, just as many advocates have risen to advertising's defense. Represented here are samples of two positions.

As with many arguments, the truth may lie somewhere between the two extreme positions. Both critics and defenders of advertising seem to agree on one thing—that advertising engages in distortion and embellishment. The critic condemns this behavior as being injurious to the consumer. The justifier argues that distortion may take the form of exaggeration—of puffery—but the sovereignty and good sense of the consumer will not permit outright falsity of claims. Consumers can defend themselves by refusing to repurchase goods that sellers misrepresent to them. Knowledge of this fact is enough to keep most advertisers honest. Furthermore, advertisers have no monopoly on the use of embellishment. Politicians thrive on it; artists of all kinds require it; storytellers depend on it to engage the listener's interest. Embellishment attracts attention. It arrests the eye and ear. That is its purpose. Is it more evil for an advertiser than others to use it? The defender of advertising says no; the critic says yes. The matter of intent and purpose may be a key factor here. The critic sees embellishment being used for monetary gain by an advertiser; the advertiser, however, fails to see that others engaging in it have any goal in mind other than personal gain.

Whether advertising achieves its purposes may indicate whether or not it manipulates people's minds. The charge that it manipulates lacks empirical verification. It is presumed that *all* advertising expenditure can't be wasted! And if, in fact, it succeeds, the advertiser wins patronage that he or she otherwise would have foregone. Whether sales are won through "manipulation" or merely from persuasion is academic. The power of the ad message presumably convinces buyers to purchase a product or service. Despite disclaimers that ad campaigns and brainwashing attempts fail, continuing expenditures on advertising offer evidence that advertisers *believe* advertising can persuade. And ample evidence exists showing the impact on sales of effective advertising campaigns. So the persuasive power of some advertising probably cannot be denied.

The Social Impact
This leaves unanswered the crucial question of the social impact of this effort. The critic argues that this manipulation (persuasion) forces the purchase of unwanted goods and the creation of "false" values. The criticism fails to distinguish between the effect of advertising that counterbalances the impact of competitors' advertising from that which attracts purchases of a class of products. In practice, the same advertising may accomplish both purposes; still, one must distinguish intent from effect of the advertising. If advertiser A "manipulates" a consumer to buy A's

---

[21]Dollard, "Fear of Advertising," pp. 310–311. Reprinted with permission of the publisher.

product rather than B's, it is hard to see how the customer suffers unless A's product is inferior or the advertising was misleading. Presumably, the Federal Trade Commission can handle the latter problem, and the consumer can handle the former through his refusal to repurchase A's product. (Ignored here is the consumer's loss from having to pay for duplicative advertising, which is another issue.)

But advertising can have an effect other than the purchase of A's or B's product. It can make chrome-laden, power-packed, high-status automobiles more attractive than expenditures on housing, health care, education, or better nutrition. The importance of value judgments in this discussion cannot be overemphasized. To evaluate whether advertising's persuasive power has forced consumers to buy the "wrong" bundle of goods requires that one knows what is the "right" bundle. Preston argues that:

> Tastes stimulated by advertising—such as tastes for alcoholic drinks, automatic dishwashers and cavity-free teeth—are not, in general, more or less admirable than tastes cultivated by family training and "informal" social contact—such as tastes for education, racism, and sex.[22]

With the outlawing of advertising, what goods will consumers purchase? In the short run, they will continue to buy the available array of consumer goods and services, most of which, prior to the ban, were presumably advertised in varying degrees. In the long run, one is not certain how purchases might vary and, more importantly, what forces might influence consumer behavior. One is struck by the impression that many of advertising's critics would prefer to see people consume more goods and services that are now little advertised (such as cultural activities) or services traditionally offered by government bodies. It is not clear, however, how preferences for these goods and services would be developed in the absence of a persuasive tool like advertising. Evidence that these preferences are inherently derived is missing.

Thus, the debate might benefit from more thought being given by both sides to the implications of reducing or eliminating advertising. If it manipulates minds, how will its elimination affect behavior? If it doesn't manipulate, what is it about advertising that annoys so many of those exposed to it?

How Should Markets Operate?

There is a final aspect of this topic. Much of the debate between the business community and critics of marketing results from their divergent perceptions of how markets should operate.[23] To the critic, competition means an emphasis on price differences. The marketer emphasizes product differentiation. To the critics, a product performs a primary function; they see consumers' needs served by this primary function. Business people visualize secondary functions that products perform. They see an expanding horizon of needs that they can fill through product differentiation. Finally, the critics see information as data that help the

---

[22]Lee E. Preston, "Advertising Effects and Public Policy," mimeo. (Paper presented to American Marketing Association Conference, Denver, Colorado, August 28-30, 1968), p. 1.

[23]Raymond A. Bauer and Stephen A. Greyser, "The Dialogue That Never Happens," reprinted in Aaker and Day, *Consumerism*, 1st ed., pp. 59-73.

consumer make rational decisions within the context of products' performing primary functions and serving uncomplicated wants. The marketer views information as messages helping to sell products that satisfy a variety of consumer demands.

People have basic needs that they must fulfill to survive. But they also possess psychological needs that they may feel are as important as the physical ones. The psychological yearnings predated the first ad man or the original critic of business. The goals of social status and ego-gratification, and the search for aesthetically satisfying experiences fall outside of humanity's primal urges; however, this does not diminish their importance. Much of what we call product differentiation tries to satisfy these psychological wants. It takes the form both of product features and advertising appeals. Thus, material goods often serve to satisfy nonmaterial goals. The consumers, and not the critics, might better determine whether they require fulfillment of nonmaterial yearnings, and what form that fulfillment might take.

When one recognizes the variety of needs that people possess and the various ways of satisfying them, understanding advertising's function becomes easier. It does more than communicate facts. It can project an image of the product as well. This facet of advertising may aid the marketer by distinguishing, in the consumer's eyes, the advertised product from the competitors'. Furthermore, argue the defenders, advertising may also attribute characteristics in the product's user that gratify his or her nonmaterial needs. And this contributes to the user's perceived welfare. Who is to say whether the pleasure a woman feels from wearing a perfume advertised to lure men is any less intense than pleasure derived from a utilitarian pair of walking shoes. Each may get the job done. Are the walking shoes "good" because they are unadvertised and utilitarian, and the perfume "bad" because it is "frivolous" and the need for it was generated by the product's advertising? It may be that the consumer is better able to answer that question than either the businessman or his critic.

Many argue, however, that young consumers (children) are particularly vulnerable and can be easily manipulated by advertising. The effect of advertising on this consumer class thus requires separate analysis.

THE EFFECT OF TV ADVERTISING ON CHILDREN

Pre-teenage children constitute over a quarter of the United States population. Television advertising touches this segment daily. Research by Nielsen indicates that children aged 2 to 11 average nearly 24 hours of television viewing time each week.[24] Commercials comprise approximately 20% of total children's television content.[25] The pros and cons of advertising to this special audience provide fodder for a lively public debate. Table 5-1 summarizes the central issues in this debate.

---

[24]Reported in John A. Howard and James Hulbert, *Advertising and the Public Interest: A Staff Report to the Federal Trade Commission* (Chicago: Crain Communications Inc., 1973), p. 59.

[25]John R. Rossiter and Thomas S. Robertson, "Children's TV Commercials: Testing the Defenses," *Journal of Communications*, 24 (Autumn 1974), p. 137.

TABLE 5-1   ADVERTISING'S EFFECT ON CHILDREN: CLAIMS AND COUNTERCLAIMS

	Claim	Counterclaim
Personal	Children unable to cope with persuasive arguments Parents forced to deny children's requests. Children become salespeople. Children's characters warped by overemphasis on materialism.	Early exposure to advertising contributes to consumer socialization and other maturation processes
Products	Products advertised are unhealthy (too much sugar) too expensive, etc.	Products advertised meet health and safety standards.
Programs	Little attention to education and reinforcement of positive social behavior. Emphasis on high ratings only.	Advertising support is necessary to maintain the great number and variety of children's programs.
Volume	Too much TV advertising.	A restriction on commercial time would fall heavily on the small advertiser.

SOURCE. Adapted from Seymour Banks, "Public Policy on Ads to Children," *Journal of Advertising Research,* 15 (August 1975), pp. 7–12.

Dominant attention has been given to three alleged effects of advertising on children:

- the child is unable to handle persuasive arguments and is easily manipulated;

- the child becomes a surrogate salesperson in the household and intrafamily tension results;

- the child develops overly materialistic values and is more inclined toward nonrational choices in a quest for instant gratification.[26]

Persuasive Ability

Children differ in their response to advertising by age level. Scott Ward reports that older children (11 to 12 years old) exhibit more sophisticated reactions to television commercials than younger children, especially 5- to 7-year-olds.[27] Older children are conscious of both the purpose of advertising and the concept of sponsorship, while younger children show low awareness the concept of commercials and often envision them as part of the program. Likewise, younger

---

[26]Ibid., p. 137.
[27]Reported in Howard and Hulbert, *Advertising and The Public Interest: A Staff Report,* p. 62.

children are more likely than older ones to believe advertisements.[28] This is frequently offered as further evidence of the limited discriminatory powers of younger children.

Family Relations

Advertising encourages children to ask their parents for specific products. Critics argue that such requests may create family tension, particularly in low-income families where the requests must often be denied. Studies show that children's attempts to influence purchases vary with the child's age and with the particular product.[29] The frequency of these attempts decreases with age. Commercials for frequently purchased products (such as cereal) were identified by mothers as the most influential on children, and mothers were most likely to yield to requests for such products. Conclusive evidence does not exist on the relationship between children's requests for products and conflict within the family.[30] In fact, Seymour Banks argues that ". . .a spirited give-and-take within the household or even an occasional exchange of open hostile interactions between parent and child may actually facilitate the child's ability to cope with the realities of independent living . . ."[31]

Socialization

Socialization is the process by which an individual learns a role and the particular values and requirements for performing that role. Critics contend that advertising encourages materialism and fosters undesirable values. In response, Robertson counters that ". . .advertising only reflects the existing values of the society and does not create these values."[32]

Does advertising facilitate consumer socialization—learning to consume? Industry representatives suggest that learning how to make consumer decisions is a useful side effect of children's advertising. Parents play an important role in this learning process. Studies show that if young children (2 to 5 years old) have an advertisement explained to them, they are able to evaluate it. Without an explanation the child has difficulty separating the advertisement from the program and is more inclined to be disappointed when the product does not meet his or her expectations.[33] Advertising is not an independent means of socialization and thus

---

[28]Scott Ward, "Children's Reactions to Commercials," *Journal of Advertising Research*, 12 (April 1972), pp. 42–43.

[29]Scott Ward and Daniel Wackman, "Children's Purchase Influence Attempts and Parental Yielding," *Journal of Marketing Research*, 9 (August 1972), pp. 316–319; see also Thomas S. Robertson and John Rossiter, "Short-Run Advertising Effects on Children: A Field Study," *Journal of Marketing Research*, 13 (February 1976), pp. 68–70.

[30]Andre Caron and Scott Ward, "Gift Decisions by Kids and Parents," *Journal of Advertising Research*, 15 (August 1975), pp. 15–20.

[31]Cited by Thomas S. Robertson, "The Impact of Television Advertising on Children," in *New Consumerism: Selected Readings*, ed. William T. Kelley (Columbus, Ohio: Grid, 1973), p. 261.

[32]Ibid., p. 262.

[33]Research conducted by Donald R. Lehmann, reported in Howard and Hulbert, *Advertising and The Public Interest: A Staff Report*, p. 65.

A Ban on Candy TV Ads?

A public-interest organization, Action for Children's Television (ACT) charges that many candy commercials contain misleading information about candy nutrition and that advertised sweets can cause tooth decay. The organization contends that children under 12 years old lack the sophistication to realize that the claims are deceptive. The group has asked the Federal Trade Commission to bar television commercials aimed at selling candy to children. Previously, the activities of ACT have led to a reduction in the length of ads on children's television programs and a ban on selling by the hosts of such programs.

SOURCE: *Wall Street Journal*, April 7, 1977, p. 4.

its relative influence varies according to family and home environment. A child who has been deprived of close family ties and whose predominant companion is television may be unduly influenced by this medium.

A number of recommendations have been made concerning children's television advertising, ranging from a complete ban to a restriction on advertising during selected time periods such as Saturday mornings. Likewise, the broadcasting industry has developed a number of guidelines for the self-regulation of commercials directed to children. For example, the National Association of Broadcasters acts as a mandatory clearance unit for all toy commercials as well as those offering a premium to children. From 1970 to 1973, 13% of the commercials submitted to the Code Authority were rejected.[34]

Despite these efforts toward self-regulation, criticism continues unabated. A balanced perspective is needed. Critics tend to exaggerate advertising's effect on children, while marketers often underestimate the potential power of the medium. If advertising does have deleterious effects on children, what should be done? A staff report to the Federal Trade Commission recommends: "Research should be encouraged—wherever and whenever possible—by industry, government and the public on the effects of television and television advertising on children. Only with better knowledge can a sound foundation for better industry and public policy be developed.'"[35]

PUBLIC'S ATTITUDE TOWARD ADVERTISING

Until now this discussion has suffered from a defect common to most analyses of advertising's social impact. It has assumed widespread disenchantment with advertising, and strong public pressure to limit its use. A research study published in

---

[34]Seymour Banks, "Public Policy on Ads to Children," *Journal of Advertising Research*, 15 (August 1975), pp. 11–12.

[35]Howard and Hulbert, *Advertising and The Public Interest: A Staff Report,* p. 67.

1968 finally substituted fact for fiction by reporting on the attitudes toward advertising of a large cross section of adult Americans.[36] Asked how they felt about advertising, 41% of the 1,846 respondents gave answers favorable to it, 34% were "mixed," 14% were unfavorable, 8% were indifferent, and 3% made no response or gave unclassifiable answers.[37]

Summing up the study's findings, the authors concluded:

> Clearly the American public would be against the abolition of advertising or even its abolition in any medium. Overwhelmingly the public produces favorable comment more often than criticism. Not only do American readers and viewers find advertising informative to them, they also find it enjoyable. The attitude that says "advertising is a necessary evil in our particular economic system, it serves to sell goods, but it annoys me" is not the prevailing attitude of the public. Much more common is the woman who enjoys thumbing through the dress ads in her newspaper or magazine, or the family that chuckles at the humor in the TV commercial. To eliminate advertising would be to eliminate one of the pleasures, as well as one of the guides, of the American public.[38]

What are the attitudes toward advertising of a specific segment of the population, such as college students? Different trends emerged for this segment in a more recent study.[39] More than 80% of the students rated television advertising as highly annoying. A similar proportion felt that over one-half of all advertising insults their intelligence. Why the apparent discrepancy between the two samples? The researcher suggests that the differences in attitudes may simply reflect opposing value systems.

SUGGESTED REMEDIES

The heated public debate over advertising's effect on the consuming public has led to several suggested remedies. Some of the remedies focus on specific regulatory mechanisms; others take a more comprehensive look at advertising in society.

The section opens with a discussion of several new remedies that have been proposed by the Federal Trade Commission (F.T.C.). These go beyond the cease-and-desist order that the F.T.C. has relied upon in the past. Next, we examine a framework that has been proposed as a guide for self-regulation in the advertising industry.

Corrective Advertising

In 1970, the F.T.C. began to use "corrective advertising" as a remedy to protect the consumer from unfair and deceptive advertising.[40] The basic purpose of the

---

[36]Raymond A. Bauer and Stephen A. Greyser, *Advertising in America: The Consumer View* (Boston: Division of Research Graduate School of Business Administration, Harvard University, 1968).

[37]Ibid., p. 91.

[38]Ibid., p. xi. Reprinted with permission.

[39]Thomas F. Haller, "What Students Think of Advertising," *Journal of Advertising Research*, 14 (February 1974), pp. 33–43.

policy is to correct former advertising copy that may have misled the consumer through questionable claims.

To illustrate, the F.T.C. alleges that Warner-Lambert falsely represented Listerine's ability to prevent colds through the use of the statement "Kills Germs by Millions on Contact." The cease-and-desist order requires the firm to include a corrective message in all Listerine advertising until it has expended an amount equal to its average annual Listerine budget for the ten-year period of April 1962 to March 1972—an estimated $10 million. The advertising must include this corrective message: "Contrary to prior advertising, Listerine will not prevent colds or sore throats or lessen their severity." A court battle is predicted.[41]

Robert Dyer and Philip Kuehl note that corrective advertising policies should be recognized as a complex communication system that includes: (1) message content factors, (2) media selection variables, and (3) consumer response characteristics.[42] Because of the intricate nature of this communication mix, "FTC decisions can result in penalties to the respondent firm beyond appropriate statutory limitations."[43] A more complete understanding of the consumer response characteristics is needed for effective and nonpunitive corrective advertising orders.

Substantiation of Claims

Since 1971, the F.T.C. has embarked upon a policy that requires substantiation of claims made by advertisers. Upon demand, the firm must submit to the commission data that support advertising claims relative to product safety, performance, efficacy, quality, or comparative price. A recent case illustrates the program.

The F.T.C. alleges that the Bon Marche Company made unsubstantiated claims in advertising that its cosmetic skin preparations "will slow down the aging process by 40%." The commission requires written certification of a reasonable scientific basis for the claim.[44] The chairman of the F.T.C. feels that this program will deter unfair and deceptive advertising, but will never play a significant role in consumer education.[45] In fact, critics contend that the substantiation program may cause the consumer to receive less, not more, information as sellers become more cautious.[46]

---

[40]Robert F. Dyer and Philip G. Kuehl, "The 'Corrective Advertising' Remedy of the FTC: An Experimental Evaluation," *Journal of Marketing*, 38 (January 1974), pp. 48–54.

[41]In re Warner-Lambert Co., F.T.C. Dkt. 8891 (December 1975); also "Legal Developments in Marketing" section, *Journal of Marketing*, 40 (July 1976), pp. 101–102.

[42]Dyer and Kuehl, "Corrective Advertising," p. 54.

[43]Ibid., p. 54; see also Michael B. Mazis and Janice E. Adkinson, "An Experimental Evaluation of a Proposed Corrective Advertising Remedy," *Journal of Marketing Research*, 13 (May 1976), pp. 178–83.

[44]In re Allied Stores Corp et al., F.T.C. File No. 742 3119 (November 1975); also "Legal Developments in Marketing" section, *Journal of Marketing*, 40 (July 1976), p. 104.

[45]Reported in Dorothy Cohen, "Remedies for Consumer Protection: Prevention, Restitution or Punishment," *Journal of Marketing*, 39 (October 1975), p. 26.

[46]"F.T.C. to Require Public Proof of Ad Claims," *Wall Street Journal*, June 11, 1971, p. 2.

THE F.T.C. IMPROVEMENT ACT OF 1975: SIGNALLING A NEW DIRECTION?

A new set of expectations has been placed before the Federal Trade Commission by Congress in enacting the F.T.C. Improvement Act of 1975. Specifically, this legislation: (1) expands the F.T.C.'s interstate commerce authority; (2) clarifies the body's rule-making authority; (3) provides for the participation of consumer groups in F.T.C. proceedings; (4) provides new power for cease-and-desist orders, and (5) broadens the F.T.C.'s power to order restitution.

To illustrate the clout of the improvement act, let's look at the offensive weapons now available to the F.T.C. The Commission can now seek equitable relief for consumers through the following remedies:

1. Refund of money or return of property;
2. Cancellation or rewriting of contracts;
3. Payment of compensatory damage;
4. Notification of the public.

How will these new tools be used? A careful analysis can be made only when these provisions have been translated into Commission policy.

SOURCE: Gerald G. Udell and Philip J. Fisher, "The FTC Improvement Act," *Journal of Marketing,* 41(April 1977), pp. 81–86.

The F.T.C. order falls short of recommendations by Ralph Nader and others which called for *all* claims to be substantiated and not just those challenged by the commission.[47] The commission, on the other hand, hopes that industry, as a result of its move, will police itself more effectively than before. Meanwhile, a bill—the Truth-in-Advertising bill—if enacted, would make illegal the advertising of products for which adequate documentation of claims is unavailable. The F.T.C. regulation may postpone this type of legislation pending a review of the regulation's effectiveness.

The F.T.C.'s approach to regulating advertising views the consumer as an economic person who makes purchase decisions rationally on the basis of objective data. But, Dorothy Cohen argues, the buyer is as much a behavioral as an economic person.[48] Full disclosure helps to protect this economic individual and improve his or her buying performance, but it is inadequate. Opinion leaders, brand loyalty and brand images, social group norms, and other noneconomic factors may be as important as objective data in regulating buyer behavior. Cohen

---

[47]Ralph Nader and Aileen Adams, *Petition for Trade Regulation Rule Proceeding and Issuance of Enforcement Policies before Federal Trade Commission.*
[48]Dorothy Cohen, "The Federal Trade Commission and the Regulation of Advertising in the Consumer Interest," *Journal of Marketing,* 33 (January 1969), pp. 40–44.

reminds us also that people accept information selectively, blocking some messages and letting others filter through. Habits, biases, attitudes, and social relationships may influence one's receptivity to consumer information as much as one's intelligence does. Thus, a policy that is based on disclosure of objective facts and ignores subjective considerations may be ineffective.

There is another problem, even when objective information is made available. "Technological change is so rapid that the consumer who bothers to learn about a commodity or service soon finds his knowledge obsolete. In addition, many improvements in quality and performance are below the threshold of perception, and imaginative marketing often makes rational choice even more of a problem."[49]

Affirmative Disclosure

An affirmative disclosure order may be issued by the F.T.C. when an advertisement fails to provide sufficient facts for an informed decision. The intent here is to provide additional information to the consumer regarding the positive and negative attributes of products or services.[50]

The impact of the affirmative disclosure requirement can be seen in a complaint against three computer schools. The schools were charged with misrepresentation of career opportunities and were required to disclose the following information in future advertisements: starting salaries, placement success rates, and employers who hire graduates.[51]

Self-Regulation

The discussion to this point has centered on the regulatory mechanisms of the Federal Trade Commission and remedies for specific advertising problem areas. Must the advertising industry surrender all responsibility to the government, allowing it to build the necessary institutions to protect the consumer? Howard and Hulbert emphasize that this alternative is full of risk and could damage the interests of consumers as well as industry.[52]

A more viable option is a concerted individual and collective effort within the advertising industry to provide adequate information to consumers. Howard and Hulbert feel that the following criteria should guide such an effort.

1. *Timeliness*—Is the information available when the consumer needs it?

2. *Intelligibility*—Is the information clear and understandable to the consumer?

3. *Relevance*—Does the advertisement contain information about the

---

[49]*Consumer Issues '66,* A Report Prepared by the Consumer Advisory Council (Washington, D.C.: U.S. Government Printing Office, 1966), p. 6, quoted in Cohen, ibid.

[50]Cohen, ibid., pp. 26–27.

[51]Cited by Robert E. Wilkes and James B. Wilcox, "Recent FTC Actions: Implications for the Advertising Strategist," *Journal of Marketing,* 38 (January 1974), p. 58.

[52]John A. Howard and James Hulbert, "Advertising and the Public Interest," *Journal of Advertising Research,* 14 (December 1974), pp. 33–39; see also Howard and Hulbert, *Advertising and the Public Interest: A Staff Report,* chapter 8.

relevant dimensions that are important to consumers in choosing among competing brands?

4. *Truthfulness*—Does the communication tell the truth?

5. *Completeness*—Does the consumer have enough information to choose among brands?

6. *Proper Segmentation*—Do advertisements reach the right audience, and *only* the right audience?[53]

While one can obviously find exceptions, the researchers feel that substantial progress has been made in the application of these criteria by marketing practitioners. In the case of the *completeness* dimension, more care is required. Such an industry effort ". . .would increase the credibility of advertising as an institution and as a source of consumer information."[54] Discussion of specific industry attempts at the self-regulation of advertising and other marketing practices is included in chapter 8.

Let's turn to other dimensions of promotion. How credible, for example, are personal selling practices?

SELLING PRACTICES

Salespeople have taken more than their share of criticism. Whether selling attracts more charlatans and slick operators than other occupations is unknown. People seem to think so since selling as an occupation traditionally ranks low in prestige and salespeople often are the butt of jokes.

Objections to salespeople and their tactics run the gamut from displeasure with high pressure tactics at one extreme to outright fraud at the other. Public policy probably cannot deal with the former; existing law covers the latter. Concern here lies less with salespeople's shortcomings and more with selling *procedures* with which public policy might deal. First, selected practices are singled out for further study: a brief look at negative option selling, then door-to-door selling, which commands more attention. Second, we examine an important aspect of marketing that often goes unnoticed by the consumer—selling in the channel of distribution.

Negative-Option Selling

Ten million subscribers pay $250 million a year for negative-option purchases.[55] Under this arrangement, the buyer agrees to accept and pay for merchandise unless he or she rejects it within a specified period of time. Record companies and book publishers account for most sales of this type. A Federal Trade Commission hearing revealed a number of abuses of the system, including inadequate time for

---

[53]Ibid.

[54]Howard and Hulbert, "Advertising and the Public Interest," *Journal of Advertising Research*, p. 38.

[55]John D. Morris, "Apathy Perils U.S. Plan to Ban 'Negative Option' Sales Method," *New York Times*, November 23, 1970, p. 32.

subscribers to return negative-option cards, insufficient advance information on how the plans operate, the delivery of unwanted merchandise in place of what the subscribers ordered, the use of deception in trying to collect on phony bills, and inadequate attention to customers' complaints. The commission also sees a fundamental drawback to negative-option selling, in addition to specific abuses. They view the practice as playing on people's traits of forgetfulness and procrastination and exploiting their preoccupation with more pressing personal matters. Dr. Ernest van den Haag, a psychiatrist supporting the industry, counters this assertion. He thinks "subscribers may be aware of their own weaknesses and of their tendency to be diverted and to procrastinate, and they may subscribe as a result of their awareness. Thus, they may cause themselves to do what the spirit is willing to do but what the flesh may be too weak to carry out."[56]

Hearings to consider regulations banning negative-option selling as an unfair and deceptive trade practice created expected industry opposition but little public interest in the restriction. This absence of support may confirm Dr. van den Haag's position or may indicate that the alleged annoyance of negative option is insufficient to get many people excited about the issue.

Door-To-Door Selling

Door-to-door selling has been under attack for a number of years. Agitation for its control springs from two sources: disgruntled consumers who have been bilked by door-to-door salespeople or annoyed by the practice, and local retailers who resent the competition. The courts have supported an F.T.C. order that requires sales personnel of companies selling encyclopedias door-to-door to identify themselves as the companies' representatives when seeking admission to the prospect's office or home.[57] Pressure from retailers has led, in some communities, to licensing requirements controlling the quality of people engaged in door-to-door selling. A more severe restriction is the "Green River" ordinance, which exists in many communities. This type of ordinance forbids solicitation in the home without consent of the resident. Use of the ordinance may limit what some consumers regard as an objectionable sales procedure, but it also curtails competition by eliminating rivals of established local retailers. Local merchants usually provide the impetus for passage of these ordinances, although companies practicing door-to-door selling have succeeded in limiting the spread of the restrictive ordinance.

Other legislation seeks not to abolish door-to-door selling, but to curtail some of its objectionable features. To illustrate, approximately 30 states have a consumer protection statute that provides buyers of merchandise sold door-to-door an opportunity to reconsider their purchases.[58] Thus, the consumer is given time, a cooling-off period, to reevaluate and perhaps cancel certain purchases they have already made from door-to-door salespeople. The Federal Trade Commission has likewise proposed cooling-off periods in regulating door-to-door sales.

---

[56]Ibid.

[57]Cited by Cohen, "Remedies for Consumer Protection," p. 25.

[58]Dennis H. Tootelian, "Attitudinal and Cognitive Readiness: Key Dimensions for Consumer Legislation," *Journal of Marketing*, 39 (July 1975), pp. 61–64.

The "cooling-off" feature seeks to control what many see as objectionable features of house-to-house selling—the combination of high pressure and, often, unethical selling and the unsolicited character of the transaction. Unethical persuasion may take countless forms. Tricks of the trade include: "bait and switch tactics, bogus contests, the model home pitch, the free gifts and sample offer, the official inspector impersonation, the specially selected household gimmick, verbal promises or implications, phony bargains, trick financing, guarantees not honored, materials misrepresented, misleading pictorial renderings, social pressures, exaggerated product performance and scare tactics."[59]

Opponents of this legislation to curb door-to-door selling object on several grounds.[60] They view it as discrimination against door-to-door marketing without dealing with other forms of unethical selling. They also feel it penalizes an entire industry to correct the abuses of a minority. Moreover, they see a "cooling-off" period weakening the concept of a contract. Implying that door-to-door selling is a shady occupation will make it even harder, it is argued, to recruit reputable solicitors—thus exacerbating the problems that led to the legislation. Finally, opponents would rather see laws aimed at abuses of this kind of marketing than punitive legislation against the entire industry.

The F.T.C. is examining the practices of door-to-door marketers of encyclopedias and other reference works to determine if they are engaged in unlawful activities. Three questions establish the focus of the inquiry. Are salespeople misrepresenting the purpose of their visit? Are they informing consumers that they have been specially selected to receive an offer? Are customers told that they will be given products free (or for almost no charge) if certain acts are performed?[61]

Neither legislation of this type nor a similar F.T.C. regulation on door-to-door selling would deal with the invasion-of-privacy issue. Solicitation by a door-to-door canvasser involves an unsolicited disturbance of one's privacy. Not unlike the unwanted guest, such an individual intrudes into the household or, at a minimum, interrupts activity (or inactivity) long enough to have the doorbell answered. A similar problem exists with respect to telephone solicitation, which remains pretty well unchecked. In both cases one may ask which should be paramount: the right of sellers to ply their trade in a particular way or the right of citizens to protect themselves from unsought invasions of privacy by vendors? Limiting telephone and door-to-door solicitation does not rule out alternative ways of selling.

Selling in the Channel: A Lingering Efficiency Question

The typical consumer is familiar with personal selling situations that involve direct contact with a salesperson. The consumer may be unaware of selling that takes place down the channel of distribution—for example, wholesalers selling to retailers, or industrial salespeople selling to jobbers or other wholesale intermediar-

---

[59]Marvin A. Jolson, "Cooling Off the Door-to-Door Salesman," *Business and Economic Dimensions,* Bureau of Business and Economic Research, University of Florida, February 1971, p. 17.
[60]See ibid., pp. 13–17.
[61]"Legal Developments in Marketing" section, *Journal of Marketing,* 40 (October, 1976), p. 119.

ies. While advertising is the obvious and inviting target of marketing critics, the marketing manager may assign as much or more attention to this aspect of promotion.

There are various ways to reduce selling expenses. One is to change the organizational structure in distribution. Establishing corporate chains and retailer co-ops can eliminate some of the selling effort among channel members. So too can other efforts to rationalize distribution through vertical integration. Increasing concentration of sellers at the manufacturing level may also reduce the total selling effort. These moves, however, may exact a toll in the form of higher prices that grow out of increased market power. Much could undoubtedly be accomplished to reduce firms' personal selling costs through improved routing of salespeople, better call-account management, and alternative ways of handling small orders. Some firms have cut selling costs substantially by using operations research techniques and distribution cost analysis, but much remains to be done.[62] The failure of many firms to control selling costs as effectively as they control factory costs undoubtedly leads to higher than necessary selling expenditures.

Summarizing, firms may reduce personal selling costs in two ways: (1) by improving efficiency at the firm level through better management, and (2) by rationalization of the institutional structure through vertical integration within the channel, or through horizontal integration of producers or distributors. Again, the second of these alternatives creates the same dilemma as before: How do we accomplish marketing economies without unduly weakening competition?

Discussion Questions

1. Is advertising "wasteful"? If so, is *all* of it wasted or just some of it? If some, which is and which isn't? What criteria of waste do you use? What does advertising waste?

2. Distinguish, if possible, between advertising "puffery" and deception. Can you cite specific examples of advertising that fall into each category?

3. Some critics of advertising argue that it should be limited "to protect people from themselves." This is especially said to apply to less well-educated people. Evaluate this argument.

4. Analyze this statement: All advertisements have the capacity to deceive some members of an audience.

5. Some critics argue that advertising directed to children should be banned entirely, while others have proposed special restrictions on this type of advertising. Agree or disagree? Explain.

6. Legislators and consumer advocates have proposed "Truth-in-Advertising" legislation that would require marketers, prior to an ad's publication, to file information with the Federal Trade Commission substantiating their claims. Evaluate this proposal.

---

[62]See, for example, Charles H. Sevin, *How Manufacturers Reduce Their Distribution Costs* (U.S. Department of Commerce, 1948); and Arthur A. Brown, Frank T. Hulswit, and John D. Kettelle, "A Study of Sales Operations," *Operations Research*, June 1956, pp. 296–308.

7. Select a recent magazine advertisement for a consumer product and rate it, using the six criteria proposed by Howard and Hulbert: timeliness, intelligibility, relevance, truthfulness, completeness, and proper segmentation.

Suggested Exercises: Class or Small Group Assignments

1. A hotly debated issue in the advertising industry centers on comparative advertising, that is, advertising that compares the sponsor's product with that of a competitor, by name. Advocates contend that comparative advertising is the industry's own brand of consumerism. Consumers are encouraged to compare brands before buying, and manufacturers are given an incentive to produce better products. Critics argue that comparative advertising confuses the consumers, focuses on trivial product features, and reduces the credibility of advertising. Develop a position in this debate.

2. David Gardner identifies three categories of deceptive advertising: (1) unconscionable lie; (2) claim-fact discrepancy, and (3) claim-belief interaction. Attempt to identify an ad that falls into one of these categories.

SIX
Price:
Ethical
and Legal
Dimensions

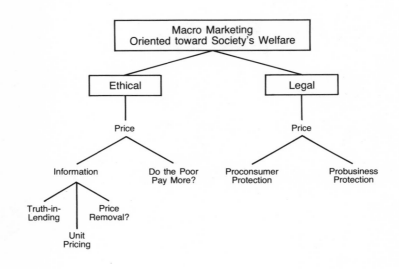

Three objectives motivate the discussion in this chapter. First, the legal environment of pricing is considered. You will learn that some pricing laws protect consumers while others protect business. Second, the availability and use of price information are examined from a consumer decision-making perspective. From the figure above, note that we will examine truth-in-lending and unit pricing information as well as the controversy surrounding price removal in selected supermarkets. Third, ghetto prices will be examined. Are prices higher in ghetto stores? Available evidence is reviewed.

SIX

Price: Ethical and Legal Dimensions

Public outcries over the increased costs of food, medical services, automobiles, and a range of products and services continually challenge the marketing manager. Critics argue that prices and profits are exorbitant and that increased governmental regulation is the only remedy to the problem. Proponents of business counter that such regulation will only aggravate the problem by shielding a greater number of industries from the free forces of a competitive market. The consumer, who has the most to lose in debates of this subject, is not overlooked.

Consumer advocates contend that expanded price information is the buyer's key weapon for survival in the marketplace. This information reduces buying mistakes and enhances competition among various brands. In this chapter, we examine the complex forces that surround pricing decisions in our contemporary society. For perspective, let's begin by examining pricing legislation and its implications for both consumers and business.

PRICING: THE LEGAL ENVIRONMENT

The stereotypical conception of the American economic system runs as follows: it is a free enterprise, capitalistic economy; competition lies at the heart of free enterprise; since freely fluctuating, market-determined prices form the cornerstone of competition, the American consumer reaps the benefits of vigorous price competition. Of course, this conception falls short of reality. The United States has a mixed system, with active government influence and participation in many sectors of the economy mixed with free enterprise sectors exhibiting various degrees of competitive behavior. Some sectors witness vigorous price competition; in others, government or industry price-fixing arrangements nullify the competition.

The rationale for government intervention in price-making is ambiguous. On the one hand, government seeks to maintain vigorous price competition; on the other its actions limit it. This ambiguous posture undoubtedly reflects the conflicting pressures exerted on government by private interests. The result is a crazyquilt pattern of interference which strengthens competition with the left hand and weakens it with the right. This section on pricing focuses on this ambivalent policy to see whether, on balance, government intervention in the price-making process benefits or hinders the consumer.

Proconsumer Pricing Protection

Government intervention in the pricing process on the consumer's side takes four forms: antitrust enforcement, prohibition of deceptive business practices, regulatory control, and price control and wage freezes. All of the remaining government measures in this area—and there are many—aim to protect competitors from each other and in so doing constitute probusiness, anticonsumer measures. Of the four proconsumer measures, three are more or less permanent, embedded into law or court decisions; the fourth is an emergency remedy that protects consumers when conditions warrant its use.

Antitrust Enforcement   The strongest protection that consumers may receive against unfair prices is a competitive economy. Often, however, sellers try to seal off markets and artificially raise prices through collusive price-

fixing agreements. Fortunately for consumers, price fixing is a violation per se of the antitrust laws. Protection comes not from statutory language outlawing price rigging, but from court cases against the practice, which date back to the end of the nineteenth century. The rulings derive from authority in Section 1 of the Sherman Act, which outlaws "every contract, combination in the form of trust or otherwise, or conspiracy, in restraint of trade or commerce among the several states. . . ." Few would claim that antitrust enforcement of price fixing eliminates the practice from the American business scene. Nonetheless, it is bound to be a deterrent, especially in the aftermath of such highly publicized price-fixing cases as the electrical equipment conspiracy in the early 1960s, in which several top company officials served prison terms for their roles in the arrangement.

Wheeler-Lea Act   Consumer price protection also flows from the Wheeler-Lea Act of 1938, which amends Section 5 of the Federal Trade Commission Act to prohibit "unfair or deceptive acts or practices in commerce." The law applies to deception of several kinds including deceptive pricing practices. Price deception usually involves offering the consumer a better price deal than he or she actually receives. Fictitious reductions from inflated "original" prices are a typical case. The F.T.C. has issued "Guides against Fictitious Pricing," a publication which spells out guidelines to prevent such an abuse. For industries generating many deceptive pricing complaints, the commission publishes special regulations to limit deception in the consumer's interest.

Regulatory Control   The third area of government intervention to maintain fair pricing occurs in public utility regulation. The monopolistic character of most utilities dictates the control of their pricing power by regulatory agencies. These are state or federal commissions, depending on the geographical scope of the utilities' operations.

Price Control and Freezes   Government price controls and freezes represent the fourth type of intervention on behalf of consumers. This authority is generally used in emergency wartime situations to control threatened or actual price inflation. Thus World Wars I and II and the Korean conflict witnessed federal price controls that lasted through each of the emergency periods. President Nixon's 90-day wage and price freeze, introduced in August 1971, sought to cope with a similar problem but in a modified peacetime environment. Each of our wartime experiences with controls—especially the 1971 freeze—points up an interesting aspect of our attitude toward inflation protection. Over the long run, the American economy has experienced an increase in the average price level. There have been brief periods of sharp increase and, at times, reductions in the general level of prices, but the overall pattern of prices has been gradually upward. Public pressure to control prices is virtually nonexistent when the uptrend is gradual; it is only when accelerated inflation threatens or exists that public opinion swings toward support for controls. Whether consumers suffer from price inflation depends largely on their ability to increase their income correspondingly. The enormous administrative burden of price controls and the rigidities in the economic system that they create are enough to discourage their use except in emergencies, even though some consumers suffer inequities.[1]

Probusiness Pricing Protection

The foregoing measures provide formidable consumer protection from unfair and anticompetitive pricing. But the pressure of special business interests has also created an impressive umbrella of anticompetitive devices that shelter sellers from the full impact of market forces. What follows is a brief account of some of these measures.

In some instances government intervention on behalf of sellers has an indirect rather than direct effect on prices. However, the impact is no less real. Examples are tariffs and quotas that discourage competition from foreign producers and reduce pressure on domestic producers to lower prices. No industry has done a more effective job of regulating competition by controlling supply than the petroleum industry. State proration laws plus the Interstate Oil Compact effectively curb domestic output. Matching supply to changing demand levels keeps control of the market price level in the producers' hands rather than letting it be determined by the unpredictable forces of the marketplace.

Over the years, many states have enacted a variety of laws to curtail price cutting. These include:

1. Fair trade laws that permit contracts requiring retailers to charge a price no lower than a prescribed level. For a number of years, these laws were exempted from the price-fixing prohibition of the Sherman Antitrust Act (1890). A 1976 federal law nullifies fair trade laws by again making them subject to the Sherman Act.[2]

2. Minimum markup laws ("Unfair Practices" Acts) designed principally to eliminate the use of "loss leaders." Almost two-thirds of the states at one time had passed laws of this type, but in a number of instances the courts have ruled against them. They also have invalidated fair trade laws.

3. State laws regulating the sale of specific commodities such as milk or liquor. These laws vary from state to state where they exist, but the intent and effect are pretty much the same. They protect the interests of the retailers (and, often, producers, especially of milk) from price competition. The protection usually shelters the small, higher cost retailers from the rigors of price cutting. Society suffers from a misallocation of resources; consumers lose the benefits of price competition.

---

[1]A quibbler might suggest that presidential exhortation is a fifth protection against price inequities. President Kennedy's successful effort to roll back steel prices in 1962 is a case in point. These efforts are very spasmodic and represent brief forays in the price battle rather than full-fledged and longer lasting protection.

[2]In "Legal Developments in Marketing" section, *Journal of Marketing,* 40 (July 1976), p. 101. At the time of passage, 21 states, including Illinois, Michigan, Indiana, Pennsylvania, and Maryland, had fair trade laws.

Historical Perspective Most of these three kinds of state laws trace their origin to the great Depression, when the pressure was intense from beleaguered retailers for protection against the ravages of competition. At the federal level, protection during the same period took the form of agricultural price supports, the Robinson-Patman Act, and the National Industrial Recovery Act of 1933. Under the latter act, industry codes provided for minimum prices designed to alleviate ruinous competition. The act was declared unconstitutional in 1935, but the other two measures continue in effect, even though conditions today are vastly different from those existing when they were introduced.

The Robinson-Patman Act seeks to prevent certain kinds of price discrimination; however, the focus is on protection of sellers from one another rather than on protection of the consumer. As with the various state laws, it grew out of small retailers' complaints. They felt threatened by large distributors who had grown to prominence in the 1920s and 1930s. Specifically, the Robinson-Patman Act defined price discrimination as unlawful and empowered the F.T.C. to (1) set limits on quantity discounts, (2) forbid brokerage allowances except to independent brokers, and (3) prohibit promotional allowances and services or facilities not made available to all buyers on proportionately equal terms.[3]

This brief summary of the major government-supported devices to protect sellers from price competition gives some idea of the forces arrayed against the consumer who looks to a free market system for competitively determined prices. Fortunately for the consumer, many of the state laws designed to stifle price competition have been ineffective, unenforceable, or declared unconstitutional. This nullification has been especially true with the fair trade laws and minimum markup laws. Furthermore, not every state has enacted these protective laws. Where commodity control laws protecting cigarettes, milk, liquor, and so on exist, the consumer undoubtedly loses out to protected retailers. No one has studied the combined effect of these laws, but they artificially raise retail prices on goods with annual sales volume running into billions of dollars. One can assume that the effect on prices of the other restrictive measures is substantial but, here again, an accurate estimate of the consumers' "losses" is unavailable and probably impossible to ascertain with any degree of precision.

It is tempting to think that the deterrent effect of the illegality per se of price fixing is adequate to compensate for these losses. But anyone who has been exposed to industrial price making and has had extensive contacts with marketing executives must be pessimistic. It is hard to imagine any action that would reap greater pecuniary benefits for the consumer than *consistently* vigorous antitrust enforcement on a scale far exceeding anything witnessed in the past. Political realism may nullify the possibility of such a reform, but that does not diminish its exciting possibilities.

Marketing Efficiency and the Law: A Complexity
Many of these pricing laws create a number of interesting and rather complex trade-offs for consumers and business people. Both parties would agree that increased marketing efficiency is favorable to their own interests, spelling higher

---

[3]Philip Kotler, *Marketing Management: Analysis, Planning and Control* (Englewood Cliffs, N.J.: Prentice-Hall, 1976), p. 41.

profits for business and lower prices for consumers. Gordon Bloom isolates the Robinson-Patman Act and applies this point to food retailing.[4]

Assume that a retailer approaches a manufacturer of paper bags with this proposal:

"I want to reduce my buying expense and you want to reduce your selling expense, and even out fluctuations in production. I don't care when you deliver bags to me or in what amounts provided that at all times my inventory of bags does not fall below x bags nor exceed y bags. You can schedule production of my bags when convenient to you and ship when convenient to you. You will be responsible for maintaining my inventory; billing and notification will be handled automatically. I will concentrate all my purchases with you. Now what kind of a discount can you give me?"[5]

None! Bloom notes that the existing interpretation of the Robinson-Patman Act prohibits buyers and sellers from entering into such mutually advantageous agreements for two reasons. First, the manufacturer would have difficulty in proving the cost-savings to the satisfaction of the Federal Trade Commission. (Cost justification is an argument available to a seller accused of illegal price discrimination.) Second, in return for giving the manufacturer the opportunity to fill this order during slack periods, the retailer expects a larger discount than other buyers receive. While not permitted under the law, Bloom argues that such agreements should be encouraged because they make improvements in productivity possible.

INFORMATION: PRICE AND TERMS OF SALE

The efficient functioning of a free market system depends upon the availability of adequate market information. Making rational buying decisions where choice is available requires that shoppers have access to accurate product information, and knowledge of terms and conditions of sales. Much of the current interest in consumerism centers on the improvement in the quality and amount of information available to the consumer. This section studies some of the issues in this area that have captured the attention of consumer advocates.

Truth-in-Lending

Usury and objections to it have an ancient lineage. In the Middle Ages the Church took a strong stand against the practice. Moneylenders have always been suspect, and continual measures have been taken to limit the interest they may charge on loans. The laws in many states today control usury through statutory maxima of interest rates.

In recent years consumer protection in this area has taken a new direction. The so-called Truth-in-Lending Law seeks to protect consumer interests by providing full disclosure of interest rates and credit terms on the premise that disclosure lets the consumer protect him or herself from credit abuse. Passed in 1968, the Consumer Credit Protection Act (the official title) provides for dis-

---

[4]Gordon F. Bloom, *Productivity in the Food Industry: Problems and Potential* (Cambridge, Mass.: MIT Press, 1972), pp. 251–252.

[5]Ibid., p. 252, reprinted with permission of the MIT Press, Cambridge, Mass.

closure of: the annual rate of interest of all finance charges on credit transactions, the method of determining the finance charge, conditions under which additional charges may be imposed, and the minimum periodic payment that may be required.[6] Thus, when a credit transaction specifies interest at the rate of 1½% a month, it must also state the annual rate of 18%. An installment payment schedule of $X a month must be accompanied by a statement indicating the annual interest rate that underlies the schedule.

Is It Working? How effective is the law in accomplishing its purpose? A Federal Reserve Board (F.R.B.) survey in 1970 found 21% of new-car buyers with installment loans were unaware of the interest rate charged them, as were 42% of new-furniture buyers.[7] Thirty-five percent of the car buyers estimated the interest charges much too low (less than 7%, when they were nearly double that figure). The Federal Reserve Board also found a high rate of compliance with the law. The discouraging results indicate, therefore, not abuse of the law by creditors but either a failure of borrowers to remember the interest rates or their failure to learn the rates when they arranged for credit. An encouraging note is an F.R.B. finding that this survey showed a "significant improvement" in consumers' awareness of interest charges compared with results of a survey taken just prior to the act's passage.[8]

George Day and William Brandt have examined consumer usage of the Truth-in-Lending information in more depth.[9] While 57% of all credit buyers notice some credit information, only 34% correctly report the interest charges associated with a recent purchase. Overall, 10% of all credit buyers claim use of the information in their last purchase of a durable good. Day notes that the ". . . information seems to enhance confidence by assuring buyers of the correctness of their choice."[10] Interestingly, while a small proportion of consumers report actual use of the credit information, more than half (54%) of the buyers indicate that they feel better knowing the rates and the charges.

Credit and the Low-Income Consumer Homer Kripke also finds truth-in-lending ineffective.[11] He doubts the efficacy of providing low-income shoppers with information on financing. He sees the law using middle-class solutions (disclosure) to a low-income class problem. He cites evidence in the bill's hearings that many credit users failed to realize that they had to pay finance

---

[6]Some of these specific requirements come from Federal Reserve Board regulations provided by the act and not directly from the wording of the act itself.

[7]"Loan Rates Confound Consumers," *Orlando* [Florida] *Sentinel,* February 7, 1971, p. 17-A.

[8]Ibid.

[9]George S. Day and William K. Brandt, *A Study of Consumer Credit Decisions: Implications for Present and Prospective Legislation* (Washington, D.C.: National Commission on Consumer Finance, 1973), reported in Day, "Assessing the Effects of Information Disclosure Requirements," *Journal of Marketing,* 40 (April 1976), p. 46.

[10]Ibid., p. 46.

[11]Homer Kripke, "Gesture and Reality in Consumer Credit Reform," in *Consumerism: Search for the Consumer Interest,* 2nd ed., ed. David A. Aaker and George S. Day (New York: The Free Press, 1974), pp. 218–224.

charges even though they had signed documents that indicated the charges. Furthermore, he sees many low-income buyers trapped into using credit because of their low or nonexistent cash resources. They may realize full well the crushing credit burden that they undertake but remain powerless to overcome it. Kripke complains also that the Consumer Credit Protection Act fails to cover fraud and deception in selling—a more serious problem, as he sees it.

The evidence to date indicates that truth-in-lending has only marginal effects on buyer behavior. As with other consumer information proposals, the success of truth-in-lending depends upon the consumers' *use* of the information that the legislation provides. Kripke has perceived what may be a bitter irony—that those with low incomes, who most need the law's protection, may benefit little; instead the gains, if any, may accrue to those with less need and more income.

Unit Pricing

The billions of dollars spent on grocery shopping create an enormous potential for improvement through consumer-oriented reform. One of these reforms that commands considerable interest is the unit pricing of food products.

Those pleading for reform of grocery store pricing charge that the shopper faces an impossible task in calculating values correctly and quickly. Confronted with a proliferation of products, package sizes, and price offerings, the average shopper is hard-pressed to determine the best buys. Which is the better buy: a 6½-ounce can of pineapple for 21 cents or the 20-ounce size for 57 cents?

Unit pricing is suggested as a partial solution to this dilemma. It calls for dual pricing of grocery products: one price for the full package or can, the other on a price per unit (for example, ounce) basis. The unit measurement gives the shopper a standard for comparing competitive product prices. Thus, in the foregoing example, the unit prices for the two sizes, respectively, would be 3.23 cents and 2.85 cents per ounce.

Consumer Usage   A number of states require unit pricing; among them are Massachusetts, Vermont, Maryland, Rhode Island, and Connecticut. Several other states have similar legislative proposals pending. Do shoppers understand and use this form of price information? Let's look at the evidence. Over 60% of the consumers questioned in a survey on this subject reported an awareness of unit pricing information, while 50% comprehended the meaning of the concept.[12] In terms of actual usage, the results were mixed but generally indicated that 30 to 40% of consumers used the information for selected purchases.[13] This usage appeared to vary by income group.

Research indicates that low-income shoppers do not make significant use of unit pricing, in contrast to middle- and high-income shoppers.[14] Similarly, the elderly shopper makes little use of this information.[15] Thus, those standing to profit most from its use—low-income groups and the aged—apply it the least. Many argue that educational efforts are needed to correct this discrepancy.

Unit pricing programs have other problems. The costs of introducing and maintaining unit pricing are relatively high. For example, Jewel Tea Company estimated the cost per store of introducing unit pricing to be $1,000.[16] Small independent retailers may suffer a special handicap since they are less able than large chains to absorb the additional expense. They face a dilemma—unable to afford the additional expense, but subject to a competitive disadvantage if they do not. There may also be a problem of keeping price labels up to date.

Are They Switching?   With the introduction of unit pricing, some policy makers forecasted that consumers would switch to lower-priced alternatives. A dramatic shift is not evident. Clearly, price is but one of the criteria that consumers apply to buying decisions. Past experience with a brand, quality, taste, color, brand name, and a range of other factors may be more important than the price criterion. Indeed, the relative influence of unit price information on buying decisions likely varies by customer segment and by product category.

Price Removal Controversy[17]

As the reader is probably aware, most of the products available in supermarkets now contain a bar code symbol—a Universal Product Code (UPC). What is the significance of this code for retailers and consumers? Each code and symbol is unique and identifies, among other things, the manufacturer, size, contents, and

---

[12]George S. Day, "Effects of information Disclosure", p. 46.
[13]See for example, "Consumer Behavior in the Supermarket," *Progressive Grocer,* 54 (October 1975), pp. 37–48.
[14]Hans R. Isakson and Alex R. Maurizl, "The Consumer Economics of Unit Pricing," *Journal of Marketing Research,* 10 (August 1973), pp. 277–285.
[15]John S. Coulson, "New Consumerists' Breed Will Fade Away," *Marketing News,* Mid-June, 1971, p. 5.
[16]"Unit Pricing Chalks up Some Surprises," *Business Week,* October 31, 1970, p. 80.
[17]Much of the material in this section is drawn from Gilbert D. Harrell, Michael D. Hutt, and John W. Allen, *Universal Product Code: Price Removal and Consumer Behavior* (Michigan State University, Graduate School of Business Administration, Division of Research, 1976), chapters 1 and 5.

flavor of a product. The code is designed for use with UPC point-of-sale scanning systems in retailing. Let's examine how the scanning system works.

Where's the Price? The scanner is an electronic sensor capable of registering a particular item and its price without a checker manually making an entry on the traditional cash register keyboard. The checker merely passes each item over the electronic sensor, transmitting the UPC code to a computer processor, which enters a correct price and brief description of the item on the consumer's register tape. As each item is scanned, the price and product description are displayed on a screen above the checkstand. Items that are not source-marked with the UPC symbol by the manufacturer can be coded by the retailer. Since the retailer assigns a specific price to a code and can determine that price by scanning the code, individual price labels are no longer needed. If prices are not marked on each individual item, the shelf becomes the source of consumer price information prior to purchase; the view screen on the register is the source during checkout; and the expanded register tape, after the sale. Figure 6.1 displays the workings of the system.

The Debate The potential removal of price labels from individual items stands at the center of a lively debate between food industry executives on the one side and consumer and labor union representatives on the other. Several states have already passed mandatory price-marking legislation—among them are Connecticut, Massachusetts, California, and Rhode Island. Similar legislation

Figure 6-1   How Does the System Work? Courtesy of the Grocery Manufacturers of America.

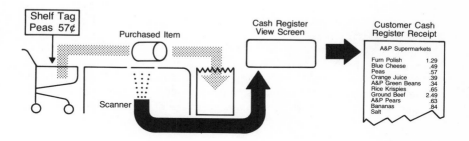

is being proposed in other states, as well as in both houses of Congress. Several issues emerge in the debate over price removal.

Critics contend that shoppers in the UPC-prices-off environment will: (1) have difficulty in determining and comparing prices; (2) suffer a reduction in price awareness; and (3) find shopping more inconvenient and time-consuming (for instance, matching product to shelf price) than shoppers in conventional stores. Industry representatives counter that consumers will readily adjust to the system, shop as efficiently as before, and enjoy new benefits. They contend that the more complete register tape provided through the scanning system has the potential for increasing the sensitivity of the consumers to price changes over time. Likewise, supporters maintain that the scanning system is not only faster, but also more accurate than manual checkout methods.

Impact on Price Awareness A public policy committee on the Universal Product Code, which includes representatives of the diverse viewpoints in the debate—industry, labor, and consumer—commissioned a study to examine the issues. The research indicates that shoppers in the UPC-prices-off environment display less ability to determine the correct price at the point-of-purchase than consumers in conventional stores. Another facet of the research centers on the price recall ability of shoppers in the store. Before checking out, shoppers were asked to report the prices of items selected that day. UPC store shoppers, on the average, erred more frequently and by a larger margin than their conventional store counterparts. For several measures no significant differences emerge between shoppers in the two store types: conventional versus UPC-prices-off. To illustrate, the change in the consumer information environment (item prices on versus item prices off) does not appear to influence unit price usage or the length of time required by consumers to complete the shopping task. New technology often brings trade-offs, and the UPC scanning system is no exception. Compared with conventional store shoppers, customers in the UPC stores were clearly more satisfied with checkout speed, but less satisfied with the availability of price information.

Further Tests Needed Given the problems that the system poses for consumers, the food industry has adopted the position that item pricing should be retained pending further experimentation with alternate methods of conveying price information. The potential managerial benefits of the UPC scanning system provide a stimulus for the retail food industry to test and implement the technology further. These benefits include few checker mistakes, improved labor productivity (checker, price-marking, reordering), tighter inventory control, and an expanded base of transaction information for more informed managerial decisions. Note that some of the productivity advantages can be realized by implementing the system, but retaining individual item prices.

THE POOR: DO THEY PAY MORE?

Critics charge that marketing institutions levy exorbitant prices and credit terms on ghetto residents. As a social issue confronting marketing, ghetto marketing is sufficiently important to warrant careful examination. Since the United States is characterized as an affluent society, why has this topic commanded so much attention and concern in recent years? Clearly, statistics on per capita income, consumption of durable goods, and the share of the world's wealth controlled by Americans confirm the affluence of the United States. But the totals and averages mislead. They hide the existence of a large core of impoverished people to whom, for one reason or another, the hope for affluence is a myth. In fact, these Americans fall short of achieving even a minimal standard of living. More than two-thirds of the people with incomes below a poverty level are white, but the nonwhites, mostly blacks, are more numerous than their share of the total population would warrant. Increasingly, these poor nonwhites concentrate in the ghettos in our major cities. Several factors have led to the increased concern for the poor, not least of which is the incongruity of the presence of poverty in a land of plenty.

Ghetto residents spend a large share of their income in neighborhood stores; therefore, improvement in marketing conditions could alleviate their financial plight. This is especially true of food marketing, since it is estimated that the poor pay from 29 to 36% of their income on food, compared with 18% so spent by the average household.[18] To appraise the performance of marketing in the ghetto, we need to investigate prices there and compare them with those outside of the ghetto. Of prime interest are food prices, and secondarily, prices of nonfood items, particularly appliances.

Ghetto Food Prices

The Bureau of Labor Statistics "found no significant differences in prices charged by food stores located in low-income areas versus those charged by stores in higher income areas, when the same types of stores (chains, large independents, small independents), the same qualities of foods, and the same sizes of packages are compared."[19] Thus, the study found no evidence to support the allegation that ghetto chain stores charge more than do chain operations in higher income areas. They did find that small independents in both ghetto and nonghetto areas charge higher prices than either large independents or chain stores. This condition handicaps ghetto dwellers since they, more than high-income people, patronize small stores. Another condition handicapping the poor is their greater inclination to buy smaller package sizes. This raises their food bill above what it would be if they were to purchase large, more economical sizes.

---

[18]Figure for poor from David Caplovitz, "On the Value of Consumer Action Programs in the War on Poverty," prepared for Office of Economic Opportunity, March 8, 1966, and reported in *Consumer Problems of the Poor,* hearings before Special Studies Committee of House Committee on Government Operations, 90th Congress, 2nd sess., October 12, November 24 and 25, 1967, p. 5; average household figure from U.S. Department of Agriculture, "National Food Situation Report," November 17, 1967, also reported in *Consumer Problems of the Poor,* p. 5.

[19]U.S. Bureau of Labor Statistics, "A Study of Prices Charged in Food Stores Located in Low and Higher Income Areas of Six Large Cities," February 1966, reproduced in *National Commission on Food Marketing, Technical Study No. 10,* June 1966, p. 122.

New Haven   Howard Kunreuther uncovers similar shopping patterns in an analysis of the consumer behavior of low-income groups in New Haven.[20] More than 60% of low-income families concentrate their shopping in small neighborhood stores, while only 15% of middle-income families rely on the small local grocer. The relative mobility of the two income groups likely accounts for the markedly different shopping patterns. Nearly half of low-income families use public transportation or walk to their local grocery store, while nearly all of the middle-income families drive automobiles to a supermarket. Additionally, the New Haven study suggests that ". . . the poor may pay more because constraints force them to buy smaller sizes on a more frequent basis than middle income shoppers."[21]

Philadelphia   Charles Goodman, in a study of the shopping behavior of Philadelphia ghetto residents, likewise examines store choice.[22] He studied prices at twelve stores, equally divided among supermarkets, medium-sized independents, and small convenience stores. All of the supermarkets lay in a region extending one-half mile from the boundary of the 160-acre residential area surveyed. The ghetto shoppers were inclined to patronize either these supermarkets or three of the four medium-sized independents whose prices were actually below the supermarkets'. They tended to shun the local, higher-priced stores. Why do low-income shoppers in New Haven (previously cited) and Philadelphia follow different shopping patterns? Kunreuther suggests that the differences stem from the relative locations of larger retail stores in the two market areas.[23] In contrast to the shopping alternatives in New Haven, larger stores were located relatively close to the low-income areas in Philadelphia.

Some Inconsistencies   While existing evidence suggests that the poor do tend to pay more when they shop at the smaller, inefficient stores and do not pay more when they shop at supermarkets, contrary evidence has been presented. To illustrate, market basket studies in three major metropolitan areas found prices from 6 to 15% higher in ghetto-area stores than in stores in higher income areas.[24] Similar comparisons support the allegation that selected ghetto chain stores raise prices on the dates ghetto residents receive welfare checks and food stamps.[25] Thus, disturbing inconsistencies emerge in past studies.

Part of the problem stems from weaknesses in the research designs. Burton Marcus's Watts study remedies these defects to some extent.[26] He studied prices on all available items included in the Consumer Price Index for a total of 49 stores in the Watts and Culver City areas of Greater Los Angeles. Watts is a recognized low-income area inhabited principally by nonwhites. Culver

---

[20]Howard Kunreuther, "Why the Poor May Pay More for Food: Theoretical and Empirical Evidence," *Journal of Business,* 46 (July 1973), pp. 368–383.

[21]Ibid., p. 377.

[22]Charles S. Goodman, "Do the Poor Pay More?" *Journal of Marketing,* 32 (January 1968), pp. 18–24.

[23]Kunreuther, "Poor May Pay More", p. 377.

[24]Reported in *Consumer Problems of the Poor,* pp. 7–40.

[25]Ibid.

[26]Burton H. Marcus, "Similarity of Ghetto and Nonghetto Food Costs," reproduced in Aaker and Day, *Consumerism,* 1st ed., pp. 382–389.

City is predominantly white and has a higher average income than Watts.

The Marcus study reveals a slightly lower average price level in the ghetto than in the nonghetto area. However, excluding meat and produce items, ghetto food prices were 4% higher. Since meat and produce quality can vary substantially, one may suspect that lower prices for these items in the ghetto stores relate to their lower quality. By taking explicit account of quality, he looks behind the raw statistics and improves our understanding of apparent price differences.

Whether the poor pay more for food is far from clear. The evidence is mixed. When one adjusts for quality and the size of stores available to the poor, the evidence points toward higher prices in the ghetto. Conclusive statements depend upon conclusive findings. Much of the available research lacked adequate controls. For example, the stores covered in the Bureau of Labor Statistics research had advance notice of the price study, and only those consenting to be studied were analyzed. There are other problems. One of the stickiest is getting comparable market baskets in ghetto and nonghetto stores since these shops often fail to carry identical brands. Different product preferences of various ethnic and racial groups also lead to stores' stocking different items.

The studies of ghetto food prices tend to agree on one thing: the limited availability of high-volume food chain operations in low-income areas. They exist, but not to the extent that they do elsewhere. This shortcoming puts the ghetto resident at a definite disadvantage in food buying.

Nonfood Prices

In contrast to food retailing, more substantial evidence has been found to indicate abuse of low-income groups by furniture and appliance retailers. David Caplovitz analyzed the marketing practices of retailers in East Harlem and the several hundred East Side New York families who patronized them.[27] In summary, his research found that:

1. Lower income families (under $3,500 a year) paid more than higher income families for television sets, record players, and washing machines.

2. Those shopping outside of the immediate neighborhood paid less than shoppers using local stores.

3. A related factor emerged—higher appliance prices were associated with traditional stores (neighborhood retailers), and lower prices with discount houses, chains, and department stores, which predominate outside of the ghetto.

4. Credit customers paid higher prices than cash customers.

Importantly, the last factor creates a greater burden for blacks and Puerto Ricans than for whites. Similar results appeared in a Federal Trade Commission survey of 96 District of Columbia furniture and appliance retailers.[28] Prices for

---

[27]David Caplovitz, *The Poor Pay More* (New York: The Free Press, 1967).
[28]Federal Trade Commission, *Economic Report on Installment Credit and Retail Sales Practices of District of Columbia Retailers*, in *The Ghetto Marketplace*, ed. Frederick D. Sturdivant (New York: The Free Press, 1969), pp. 76–107.

appliances sold by the low-income area retailers ranged from 13 to 80% higher than prices at the department stores. Likewise, installment credit was used in virtually all of the transactions of the low-income area merchants.

Sturdivant and Wilhelm looked beyond different prices charged in ghetto and nonghetto stores to study the effect of ethnicity on appliance prices.[29] They arranged for three couples—white, black, and Mexican-American—to shop for television sets at stores in Culver City, Watts, and East Los Angeles. These areas are typical middle-class white, black, and Mexican, respectively, in Greater Los Angeles.

The findings are given below.

1. Average price quotations were higher by 17 to 48% in the two lower income areas than in the Culver City stores for four television brands.

2. Installment credit costs tended to be higher when the couples shopped outside of their areas.

3. Minority couples were quoted higher prices than the white couple in two of the three white-area stores, but the prices were no greater than those in the ghetto stores and were often less. In other words, price discrimination was greater between location of store (ghetto versus nonghetto) than between ethnic group.

What do these studies add up to? Hardly *conclusive* evidence that the poor pay more for appliances. Still, what little evidence there is all points in the same direction—higher prices for the poor. All three surveys found that credit played an important part in the buying process in the ghetto stores. It influenced the effective prices substantially and also affected the ability of the poor to buy. With credit, too, comes a chain of relationships between ghetto merchants and their customers which contributes to the criticism of ghetto marketers.

Ghetto Credit Practices

The available data on credit use by the poor are mixed. Caplovitz found that about 60% of his East Harlem subjects had installment debts outstanding when he studied them.[30] This figure differed little from the percentage for all consumers. On the other hand, the F.T.C. study of ghetto shopping in Washington, D.C., revealed that 92.7% of the sales of stores in the low-income areas were installment sales; this compared with 26.5% for general market retailers outside of the ghettos.[31] These percentages are not necessarily inconsistent since some ghetto residents shop in nonghetto stores. We can infer from these figures—and other data support the inference—that many ghetto residents are trapped into using neighborhood stores for durable goods purchases. Here credit plays a dominant role in the buying process. Entrapment may take subtle forms. It results from the poor's relative lack of mobility, their lower level of education and inadequate

---

[29]Frederick D. Sturdivant and Walter T. Wilhelm, "Poverty, Minorities, and Consumer Exploitation," reprinted in Sturdivant, ibid., pp. 108–117.

[30]Caplovitz, *The Poor Pay More*, p. 101.

[31]Federal Trade Commission, *Economic Report on Installment Credit and Retail Sales Practices of District of Columbia Retailers,* March 1968, p. 23.

information sources, and their lower income, which puts many of them at the mercy of merchants who use credit as a prime selling tool. Thus, although the poor may incur no more installment debt than others, those who shop for durables in ghetto stores are almost certain to buy on time, with credit's attendant problems.

The proverbial "dollar down, dollar a week" accurately describes credit terms for ghetto retail transactions. Payments are low to reduce their burden. They are made often to keep close tabs on customers and to get them into the store. Most customers visit the store to pay on their accounts. This arrangement gives the merchant repeated opportunities to make additional sales. This tying of the customer to a store is a familiar arrangement to many ghetto residents who have emigrated from the South. There, as sharecroppers, they had similar linkages with the company store.

The granting of credit is a major competitive tool for the ghetto merchant and overshadows price as a determinant of sales, especially for hard goods. Credit exists in the sale of food, but to a lesser extent than in the sale of durables. Some of the credit collection problems of ghetto merchants stem from their willingness to grant liberal credit terms as a sales inducement. This behavior harms the improvident customer, who gets deeply into debt. Thus, the system gives both customer and seller a tool with which each can satisfy a need, but it simultaneously creates problems for them both.

Stacked Deck Unfortunately for the customers, most of the cards are stacked against them. The merchants possess more market knowledge, better access to legal remedies, and the ability to confuse the customer and extract credit terms that compensate them for the risks they incur. Many ghetto shoppers lack the knowledge and, often, the reading ability to realize the credit terms they have agreed to when they make a durable goods purchase. Congressional hearings reveal numerous instances of ghetto shoppers being unaware of having to pay finance charges even though the papers that they signed indicated a total cost in excess of the price quoted them.[32]

The ghetto shopper pays dearly for the use of credit. Sturdivant and Wilhelm report their experimental shoppers being quoted prices, including credit charges, for television sets that ran up to 87% above the regular list price.[33] The F.T.C. study reveals average annual finance charges of 23 to 25% in ghetto stores, four percentage points above the rates in nonghetto stores.[34]

Ghetto Merchant Practices
The low-income shopper suffers from more than the extortionate finance charges imposed by ghetto merchants. He or she is victimized by other merchant practices.[35] Often durable goods have no price marks. The price may hinge upon whether the shopper is judged a good or bad credit risk. The same phenomenon

---

[32]Homer Kripke, "Gesture and Reality in Consumer Credit Reform," reprinted in Aaker and Day, *Consumerism,* 2nd ed., pp. 218–224.
[33]Sturdivant and Wilhelm, "Consumer Exploitation," p. 114.
[34]Federal Trade Commission, *District of Columbia Retailers,* p. 26.
[35]See Caplovitz, *The Poor Pay More.*

occurred in the shopping study in Watts, East Los Angeles, and Culver City. Price also depends on the assumed naiveté of the shopper. Sales personnel become adept at measuring the economic status of their customers. They may refer high-credit-risk shoppers to other stores specializing in such accounts—at higher prices. The store making the referral receives a kickback commission. Most furniture and appliance stores in the ghetto also lack high-quality merchandise since the use of high percentage markups would price quality merchandise out of the market.

Bait-and-Switch A widespread and nefarious ghetto merchant practice, reported by Caplovitz and others, is the use of bait-and-switch techniques. They take several forms. The "bait" may be an attractively priced bedroom suite displayed in the store's windows. Inside, the shopper is pressured into buying higher priced items. Merchandise in the window display is "unavailable" or "incomplete." The bait may take the form of an ad for a bargain. Attracted to the store, the customer again is high-pressured into buying another, more expensive, model.

Ghetto customers also complain of being quoted one price and signing sales contracts containing higher prices. They may reluctantly pay the higher price or make the down payment, refuse to make additional payments, finally default and lose the merchandise. Equally nefarious is the tactic of switching goods after the sale. Here the customer pays for a new item and receives a used or reconditioned model. The ways to defraud the gullible customer appear endless.

Bait-and-switch tactics may not be used more in the ghetto than elsewhere, but their use may be morally more reprehensible for two reasons. Ghetto residents generally have less than average education and therefore may be more susceptible to deceptive persuasion. Also, their financial straits magnify the impact of unwise buying decisions.

Shopping Behavior of the Poor

It is evident that the poor are heavily dependent on credit and often succumb to the wiles of rapacious merchants. What other buying characteristics do they exhibit? Louise G. Richards compares their buying behavior with the "rational" practices of careful shoppers.[36] Good consumership involves:

1. Buying necessities first, luxuries last. According to Richards, the poor generally do this. They tend to buy basics first, and consume fewer durables.[37] They may appear to spend more than they actually do on durables because of their conspicuous consumption of television

---

[36]Louise G. Richards, "Consumer Practices of the Poor," in Sturdivant, *The Ghetto Marketplace,* pp. 42–60.

[37]We need to treat these generalizations with caution. First, they suffer the disadvantages of all generalizations. Second, generalizations about the poor often are confused with generalizations about blacks. Raymond A. Bauer and Scott M. Cunningham (*Studies in the Negro Market,* Cambridge, Mass.: Marketing Science Institute, 1970) show the disparity between consumption patterns for whites and blacks with the same income. We associate blacks with the ghetto and low-income areas; yet low-income whites outnumber low-income blacks two to one.

sets. Given their limited expenditures on recreation, should one classify television as a luxury or a necessity? Symbolism enters into other purchases of the poor. The working-class wife dreams of a modern kitchen not only for its labor-saving features as a middle-class wife might, but as a symbolic end in itself. Black families consume twice as much scotch—a high-status drink—as do whites.[38] Caplovitz refers to this behavior as "compensatory consumption," which is the equivalent for low-income people of Veblen's conspicuous consumption.[39]

2. Getting the best quality at the lowest price. The poor score low on this count. They are less inclined to search for lower prices, are less well informed, and less willing to buy used items. Although the percentage of the poor with installment debt may be no greater than for other income groups, the *burden* of the debt may be more severe since their debt-income ratio is higher. Their failure to seek bargains and their inferior knowledge of market conditions probably stem from their lower level of education. The recent migrant status of many blacks and Puerto Ricans contributes to their problem. They tend to shop close to home in personalized surroundings until they get acclimated to their new environment. This lack of mobility reduces their purchase options and minimizes their market knowledge. On the other hand, Richards indicates that the poor tend to shop for specials in the purchase of durables, and the *very* poor are inclined to buy goods on sale—practices that give them high marks for good consumership.

3. Budgeting incomes and planning purchases ahead. Again the poor show up badly. Many of them have a negative net worth. Their lack of education affects their knowledge of money management. Planning suffers too when the immediate assumes overriding importance, as it does for those who live a hand-to-mouth existence. Richards reports a study showing that education is more important than income in predicting planning propensities.[40] Poor people's lower education level may reduce their ability to conceive of the abstraction of deferred spending when immediate gratification seems infinitely more rewarding and perhaps even necessary for survival.

4. Meeting needs through home production. The poor seem to rely less on home growing of food and home repairs than others. Living in crowded urban housing and owning fewer homes partly account for these tendencies. Education is another contributing factor. Home production depends in part upon acquiring skills and training that many poor lack. The cost of acquiring tools also deters them.

5. Taking advantage of consumer benefits. Legal, medical, and other agencies are available to the poor, but Richards reports that they fail to use them as much as they might to relieve their financial plight.

---

[38]Richards, "Consumer Practices," p. 48.
[39]Caplovitz, *The Poor Pay More*, p. 13. He borrows the term from Robert K. Merton.
[40]Richards, "Consumer Practices," p. 55.

Running through these behavioral patterns are several common threads. First is fatalism, a life theme that leads to resignation to one's condition. Related to this is poor people's orientation to the present, which calls for more immediate gratification of impulses and less planning for the future. They are also less mobile, physically and socially. Confined by tradition and lack of transportation to their neighborhood, the poor are less well equipped to "shop around." A reluctance to deal with strangers contributes to this condition. Social restrictions (immobility) heighten the desire for status objects and entertainment alternatives—hence, the tendency toward compensatory consumption. This behavior points up another characteristic—concreteness, or stressing material over intellectual things. Underlying most of their behavior is the pervading influence of education. Inadequate schooling lies at the heart of many of the poor's marketing problems. In part, it accounts for their being bilked by unscrupulous merchants. It limits their knowledge of market opportunities. It reduces their access to agencies and information which would improve their bargain-hunting batting average and would help to bail them out of the unpleasant aftermath of unwise purchases.[41] Most important, better education should beget more income, which could do much to relieve their downtrodden condition.

A CONCLUDING NOTE

At the outset of this chapter, the following question was posed: Does government intervention in the price-making process of the American economy benefit or hinder the consumer? While some legislation can be termed proconsumer, other government measures aim to protect competitors from each other, and in so doing constitute probusiness pricing protection measures. Historically, appeals for proconsumer price protection have been loudest during periods of accelerated, rather than gradual, inflation.

The consumer's right to accurate information as to price and terms of sale has received considerable attention from legislators and consumer advocates. The Truth-in-Lending Law at the federal level and unit pricing legislation passed in several states seek to aid the consumer in making rational buying decisions. Available evidence indicates that these information sources are used selectively by various customer segments. Many argue that consumer education programs are needed to increase the utilization of the information by low-income consumers.

Such consumers, specifically ghetto residents, face unique problems in their interaction with marketing institutions. First, the limited availability of high-volume food chain operations in low-income areas puts the ghetto resident at a disadvantage in food buying. Second, in nonfood retailing, the poor are disadvantaged in several ways. Forced to rely on credit, they often become victimized by unscrupulous merchants and by their ignorance of commercial practices. A number of existing and potential remedies exist, one of which is

---

[41] "When asked where they would go for help if they were being cheated by a merchant or salesman, almost two-thirds of the low-income consumers interviewed replied that they did not know." (Eric Schnapper, "Consumer Legislation and the Poor," in Aaker and Day, *Consumerism*, p. 343.)

the introduction of more low-cost retail institutions into ghetto areas. Are channels of distribution in the United States marketing system neglecting or providing marginal coverage of selected market segments? Questions such as this constitute the theme of the next chapter.

Discussion Questions

1. Distinguish between probusiness and proconsumer price protection. Can you cite specific examples of laws that fall into each category?

2. Is the consumer better or worse off with the repeal of fair trade laws? Explain.

3. Evaluate this statement: Many of the consumer protection measures such as truth-in-lending and unit pricing seem to be more beneficial to high- rather than low-income shoppers.

4. Many ghetto retailers victimize shoppers with "bait-and-switch" selling tactics. Define the term. As a consumer, have you been exposed to this approach? Describe the situation.

5. Can legislation feasibly limit the use of "bait-and-switch" tactics? How would it work?

6. What obligation, if any, does the municipal government have to improve ghetto marketing conditions?

7. A company's board of directors represents its stockholders. What is your reaction to the suggestion that companies also have a board of consumers to represent consumers and the public in general?

Suggested Exercises: Class or Small Group Assignments

1. There seems to be some uncertainty as to whether ghetto-area food prices are or are not higher than prices outside the ghetto. Draw up a research design that would answer this question.

2. Using a carefully selected sample of items, compare the prices of a small independent food store with those of a large chain market. Are the prices different? If so, why?

Chapter Overview

SEVEN
Channels of Distribution: Ethical and Legal Dimensions

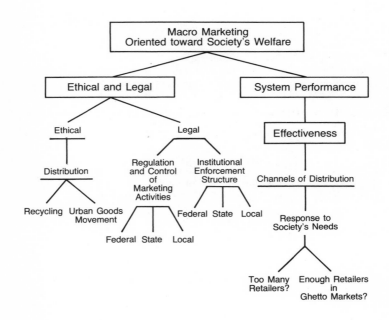

Three objectives are sought in this chapter. First, discussion centers on the effectiveness of channels of distribution in responding to society's needs. As some critics charge, are selected segments of the market ignored (for instance, ghetto consumers) by the distribution system while others receive an overabundance of attention? Second, the ecological dimensions of channels are analyzed. Here the social and economic costs of recycling and urban goods movement are examined. Third, attention is centered on the political and legal debate surrounding vertical marketing systems. The petroleum industry stands in the center of this intriguing debate.

SEVEN

Channels of Distribution: Ethical and Legal Dimensions

Channels of distribution are among the most complex phenomena encountered in an advanced economy.[1] A marketing channel can be defined as the set of institutions which participates in or facilitates the movement of goods or services from the point of production to the point of consumption. Since consumers perform important marketing functions, they too should be considered channel members along with retailers, wholesalers, and a host of other marketing intermediaries.

For centuries, middlemen—such as retailers and wholesalers—have been the frequent targets of critics. A sixth-century Roman statesman argued that when a middleman resells goods for more than their cost, "the trader must either have paid less than the goods were worth or sold them for more than their value."[2] As for retailers, Polanyi notes that the Greek word for retailer, *kapelos,* is synonymous with trickster.[3] Criticism of marketing institutions continues today.

Since most products are not consumed at the point of production, marketing functions must be performed to close the time, space, and ownership gaps that separate sellers and buyers. The marketing channels established to perform these functions take many forms, ranging from direct selling (seller to buyer) to a myriad of other combinations with varying numbers of intermediaries. Channels are an important economic mechanism in society. To illustrate, over $200 billion is spent annually in the United States in moving products from the manufacturing to the consuming level.[4]

An analysis of channels of distribution raises a number of important macro questions for the student of marketing. Are there too many retailers? Are selected segments of society, such as low-income groups, inadequately served by the distribution system? From an ecological perspective, are channels a problem (waste, pollution) or an opportunity (a recycling path)? What are the contemporary legal questions that encircle distribution? These questions establish the boundaries of the chapter.

CHANNELS: EFFICIENCY AND EFFECTIVENESS

Driving to class each day, you may come to an intersection that offers four gas stations: a self-service station, an independent outlet, and two major affiliates. Time permitting, you may prefer to take advantage of the lower-price self-service retailer. If in a hurry, you may select the most expedient alternative. Channels of distribution often deliver such trade-offs. One of the strongest indictments of marketing is that it is wasteful. Excessive advertising, unnecessary product differentiation, and contrived product obsolescence—these alleged wastes were examined in earlier chapters. Another allegation remains: excessive resources devoted to retailing. What is the evidence to confirm or deny existence

---

[1]Bert C. McCammon, Jr., and Robert W. Little, "Marketing Channels: Analytical Systems and Approaches," in *Science in Marketing,* ed. George Schwartz (New York: John Wiley and Sons, 1965), p. 322.

[2]Robert L. Steiner, "The Prejudice Against Marketing," *Journal of Marketing,* 40 (July 1976), p. 3.

[3]Reported in Steiner, ibid., p. 3.

[4]Donald J. Bowersox, *Logistical Management* (New York: The Macmillan Company, 1974), pp. 13–14.

of this factor and, if confirmed, what is the social cost of having excess retail capacity? And what social costs are associated with the high mortality rate in retailing?

Too Many Retailers?

Substantial excess capacity exists in most retail establishments. Customer shopping patterns pretty well dictate that it will exist. Living habits and working hours limit the shopping time available to many customers; this leads to peaks and valleys in weekly store sales. Seasonal factors cause additional sales fluctuations. Retailers have attempted to even out sales through such devices as "early-bird" specials, but most such efforts produce limited success. Thus, stores are burdened with almost continuous excess capacity. The extent of the excess is evident during peak periods (for example, the Christmas season) when sales volume far surpasses the levels achieved in slack times. Superfluous capacity also exists with semimechanized facilities such as vending machines, which stand idle most of the time.

Excess Store Capacity: Cost or Benefit? Measuring the extent of retail excess capacity and its social cost is almost impossible. If one views a retail establishment as a conduit through which goods flow, then certainly existing facilities are capable of enormous output expansion or, conversely, far fewer physical facilities could handle a given volume. Obviously, retailers provide more than a vehicle for transferring goods from wholesale intermediaries or producers to consumers. They sell a bundle of services that accompany the transfer of goods. Limiting surplus capacity within a store might reduce for some the psychic pleasure of shopping by creating congestion, queuing problems, and so on.

No matter what yardstick one uses to measure capacity in retailing, considerable excess continually exists. New firms add to capacity; others drop out through failure or for other reasons. So "wastes" are evident both because of a continuing overhang of excess capacity and because of repeated failures. Defenders of the prevailing system argue that this waste is the price we pay to maintain viably competitive markets. Providing consumers with alternative sources of supply strengthens price competition. Maintaining ease of market entry also buttresses the free market system. It gives would-be entrepreneurs the opportunity to try—if only to fail.

Retail Space Recycled Cox reminds us that we have little conclusive evidence of the inefficiencies involved in retailing's high mortality rate.[5] We assume that the social cost of repeated failures in retailing is high—that failures result in the loss of physical resources in addition to the misallocation of effort that might have been more productively expended in alternative employment. Although no data have been gathered concerning the dollar loss from retailers' failures, we can still analyze their impact.

---

[5]Reavis Cox, *Distribution in a High Level Economy* (Englewood Cliffs, N.J.: Prentice-Hall, 1965), p. 180.

First, we have to separate the social waste of the failure itself from the waste resulting from the aforementioned excess retail capacity. Any firm operating at less than capacity contributes to inefficiency, even though it operates successfully and is in no danger of bankruptcy. However, the unsuccessful firm is likely to encounter inadequate sales or abnormally high costs (the two are usually related), both of which reflect economic waste. Thus, excessive social costs precede failure. Do they follow from the failure itself? At first glance, they would appear to. There is visible evidence of waste when a retail establishment fails—an empty store, idle equipment, distressed merchandise, and unemployed personnel. But the retail trade structure is dynamic; firms die and new ones enter continuously. Entrants often acquire the facilities of those that have failed—even though the new firms may operate in different retail trades. Therefore, much of what appears to be wasted is recovered and reused. This recycling process apparently limits the extent of the economic loss—"apparently" because recycling may perpetuate inefficiency under new ownership. Failure may have stemmed from excessive overcapacity in the trade (as distinct from "normal" overcapacity) or from an unsatisfactory store location. If the successor firm operates in the same trade as the one that failed, economic waste is likely to continue. The same is true if the location is inadequate. Eventually the physical facilities fall into disuse and society finally writes off the assets as dead losses. In the meantime, the retailer uses more resources than necessary to function efficiently so that, until his or her demise, society is burdened with continuing economic waste.

One might argue that society is served by the process of recycling bankrupt retail trade facilities since, using a sunk-costs argument, it costs nothing to use up existing facilities. Furthermore, society gains by getting the full measure of value from existent facilities. This argument ignores the wastes that might accrue from the underutilization of the uneconomic retail capacity. Given the presence of continuing excess capacity, a better alternative would call for existing firms to take up the slack.

Too Many Gas Stations? Reducing the number of retail outlets to limit overcapacity is an appealing solution. Some years ago, Richard Lundy tackled this problem when he asked whether we had too many gas stations.[6] To answer this question requires the query: "Too many for what?" The optimum number of stations depends upon whose interest is paramount. Lundy roughly estimated the various optima, given certain assumptions. At one extreme, he postulated exaggerated conditions that would minimize the number of stations. Conditions bore little resemblance to reality. He had customers buying gas 24 hours a day, with no break between cars receiving service; only one brand was available; cars would arrive at the station with an empty tank and get filled up; stations would be located so as to equalize demand at each outlet. At the other extreme, conditions would solely favor the customers. For example, no customer would live more than one-half mile from a station. Other models called for enough sta-

---

[6]Richard D. Lundy, "How Many Service Stations Are 'Too Many'?" in *Theory in Marketing,* ed. Reavis Cox and Wroe Alderson (Homewood, Ill.: Richard D. Irwin, 1950), pp. 321–336.

tions to maximize station operators' profits by setting up a system of little monopolies, or for enough stations of a certain quality to maximize customers' welfare.

Obviously the number of stations required to meet each standard varied enormously—from a minimum of 1,906 stations (5,718 pumps) to a maximum of at least 4.4 million stations. These totals compared with the 1.5 million pumps then (1946) in existence. Lundy's estimates are rather meaningless. The assumptions were too wild to be taken seriously and he failed to trace the second-order effects on consumption of his assumptions—for example, the impact on consumption of monopoly conditions. But the exercise is useful to point out the divergent answers to the question: "How many retailers?" It depends. It depends on how one balances the diverse needs of various elements in the economic system. Answering the question hinges on the answers to other questions. What price are we willing to pay for convenience? Can we limit entry without infringing on individuals' economic freedom? How do we balance the inefficiency stemming from excess capacity against the benefits of a vigorous competitive system?

Solutions Difficult As long as barriers against entry into retailing are low, it will be hard to eliminate chronic overcapacity and to reduce substantially retailing's high mortality rate. Relieving the overcapacity problem will require reducing artificial governmental support of small retailing. Chain store taxes, minimum markup laws, and the Robinson-Patman Act buttress the atomistic structure of retailing and contribute to its inefficiency.

Better planning, more adequate financing, and improved training may reduce the mortality rate. Many franchising operations combine these advantages to the benefit of the franchisee. Available data indicate that sound franchise establishments have higher success ratios than do traditional independent retailers; however, there is a danger that overbuilding of franchises may lead to a continuation of the chronic overcapacity problem. The proliferation of fast-food outlets, many of which are essentially franchised, demonstrates that franchising is not a panacea.

Shopper Efficiency

Consumers are often called upon to assume some marketing functions formerly performed by distributors. Importantly, opportunities exist for shifting marketing functions backward in the channel toward the producer and forward toward the consumer. Someone must perform the marketing functions. What are the costs and benefits to the consumer who performs those functions?

The "Costs" of Shopping

Anthony Downs has spelled out the goals of consumers in the buying process.[7] Along with producers, consumers seek to maximize efficiency—the "efficiency of consumption." Consumption costs include money, time, and energy. Money costs consist of the cost of goods bought, transportation costs incurred in shopping, and income lost from shopping instead of engaging in remunerative work. Included in time costs are all expenditures of time in the shopping process—traveling to and from stores and time spent in selecting and paying for goods. Energy output is directly proportional to time expended in shopping, but some shoppers expend additional energy fighting traffic, arranging for baby sitters, and so on.

Consumers weigh the importance of these three elements differently, depending on varying evaluations of their relative importance. Factors affecting their importance to each consumer are the individual's income, prices of specific goods, the degree of product standardization (standardized products economize on time spent comparing various offerings), and the time pressure under which the consumer operates. What appears to be irrational buyer behavior may stem from different weights being applied to these four factors. A wasteful expenditure of time to one shopper may represent an important price saving to another.

Downs cites a number of recent developments in retailing that have increased consumers' shopping efficiency. Among them: suburban shopping centers, which save walking time and also create scale economies from shoppers' patronizing several stores on one shopping trip; scrambled merchandising, which makes more variety available in a single store; self-service, with its attendant reduction in costs and prices; longer shopping hours, which allow several members of the family to shop together—another time economizer.

Shopper Efficiency versus Marketing Efficiency

Let us examine in more detail the effect on total efficiency of some of these changes in marketing, for example, the introduction of self-service in grocery and variety stores. Here, increased efficiency at the distributor level occurs at the expense of the consumer buyer. The consumer waits on him- or herself rather than being served. Inputs under the old system consisted of labor performed by the store clerk (plus other nonlabor inputs), and shopping time expended by the customer.

---

[7]This section draws on Anthony Downs, "A Theory of Consumer Efficiency," in *Social Issues in Marketing,* ed. Lee E. Preston (Glenview, Ill.: Scott, Foresman, 1968), pp. 106–111.

Much of the so-called shopping time was, in effect, waiting time. This condition continues to exist where the customer is waited on—at a gas station pump, for example. Under self-service, it is not clear whether the customer's shopping time is increased or reduced.[8] If shoppers spend no more time shopping under self-service than they did when they were provided service, then there has been no transfer in cost from the retailer to the buyer. But there is a net efficiency gain to the buyer from the lower margins resulting from the retailer's reduced labor costs.

Several factors could modify this conclusion. Although the consumer may devote no more time to shopping with self-service, he or she performs more work and expends more energy than when service is provided. This represents a "cost" that legitimately should be balanced against the efficiency gains accruing to the retailer. Delivery is another function that is often transferred from the retailer to the customer. Again, this transfer may represent a net gain in total shopper-retailer efficiency. Avoiding delivery service reduces the retailer's costs but, since the shopper usually must return home after shopping regardless of who makes delivery, the opportunity cost of the shopper's assuming the delivery function is zero.[9] This purely economic orientation also ignores psychic "costs" to the shopper: the extra energy exerted in carrying the goods and the psychic loss from being burdened with packages.

There is another aspect to the problem. Self-service shopping thrusts a burden on the customers to increase their product knowledge. They must gain either specific product knowledge or added brand awareness. Acquiring the information involves an imputed cost measured, again, by the opportunities lost in the process. Correctly evaluating the net gain to the economy from the introduction of self-service would require an appropriate adjustment for this aggregate opportunity cost.

We face similar problems in assessing the net effect of shifting packaging functions from grocery stores, hardware stores, and other shops to the manufacturer. The shift reduces distribution costs, but at the expense of manufacturers. Since packaging lends itself to scale economies, there is probably a net gain to consumers. What they gain in lower cost, however, they lose in flexibility by having to accept a limited number of package sizes.

Self-service, as we have seen, improves marketing efficiency for distributors by shifting functional burdens to the shopper. Other marketing innovations could similarly reduce marketing costs either by curtailing services offered or transferring some of the marketing tasks to shoppers. To illustrate, individual item prices can be removed by retailers employing the Universal Product Code scanning system (discussed in chapter 6). Price removal increases the retailer's efficiency but many argue that it reduces the shopper's efficiency. Some years ago Bressler examined similar trade-offs in milk distribution. He found that costs could be cut up to 2.5 cents per quart by delivering on alternate days instead

---

[8]Comparisons here are difficult since the product assortments in self-service and nonself-service stores are usually vastly different.

[9]The conclusions reached here ignore the situation where shoppers phone in their orders.

of daily.[10] Requiring customers to buy milk in stores rather than receive alternate-day delivery could lower costs an additional 2.4 cents per quart.

Efficiency versus Competition   Still other marketing innovations could further cut distribution costs, but at the expense of viable competitive markets. Bressler also suggested the possibility of creating exclusive dealer territories in milk distribution to reduce competitive overlap, with a possible cost savings of 2 cents per quart. And an innovation in manufacturing—the creation of dairy plant monopolies—could reduce milk costs in some towns an additional 4 cents per quart. Whether or not Bressler's cost figures are correct, it is questionable whether the reduced costs would translate themselves into lower prices. The market imperfections implicit in these two innovations would certainly lead to monopoly profits in the absence of governmental regulation.

Can we achieve a reduction in the wastes of competition without resorting to the creation of monopoly markets? Is there a compromise between "too many retailers" on the one hand and "too few" on the other? Let's look at the situation in ghetto market areas and see whether we can learn from experience there. Critics argue that the ghetto retail structure offers consumers few shopping alternatives, forcing them to rely on high-cost, less efficient retailers.

Ghetto Markets: Enough Retailers?

A suggested remedy for higher prices in the ghetto is the development of a greater number of more efficient retail operations. Of course, they already exist in many locations. But critics of present ghetto marketing practices would like to see more. They feel that too many low-income residents are dependent for food and other purchases upon small, inefficient retailers. Ghetto merchants and chain store executives argue that conditions peculiar to the ghetto cause prices to rise. Among these conditions are higher pilferage rates; higher insurance costs arising out of vandalism and mistreatment of equipment; elevated land costs and rents; lower total sales volume, which increases overhead costs per unit; and smaller purchases per customer in food stores.[11] Evidence also indicates that ghetto stores have a problem of recruiting and maintaining competent management personnel, and this factor is bound to affect costs. Less vigorous competition in ghetto retailing is a noncost element that also must influence prices. Many low-income areas lack the stimulation of chain store supermarket competition. The reduced mobility of ghetto residents and their attachment to local stores where service is personalized limit shopping alternatives, with a consequent reduction in competitive pressure.

---

[10]R. G. Bressler, Jr., *City Milk Distribution* (Cambridge, Mass.: Harvard University Press, 1952).

[11]Because the per capita sale in an inner-city store averages only one-half of the typical sale in a suburban store, more help is needed to serve twice as much traffic to ring up the same sales dollars. The wear and tear on the store and its fixtures are also more a result of traffic than of sales volume." Donald S. Perkins, "The Low-Income Consumer—A Human Problem and a Selling Problem," speech in Executive Lecture Series, University of Notre Dame, March 2, 1970.

Donald S. Perkins says that attempts to cut the cost of food in retailing in the ghetto leads to an irony. "Most of the efforts to make sure that the poor don't pay more, may in fact be insuring that the poor will pay more."[12] Perkins, president of a food retailing chain, claims that multichain-store operators with ghetto stores try to charge the same prices in the ghetto that they do outside. Evidence from congressional hearings on ghetto food prices reveals the same pattern. Operating with higher costs, ghetto stores suffer a price-cost squeeze. Perkins claims that the squeeze has eliminated profits for many chain stores and left others only marginally profitable. The result: abandonment of stores, which leaves the field open to smaller, high-cost operations. Hence the irony.

Actual cost data on ghetto retailing operations are scarce. Donald Sexton reports that the gross margins for poverty area supermarkets are 3.3% higher than the average for all supermarkets.[13] A comparative study of furniture and appliance dealers in and out of the ghetto in Washington, D.C., provides more comprehensive information on this score. Table 7.1 summarizes the data. The wide disparity in gross margins accounts for the big price differentials between the two classes of stores. A small part of the difference traces to varying profit margins. Higher salary and commission expense in the ghetto stores results from their greater use of door-to-door commission salespeople, who also double as bill collectors. "Other" expenses include administration and delivery expenses, costs of processing credit, interest on borrowed funds, legal and insurance costs. Given the character of ghetto retail operations, one can understand why stores in low-income areas have higher costs. The larger bad debt loss figure for ghetto stores appears to contradict earlier evidence that the loss ratio is not appreciably higher for the poor than for higher income people. Even if the loss figure is only a little higher, the concentration of low-income shoppers' purchases in ghetto stores and their much lower relative patronage of nonghetto stores would exaggerate the difference in bad debt costs. Less use of citywide advertising media by ghetto merchants accounts for their lower ad costs.

A Bottom Line Comparison   The most significant feature of Table 7.1 is the fairly narrow difference in profit margins for the two classes of stores. Critics tend to associate higher prices with higher profits. This example is not conclusive, but it contradicts the usual impression. A larger sample of the Washington, D.C., stores revealed similar findings. Data on rates of return on stockholders' equity were mixed. For the larger sample of stores, they give the edge to the nonghetto stores; for the 20-store sample covered in Table 7.1, rates of return on equity for the ghetto stores were 12.7% compared with 8.1% for the general market retailers.[14] These data suffer from serious limitations. The cooperating stores used nonuniform accounting practices. Even if they are only

---

[12]Perkins, ibid.

[13]Donald E. Sexton, Jr., "Food Sales Mix and Profitability: Ghetto Supermarkets Revisited," *Journal of Business,* 47 (October 1974), pp. 538–542; see also Loraine Donaldson and Raymond S. Strangways, "Can Ghetto Groceries Price Competitively and Make a Profit?" *Journal of Business,* 46 (January 1973), pp. 61–65.

[14]Federal Trade Commission, *District of Columbia Retailers,* p. 21. The data covered only nine of the ten nonghetto stores.

TABLE 7–1   COMPARISON OF EXPENSES AND PROFITS FOR LOW-INCOME AND GENERAL MARKET
RETAILERS OF FURNITURE AND APPLIANCES IN WASHINGTON, D.C., 1966.

Revenue Component	10 Low-Income Retailers ($5,146,395)[c]	10 General Market Retailers ($5,405,221)[c]
Operating ratio as percent of sales	100.0	100.0
Cost of goods sold	37.8	64.5
Gross profit margin	62.2	35.5
Salary and commission expense[a]	28.2	17.8
Advertising expense	2.1	3.9
Bad debt losses	6.7	0.3
Other expenses[b]	21.3	11.2
Total expenses	58.3	33.2
Net return on sales	3.9	2.3

[a]Includes officers' salaries.
[b]Other expenses, including taxes, after deductions of other income.
[c]1966 sales.

SOURCE.   Federal Trade Commission, "Economic Report on Installment Credit and Retail
Sales Practices of District of Columbia Retailers," March 1968, p. 18.

approximate, they shed some light on an area that is shrouded in suspicion.
The absence of abnormally high profits for the ghetto stores need not surprise
us. Given reasonably free entry conditions, abnormal profits should induce
entrants into trade. This should damp down prices and restore a normal
profit equilibrium.

Considering the higher risk conditions that exist in the ghetto, merchants
there ought to expect the reward of higher profits. If other profit margin data
revealed that profits in the ghetto exceeded those outside the ghetto, critics
legitimately ought to show that they are greater than necessary to compensate
for the added risk if they are to substantiate their charges of gouging. It is unfor-
tunate that so little cost-and profit-margin data exist to help evaluate the competitive performance of ghetto retailing. Most studies emphasize prices. Until
we have more complete profit comparisons and a better idea of appropriate risk
premiums for operating in the inner city, we cannot competently judge performance there.

Suggested Remedies Having examined some of the cost constraints facing ghetto merchants, how can they be overcome? Suggested corrections take several forms, usually involving some kind of government intervention. Sturdivant proposes an investment guarantee plan to encourage investment in the ghetto. It would protect retailers against losses from riots, arson, looting, and other manifestations of civil unrest.[15] The guarantee would reimburse merchants not only for physical damage but also for loss of profits. An assessment based on the value of insured assets would provide funds for reimbursing losses. This proposal would cover all ghetto retail operations and not just food stores. Sturdivant would couple the arrangement with a proviso cancelling the guarantee if a retailer violated laws designed to protect consumers, for example, if installment loan interest ceilings were exceeded. The guarantee would insure against the added investment risks in the ghetto. To compensate for higher costs, Sturdivant would offer investment tax credits. It is hard to imagine how this incentive would help the retailer who is unable to earn a profit because of elevated costs.

Others suggest tax incentives and investment guarantees.[16] Among additional remedies proposed to make new retailing investments in the inner city more attractive are lower insurance rates (presumably through government subsidy), better police protection, an arrangement for noncancellable insurance policies, and provision for land clearance for store sites.

Perkins suggests a unique subsidy scheme to encourage the introduction of large food stores into the ghetto in spite of higher costs there.[17] He would offer the merchant the subsidy in return for his banking food stamps that are spent in his store. This not only induces the merchant to serve an area that he might otherwise shun but it also encourages the merchant to woo the poor—a refreshing contrast to the existing situation. Undoubtedly, subsidies could take other forms. This is only one example of their use. Subsidies can be effective in encouraging economic activity which, in their absence, would not occur; however, they may induce an "inefficient" allocation of resources. They call forth activity that does not occur in response to normal market forces. Bringing them into play requires a public policy determination that their benefits exceed the possible inefficiencies in resource allocation that their use may create.[18]

To this point, our discussion has focused on both the efficiency and the effectiveness of the retail trade structure. The former centers on chronic overcapacity, the latter on the alleged inadequate channel coverage for low-income segments. If, indeed, retail coverage is insufficient, *shopper* efficiency questions emerge. To reach the more efficient high-volume, low-price retailers, the ghetto consumer faces higher shopping "costs"—time, transportation, and so on.

---

[15]Frederick D. Sturdivant, "Better Deal for the Ghetto Shoppers," in *The Ghetto Marketplace,* ed. Sturdivant (New York: The Free Press, 1969), p. 153.

[16]For example, see "Should Supermarkets Take a New Look at Urban Areas?" in Sturdivant, *The Ghetto Marketplace,* p. 180.

[17]Perkins, "The Low-Income Consumer."

[18]We need to stress the possible inefficient allocation of resources. Whether it is efficient or inefficient depends on the cost functions that result from the subsidies' use. They may create a situation in which the scale of output is enlarged sufficiently to move the firm down its long-run cost curve, hence improve its technical efficiency.

CHANNELS: ECOLOGICAL DIMENSIONS

The ecological dimensions of channels of distribution often go unnoticed. Let's explore two specific linkage problems in the channel. The first concerns the significant and costly problems of moving goods in crowded urban centers, while the second examines the potential use of the channel of distribution as a recycling path.

Urban Goods Movement

The congested trade structure in many urban centers creates unique obstacles in the channel of distribution. Traffic congestion in urban areas is often blamed on the automobile, but vehicles carrying goods to central markets add significantly to the problem. This movement is costly from both an economic and a social standpoint. The economic costs include the inefficiencies that result from moving small shipments of goods through congested urban centers. Social costs are noise and air pollution created by the vehicles. Specific examples point up the problem.

The New York Trucking Association estimates that the average truck operating in midtown Manhattan loses four hours in earning time daily because of congestion.[19] To maintain a given level of customer service, there is an increased need for vehicles, manpower, and related capital as well as rising operating, maintenance, insurance, and wage expenses. Trucks carrying small shipments cross paths and get in each others' way. The resulting congestion adds to the morning rush hour traffic and increases costs and frustration for all members of the channel—shippers, receivers, and consumers.

Degree of Congestion   The magnitude of the problem is dramatized by what occurs on a typical weekday in a small section of downtown Brooklyn. Commodities are brought into the area by 28 carriers, but are redistributed by 4,200 smaller delivery vehicles.[20] Similar results appear in an analysis of truck movement in the central business district (CBD) of Columbus, Ohio.[21] Dennis McDermott and James Robeson focus on vehicles delivering or picking up freight in the under-5,000-pound range (less than a truckload). Approximately 660 vehicles fitting this description enter the Columbus CBD daily. Some intriguing examples of the "costs" of this goods movement are summarized below:

1. Average speed of vehicles in urban center—5.2 m.p.h.

2. Total vehicle time in CBD—986 hours (25% of time in transit; 25% queuing time)

3. Air pollution emitted by vehicles—460 pounds of carbon monoxide, 108 pounds of hydrocarbons, and 36 pounds of nitrogen oxide

---

[19]*Urban Goods Movement Projects and Data Sources,* Department of Transportation, Office of Systems Analysis and Information, Washington, D.C., June 1973.
[20]Robert A. Leighton and Robert T. Wood, "A Rational Urban Cartage System," *Transportation and Distribution Management,* October 1971, pp. 15–20.
[21]Dennis R. McDermott and James F. Robeson, "The Role of Terminal Consolidation in Urban Goods Distribution" (Unpublished working paper, the Ohio State University, 1974).

4. Daily cost of providing pickup and delivery in area—$11,750 per day.[22]

Any Solutions? Are there any remedies to the urban congestion/small shipment problem? Several proposed solutions are offered—among them are the temporal and spatial separation of passenger and freight movement, improvements in traffic engineering, and the consolidation of small shipments through a centralized terminal. McDermott and Robeson examine the feasibility of the consolidated approach to urban small shipment pickup and delivery service and uncover encouraging results.[23] If all shipments under 5,000 pounds were routed through a consolidation terminal in Columbus, the researchers forecast a vehicle flow reduction of 90% and an annual savings of over $2 million. The costs of building, maintaining, and operating the consolidation terminal are not included in this analysis.

Roadblocks While the benefits appear to be great, a number of obstacles block immediate implementation of the concept. First, the plan requires close cooperation among several publics: shippers, receivers, and carriers, as well as city planners and other government officials. Jurisdictional disputes between localities or competing labor unions can erect a formidable obstacle. Second, the effectiveness of the consolidation terminal concept depends upon the successful management of the facility. To illustrate, a manufacturer might not surrender control of the transportation function unless the same level of customer service was provided at a lower cost. Local legislation could *require* participation in the consolidation concept, but the enforcement problems would be enormous. Third, the urban center constitutes only one component in the national transportation network. Given the myriad controls within the system, can the initiative for an improvement in network efficiency originate at the municipal level?

Often, seemingly obvious and significant problems are clouded by daily routine and receive surprisingly little recognition. The urban goods movement problem is no exception—this important channel problem requires attention.

Recycling

Every year each American throws away over a ton of solid waste (industrial construction, commercial and household use).[24] The declining supply of natural resources, coupled with an increasing recognition of the social costs of solid waste pollution, has stimulated business and governmental interest in recycling efforts. Glass and aluminum containers, paper, and related packaging materials retain value after product use—value that often goes untapped. In most cases, such materials are discarded but, occasionally, the consumer may put the materials to another use (jelly jar to drinking glass), or take advantage of a recycling alternative (a returnable container). The recycling alternative has the

---

[22]Ibid.

[23]Ibid.

[24]Reported in William G. Zikmund and William J. Stanton, "Recycling Solid Wastes: A Channels-of-Distribution Problem," *Journal of Marketing,* 35 (July 1971), p. 34.

greatest promise of reclaiming vital resources, but poses unique challenges for all members in the channel of distribution.

Reverse Distribution   William Zikmund and William Stanton note that recycling is unusual from a marketing perspective because the consumer is the first link in the "reverse-distribution" process and must assume the role of a seller.[25] The consumer's (seller's) role is to distribute his waste materials to the market that demands his product."[26] Two important problems are inherent in this reverse distribution process. First, the consumer must be motivated to initiate the recycling process and assume specific marketing functions. Sorting (for example, aluminum, paper, glass), storing, and transporting waste materials from the household to a recycling point require an expenditure of time and energy. Will the social and financial rewards outweigh the costs? Likely, the degree of participation will vary with the extent of the recycling effort (all solid waste materials versus beverage containers) and the rewards. Second, similar trade-offs emerge for other members of the channel. Retailers, other middlemen, and manufacturers must create and maintain the recycling path. All members incur costs in handling, sorting, and transporting the solid waste materials. Again, the incentives must be sufficient to encourage participation and cooperation in the channel. Alternatively, new types of middlemen may evolve to facilitate this backward flow.

Limited evidence is available on recycling programs for specific materials, such as beverage containers. Oregon, Vermont, Maine, and Michigan and a number of localities have passed legislation to encourage the use of returnable bottles. The Vermont law, for example, requires a 5-cent deposit on all beverage containers—bottles and cans. The law calls for a gradual elimination of all beverage containers that are not refillable. Such legislation is endorsed by environmental groups as a way to reduce litter, while others point to the energy savings that may result from extending the useful life of bottles. A Federal Energy Administration study estimates that the exclusive use of returnable containers by 1982 could reduce by 44% the amount of energy consumed by the beverage industry.[27] Indeed, such projections are dependent upon consumer and channel support of recycling programs.

VERTICAL MARKETING SYSTEMS: POLITICAL AND LEGAL DEBATE

Vertical marketing systems are ". . . professionally managed and centrally programmed networks, pre-engineered to achieve operating economies and maximum market impact."[28] These systems take several forms and are increasing rapidly in the United States and other advanced economic systems. The

---

[25]Ibid., pp. 34–39.
[26]Ibid., p. 35.
[27]Preliminary report by the Federal Energy Administration, October 9, 1976.
[28]From Bert McCammon, Jr., "Perspectives for Distribution Programming," reported in Philip Kotler, *Marketing Management: Analysis, Planning, and Control,* 3rd ed. (Englewood Cliffs, N.J.: Prentice-Hall, 1976), p. 282.

impressive economies in purchasing, distribution, management training, mass advertising, and related areas account for this growth. Critics argue that in selected industries the consolidation of successive stages of production and distribution under single ownership weakens competition.

Petroleum—A Prime Target

The petroleum industry is a key target of this criticism and is under the strongest attack by government since 1911, when the Justice Department succeeded in taking apart the Standard Oil Trust. Proposed federal legislation, seeking divestiture of the operations of the vertically integrated petroleum companies, is stimulating heated public debate.[29] Table 7.2 outlines core issues in the debate.

The Battle All of the issues focus on a central question: does vertical integration play an anticompetitive role in the petroleum industry? Critics "claim that integrated petroleum companies have used profits from the production level to subsidize refining and marketing operations and, in this way, have discouraged entry by non-integrated refiners and marketers."[30] Economists generally hold that such complaints against vertical integration are groundless—shifting profits between production and marketing stages is an accounting illusion. In this sense, the vertically integrated organization is no different from any firm that relies on *established* products to subsidize *new* products.[31]Others argue that if the oil companies use crude oil profits to subsidize other operations (refining and marketing), they are acting against their own economic self-interest. Why should the companies invest in unprofitable activities? William Johnson and Richard Messick note that ". . . most integrated oil refiners have, for this reason, relied increasingly on independent oil jobbers and marketers for the sale of their products."[32]

A second major attack on vertical integration centers on the market power derived from the relatively concentrated segments of the petroleum industry such as pipelines. The petroleum industry is not as concentrated as the automobile, tire, steel, or a range of other industries. In fact, no marketer has as much as 11% of the market.[33] Critics contend that such measures fail to capture the complex web of crisscrossing business deals and cooperative agreements that tie the largest petroleum companies together in production, transportation, and marketing. Fred Allvine and James Patterson argue that the petroleum industry overinvested in branded retail outlets and underinvested in refining

---

[29]See, for example, testimony before Senate Subcommittee on Antitrust and Monopoly, *Hearings on Vertical Integration in the Petroleum Industry,* 94th Congress, 1st sess.

[30]Reprinted statement of William A. Johnson and Richard E. Messick before the Senate Subcommittee on Antitrust and Monopoly, 94th Congress, 1st sess., January 21, 1976, p. 3.

[31]Fred C. Allvine and James M. Patterson, *Highway Robbery: An Analysis of the Gasoline Crisis* (Bloomington, Indiana: Indiana University Press, 1974), pp. 214–216.

[32]Johnson and Messick, Statement before Senate Subcommittee, p. 3.

[33]H. C. Kauffmann, president, Exxon Corporation, "A View of Divestiture" (Speech to the National Press Club, Washington, D.C., April 8, 1976).

TABLE 7-2 THE DEBATE OVER DIVESTITURE OF THE PETROLEUM INDUSTRY: SELECTED ISSUES.

Charge	Counter
Oil industry is not workably competitive.	Oil industry is one of the least concentrated industries in the U.S.—top 4 companies account for only 31% of market
Major oil companies have driven independent oil refiners and marketers out of business through collusive practices.	Independents market share actually rising:
Arab oil embargo used by industry for profiteering at expense of consumers.	Profits rose sharply in 1974 but have since leveled off to preembargo levels.
Industry uses joint venture agreements to set prices and control output.	Joint ventures enhance competition, spread risk, and make very costly projects (e.g., North Sea) feasible.

Within the second charge/counter row, the following data appears:

	1965	1975
refiners:	19%	30%
marketers:	18%	30%

SOURCES. Statement of William A. Johnson and Richard C. Messick before the Senate Subcommittee on Antitrust and Monopoly, 94th Congress, 1st sess., January 21, 1976; and H. C. Kauffmann, president, Exxon Corporation, "A View of Divestiture," speech to the National Press Club, Washington, D.C., April 8, 1976.

capacity, even in the face of a predictable increase in demand.[34] They contend that inadequate refining capacity alone would have created petroleum shortages in the United States even without the Arab oil embargo. Allvine and Patterson recommend that ". . . the vertically integrated structure of the industry should be modified to prevent common ownership or control of crude and refining" operations.[35] New firms could then enter the industry and compete in an open market for crude oil, thereby countering decisions by existing refiners to restrict expansion.

Consequences What would be the consequences of breaking up the petroleum industry? The industry contends that such a move would damage the United States oil industry's efficiency, weaken its ability to counter stiff foreign competition, and discourage development of new petroleum supplies. The economies inherent in vertically integrated systems would give way to duplicated efforts and other inefficiencies.[36] Others warn that without the major integrated companies, greater concentration would be needed in all segments of the industry. "Barring this, there would have to be substantial price increases to allow the less efficient members of each segment to survive."[37] Thus, the implications of divestiture are clouded with uncertainty.

---

[34]Allvine and Patterson, *Highway Robbery,* p. 210.
[35]Ibid., p. 225.
[36]Kauffmann, "Divestiture."
[37]Johnson and Messick, Statement before Senate Subcommittee.

Drawing by H. Martin; © 1977. The New Yorker Magazine, Inc. Reprinted by permission.

An Unresolved Issue

The discussion to this point has centered on vertical integration in the petroleum industry. In general, disputes remain over its legality. The courts apply a "rule of reason" as opposed to a *per se* approach in regulating vertical integration.[38] Both the purpose and effects are important here. Does vertical integration seek to foreclose markets and destroy competition, or is it merely an attempt to introduce production and marketing efficiencies? The integrated firms clearly pose a competitive threat to the nonintegrated firms on the one hand but, the integrated companies allege, they offer lower consumer prices on the other. Whether the net effect is favorable or unfavorable is an unresolved issue.

Discussion Questions

1. Think of a retail establishment in your locality that has changed hands in recent years, apparently from financial failure. How much economic waste attended the failure, and what form did it take?

2. Why do hourly, daily, and seasonal peaks and valleys occur in retailing? Can you think of feasible ways to even out the fluctuations? Would your suggestions improve customer welfare?

3. Think of a retailer in your locality whom you would characterize as inefficient. Think of another whom you would label "efficient." What makes the one efficient and the other inefficient? Do you patronize both? If you shop at the inefficient store, why do you do so?

---

[38]Allvine and Patterson, *Highway Robbery,* pp. 215–216.

4. Assume that you are president of a large retail food chain. You are concerned about inadequate supermarket facilities in the ghettos but you are also troubled about adverse operating conditions there, for example, high pilferage rates and high insurance costs. What recommendations would you make to your board of directors about opening stores in those areas?

5. "Risks are higher in the ghetto than they are outside of the ghetto; therefore businesses operating there deserve higher rates of return." Evaluate.

6. What steps should be taken by policy makers to improve the efficiency of urban goods movement? Why haven't such proposals been effective in the past?

Suggested Exercises: Class or Small Group Assignments

1. What is your judgment about the charges that have been lodged against the petroleum industry? Develop a position in this debate.

2. National legislation has been introduced that would require a minimum 5-cent deposit on beverage containers (refillable bottles, nonrefillable bottles, and metal cans). Examine the implications of this proposal from a channel of distribution perspective. What impact would the law have on consumers? Retailers? Distributors? Bottlers?

3

Societal Monitors
of the
Marketing Process

EIGHT

Consumerism

The modern consumer movement is a dominant force in the market-place. This chapter traces the historical evolution of consumerism and takes a searching look at the current movement. Three questions guide the discussion:

- What factors contributed to the rise of consumerism?

- How does the present consumer movement differ from previous efforts?

- What has been the legal and corporate response to consumerism?

EIGHT
Consumerism

One of the abiding questions confronting a democratic society is the extent to which it tolerates or encourages government intervention in the marketplace. The response to this issue may well change over time. In the United States—following the English tradition—the trend has moved toward increased government interference. The laissez-faire attitude of the nineteenth century has made way for the welfare state of the mid-twentieth century. The shift has been uneven. Moves toward government intervention have come in spurts, with occasional bursts of legislative activity followed by a period of quiescence. Increased interest in consumerism has often preceded legislative action designed to protect the consumer from the perils of the marketplace.

The modern consumer movement, originating in the 1960s, continues to assert the rights and power of buyers in relation to sellers. Since consumerism mirrors frustration or dissatisfaction with the marketing system, the movement is a force that cannot be ignored. Consumerism ". . . encompasses the evolving set of activities of government, business, independent organizations, and concerned consumers that are designed to protect the rights of consumers."[1] The field is too broad to permit an encyclopedic account of the deficiencies in the marketing system or the myriad consumer issues which were spawned by these deficiencies. The scope and focus of the consumer movement is continually shifting. Our focus, therefore, is on the origin of consumerism, the forces behind it, and the contemporary response by government and business.

HISTORICAL PERSPECTIVE

Consumerism is not new. In fact, the roots of the consumer movement were forming at the turn of the century. An understanding of its evolution and of the parallel developments in governmental regulation of business is fundamental to an understanding of the current consumer movement. Table 8.1 provides a historical overview of key governmental influences on business practices.

The 19th Century

For centuries the rule of the market was caveat emptor (let the buyer beware). This concept, which we tend to associate with nineteenth-century economic liberalism, actually dates back to the Middle Ages. Trade then was sparse and usually occurred in local markets and at fairs. Buyers could inspect goods they intended to buy. Their judgment and visual inspections served them better than the integrity of the sellers, who might move on and never be seen again. Caveat emptor summed up the ground rules that governed these occasional transactions. A buyer might secure legal relief from fraudulent transactions only if the seller gave express warranties that were violated; yet, even in these cases, the seller was not liable if the buyer's inspection could reveal the falsity of the warranties. Thus, if inspection would have revealed the animal's deficiency, the buyer of an obviously lame horse had no legal redress against a seller who warranted the horse's physical soundness.

---

[1]David A. Aaker and George S. Day, "Introduction: A Guide to Consumerism," in *Consumerism, Search for the Consumer Interest,* 2d. ed., ed. Aaker and Day, (New York: The Free Press, 1974), p. xvii.

TABLE 8–1 A CHRONOLOGICAL LISTING OF GOVERNMENTAL REGULATION OF BUSINESS PRIOR TO 1940.

19th Century	
	Caveat Emptor
	Doctrine of Implied Warranty
1872	Mail Fraud Act
1887	Interstate Commerce Commission Act
1890	Sherman Act
Early 1900s	
1906	Pure Food and Drug Act
1907	Meat Inspection Act
1914	Federal Trade Commission Act
1914	Clayton Act
The 1930s	
1934	Securities and Exchange Commission Act
1938	Federal Food, Drug, and Cosmetic Act
1938	Wheeler Lea Amendment to the F.T.C. Act

By the early part of the nineteenth century, conditions had modified the concept of caveat emptor. By then, trade had greatly increased, especially in England, whose economy burgeoned following the onset of the Industrial Revolution. Increasingly, goods were sold on the basis of samples or by description, without benefit of inspection. As opportunities for fraud increased, so did the need to protect innocent buyers. Although caveat emptor continued to survive, the increasing number of court victories for plaintiffs in misrepresentation cases weakened it. The courts moved farther away from caveat emptor by invoking the doctrine of implied warranty, which imputed a warranty to goods purchased even when sellers avoided an expressed guarantee. In England, the Sales of Goods Act in 1893 codified protection of the consumer and pretty effectively killed caveat emptor. Court decisions in the United States accomplished the same end.

Although we can trace caveat emptor back to the Middle Ages, we associate it with more recent commercial history, when trading activity increased. Indeed, caveat emptor and the doctrine of laissez-faire, which dominated economic thought through much of the nineteenth century, are quite compatible. As long as laissez-faire ruled economic thinking, there was little room for consumer-protection legislation. The breakthrough on this front in the United States came in 1872 with passage of the Mail Fraud Act. This act, designed to protect consumers from fraudulent schemes peddled through the mails, was the only piece of consumer legislation passed in the United States in the nineteenth century.[2]

Aside from the Mail Fraud Act, other early departures from laissez-faire were designed more to protect industry from itself than to protect the consumer. The Interstate Commerce Commission (I.C.C.) Act of 1887 grew out of attempts at collusion among railroads and discrimination in rate-making, but its passage

[2]James Bishop, Jr., and Henry W. Hubbard, *Let the Seller Beware* (Washington: The National Press, 1969), p. 25.

also followed a period of ruinous competition among carriers which weakened them economically. Similarly, the Sherman Act of 1890, designed to control monopolies, stemmed from a history of predatory tactics and collusion practiced by powerful trusts that dominated several industries toward the end of the nineteenth century.

Near the turn of the century, a variety of local reform groups appeared and centered their attention on social problems and political reform. In 1898, these local organizations joined forces to form the first national consumers' organization, the National Consumers' League.[3]

The Early 1900s

All the bursts of consumerism in the United States have had one thing in common: extensive publicity concerning the alleged business and market evils, which has stimulated government action. Publicity has been generated either by events that outraged the public or books demonstrating the need for reform. Upton Sinclair's novel, *The Jungle,* which dramatized the unsavory aspects of meat packing at the beginning of the twentieth century, led to passage of the Meat Inspection Act (1907). His accounts of filth in the meat packing plants and the sale of diseased cattle as clean meat were designed to elicit support for Sinclair's socialist causes. His efforts bore fruit but missed his target. Sinclair later lamented, "I aimed for the nation's heart and hit its stomach instead."[4] During the same period the persistent efforts of Dr. Harvey W. Wiley to publicize the adulteration of food products paid off with the passage of the Pure Food and Drug Act (1906).

Other pieces of legislation enacted during this period did not focus exclusively on consumer protection. The Federal Trade Commission (F.T.C.) Act and the Clayton Act, both passed in 1914, sought to regulate competition. Although they indirectly benefited consumers, their immediate impact was felt by business firms. Thus, the only laws developed during this era to aid the consumer directly were the Pure Food and Drug Act and the Meat Inspection Act. These laws ended legislative activity in the consumer area until the 1930s. In the intervening period, America's preoccupation with World War I followed by the prosperity and relatively stable prices of the 1920s insulated its citizens from reform proposals.

The 1930s

The next wave of interest in consumerism owed much to the publication of two books, *Your Money's Worth* (1927) by Stuart Chase and F. J. Schlink, and *100,000,000 Guinea Pigs* by Schlink and Arthur Kallet. The authors attacked advertising and focused on the lack of information available for consumer decision-making. Consumer's Research, Inc., and the Consumers' Union, both designed to help consumers with their buying decisions, grew out of these publications. The deaths of 100 people who consumed a legal patent medicine provided another stimulus for change during this era. The combination of these

---

[3]Robert O. Herrmann, "The Consumer Movement in Historical Perspective," in *Consumerism,* ed. Aaker and Day, p. 10.
[4]Reported in Bishop and Hubbard, *Let the Seller Beware,* p. 35.

forces resulted in bills passed in 1938 that expanded and strengthened the Food and Drug Administration (F.D.A.) and the Federal Trade Commission.

The depression of the 1930s spawned several pieces of legislation protecting consumers' interests. The Securities and Exchange Commission (S.E.C.) Act of 1934, among other things, increased information available to purchasers of securities, and the 1938 Federal Food, Drug, and Cosmetic Act sought to prevent adulteration and misbranding of products covered by the law. The latter also required drug companies to prove the safety of their products before the F.D.A. would authorize their use. The Wheeler Lea Amendment (1938) to the F.T.C. Act empowered the regulatory body to act in the public interest in response to "unfair" or "deceptive" business practices. Proof that competition had been impaired was no longer a necessary prerequisite for action. If business practices resulted in injury to the public, the commission was free to respond.

What was the public attitude toward business during this era? A 1940 national survey by George Gallup captured the climate of the times.[5] Approximately half of those questioned in the study favored tighter regulation of advertising content and about 20% had read research reports of one of the new product rating services. The idea of a new federal cabinet position designed to represent the interests of consumers was supported by nearly 50% of those sampled.

World War II diverted attention from the consumer movement. In the 1950s several labeling and price disclosure acts were passed covering fur products (1951), textile fibers (1958), and automobiles (1958).

CURRENT CONSUMER MOVEMENT

Some trace the beginning of the present consumer movement to President Kennedy's special message in March 1962, on Protecting the Consumer Interest, when he enunciated the consumer's four "rights." These rights, to be ensured by the government, were:[6]

1. *"The right to safety*—to be protected against the marketing of goods which are hazardous to health or life." This is a partial recognition of the move away from caveat emptor to a philosophy that holds sellers accountable for the consequences of their actions. It articulates the rationale for legislation concerning food, drugs, cosmetics, and other goods which is designed to protect consumer health and welfare.

2. *"The right to be informed*—to be protected against fraudulent, deceitful or grossly misleading information, advertising, labeling or other practices, and to be given the facts he needs to make an informed choice." Over the years this right has been secured for the consumer under the free disclosure provisions of the Securities and Exchange Commission Act; the specification of standard weights and measures; grade labeling requirements; labeling acts; provisions for the identity, product composition, and quality of insecticides, drugs, poisons, alcoholic beverages, and so on.

---

[5]Herrmann, "The Consumer Movement," p. 14.
[6]"Consumer Advisory Council First Report," October 1963, pp. 6–28.

3. *"The right to choose*—to be assured, whenever possible, of access to a variety of products and services at competitive prices, and in those industries in which competition is not workable and government regulation is substituted, to be assured satisfactory quality and service at fair prices."* Most of the legislation providing this protection dates back a number of years, beginning with the Interstate Commerce Commission Act and including the Sherman, Clayton, Federal Trade Commission, Robinson-Patman, and Wheeler-Lea Acts, and the Celler amendment to the Clayton Act.

4. *"The right to be heard*—to be assured that consumer interests will receive full and sympathetic consideration in the formulation of governmental policy, and fair and expeditious treatment in its administrative tribunals."* The existence of millions of consumers and billions of annual transactions makes the guarantee of this right difficult to achieve. Consumers generally lack the organization to make their collective voices heard in the executive and legislative branches of government. The office of the Special Assistant to the President for Consumer Affairs represents a forum that gives the consumer a say in consumer matters. More effective probably are groups such as "Nader's Raiders" which, through a few activists, seek remedies for the mass of consumers. Their success with several issues points up the potential influence that a small, organized, informed consumer group can have on government policies.

In broad outline, President Kennedy's statement sets forth the dimensions of the current consumer movement.

In analyzing the earlier waves of interest in consumerism, causal factors that rallied the movement were discussed. Is the present consumer movement different? David Aaker and George Day note a striking paradox. "Today's consumerism is embedded in a society of great affluence. . . . The consumer is better off in terms of education, income, and variety and quality of goods, yet he is obviously unhappy about aspects of the marketplace."[7]

Contributing Factors

Philip Kotler takes a searching look at the factors contributing to the rise of this uneasiness.[8] He contends that the consumer movement originating in the 1960s was inevitable and not due to any single person or event. Interest in consumerism was rekindled by the presence of all the conditions normally associated with a viable social movement. The six conditions presented in table 8.2 provide the structure for Kotler's incisive analysis: structural conduciveness, structural strains, growth of a generalized belief, precipitating factors, mobilization for action, and social control. Note how the current consumer movement is linked to these conditions.

---

[7]Aaker and Day, *Consumerism,* p. xxvii.
[8]Philip Kotler, "What Consumerism Means for Marketers," *Harvard Business Review,* 50 (May–June 1972), pp. 48–57.

TABLE 8-2 FACTORS CONTRIBUTING TO THE RISE OF CONSUMERISM IN THE 1960s.

1. **Structural Conduciveness**
   Advancing incomes and education
   Advancing complexity of technology and marketing
   Advancing exploitation of the environment

2. **Structural Strains**
   Economic discontent (inflation)
   Social discontent (war and race)
   Ecological discontent (pollution)
   Marketing system discontent (shoddy products, gimmickry, dishonesty)
   Political discontent (unresponsive politicians and institutions)

3. **Growth of a Generalized Belief**
   Social critics' writings (Galbraith, Packard, Carson)
   Consumer-oriented legislators (Kefauver, Douglas)
   Presidential messages
   Consumer organizations

4. **Precipitating Factors**
   Professional agitation (Nader)
   Spontaneous agitation (housewife picketing)

5. **Mobilization for Action**
   Mass media coverage
   Vote-seeking politicians
   New consumer interest groups and organizations

6. **Social Control**
   Business resistance or indifference
   Legislative resistance or indifference

SOURCE. Philip Kotler, "What Consumerism Means for Marketers," *Harvard Business Review,* 50 (May–June 1972), pp. 48–57. Reprinted by permission.

Structural conduciveness refers to those societal developments that generate inherent contradictions.[9] As material well-being improved for broad segments of the United States population, attention shifted to the more qualitative aspects of life. The complex technology and marketing forces that delivered the abundance to consumers also delivered weighty problems. The proliferation of new products and the constant modification of existing brands, coupled with the subtleties of promotion (trading stamps, coupons), mystified many consumers. Likewise, experts related material abundance to environmental shortages—clean air and water. These developments intensified the frustrations of the consumer in the 1960s and helped produce important *structural strains.* In addition, other political and social strains were present.

Kotler emphasizes that the consumer movement was not sparked by discontent alone. A *generalized belief* about both the problems and possible solutions was needed. Encouraged by social critics, consumer organizations, and

---

[9]Ibid.

selected presidential messages, interest in consumer action programs was activated. Ralph Nader, bursting on the scene with his condemnation of auto manufacturers, further ignited the force of the movement (*precipitating factor*). Mass media coverage and the growing political appeal of consumerism provided *mobilization for action.* Kotler suggests that a quick response by government and business (those in *social control*) could have drained the early movement of its force. In his view, the movement continues because the political and corporate response remains inadequate.[10]

Marketing observers with long memories have a feeling of *déjà vu* as they study the current consumerism movement. Several of the factors accounting for today's version of consumerism contributed to growth of the consumer movement during the 1930s. Looking back to that period, Duddy and Revzan noted the increased number and variety of products, "the pressures of advertising, much of it misleading, some of it untruthful, all of it aggressive."[11] The depression of the 1930s also made the consumer more aware of prices. Undoubtedly, the "Nixon recession" in the 1960s and the accompanying accelerated inflation have had a similar impact.

The Shape of Consumerism: Nader's View
Ralph Nader, who is on the front line of the battle, has considered the *specific* shape that consumerism ought to take. The following is a list of his goals to improve the consumer's position.[12]

1. Good, fast disclosure of product information concerning quality, quantity, and safety. The consumer needs the information to help evaluate competitive products.

2. The strengthening of efforts to recall defective products and to refund payments for unsatisfactory purchases.

3. Fairer court rules and better legal representation for the economically deprived.

4. More government safety standards and a continual updating of them as products and technology change. Needed also is improved enforcement of existing laws.

5. Government (or government-sponsored) research to improve product safety.

6. Better protection from price-fixing and "product fixing"—the calculated restraint of innovation to protect present product positions.

7. More work by technical and professional societies to improve products and aid in the solution of environmental problems.

---

[10]Ibid.

[11]Edward A. Duddy and David A. Revzan, *Marketing* (New York: McGraw-Hill, 1947), p. 138.

[12]Ralph Nader, "The Great American Gyp," in Aaker and Day, *Consumerism,* pp. 23–25.

8. More private interest groups and government agencies designed to protect the consumer.

The Response to the Current Consumer Movement: Legal and Corporate

How have government and business responded to the current consumer movement? Government's reaction is revealed by the major consumer-oriented legislative actions taken during this period. While several of the major consumer protection bills were highlighted in Part II of the text, table 8.3 provides a concise summary of recent legislative activity.

Industry Self-Regulation The corporate response to consumerism may take the form of industry self-regulation or independent action by a single firm. Often an industry group will initiate policies or impose standards that individual firms are reluctant to adopt unilaterally for fear of being handicapped competitively. Some of this has already taken place. The motion picture industry's self-regulation dates back to the 1920s. For years the industry censored itself through the so-called Hays Office. Recently Hollywood has sought to rate movies to indicate their desirability for different age groups. Criticized on several counts, the rating system nonetheless attempts to meet some of the consumer's information needs concerning the industry's "product."

On a broader scale, a Council of Better Business Bureaus (C.B.B.B.) has grown out of several national Better Business Bureau organizations, with the goal of strengthening and standardizing local bureau activities and especially improving the servicing of local consumer complaints. The local bureaus have long suffered from inadequate funding and have been accused of protecting local businesses more than the consumer. The council's extensive fund-raising drive in the early 1970s sought to relieve the bureaus' shortcomings and to make them a more responsive force for consumer protection.[13] The council seeks voluntary observance of standards governing advertising and selling. Along with three major advertising trade groups, the C.B.B.B. set up a division to monitor advertising and to review consumer complaints.

Similarly, the National Advertising Review Board, created by the advertising industry itself, was established to monitor marketing communications and to investigate consumer complaints. When a violation of standards is found, the board attempts to persuade the advertiser to change or withdraw the ad. The case is turned over to the F.T.C. if the advertiser refuses to comply with the board's recommendations.[14]

The Food Marketing Institute has responded to the pressures of the consumer movement in another way. It has appointed a Council on Consumer Affairs, which has identified potential industry problem areas related to consumer concerns. The council realized that it could not determine which of the charges leveled against the food industry were legitimate. Thus it established a Consumer Research Institute "to sponsor and/or conduct research in any area of market-

---

[13]Better Business Unit Starts National Drive to Upgrade Services," *Wall Street Journal,* December 3, 1970, p. 7.

[14]Reported in Norman Kangum et al., "Consumerism and Marketing Management," *Journal of Marketing,* 39 (April 1975), p. 10.

TABLE 8–3 SELECTED CONSUMER LEGISLATION OF THE 1960s AND 1970s.

Year	Legislation	Major Provisions
1960	Federal Hazardous Substances Act	Warning labels required on hazardous household chemicals.
1962	Kefauver-Harris Drug Amendments	Manufacturers must prove drug effectiveness as well as safety.
1966	Fair Labeling and Packaging Act	Packages must be honestly and informatively labeled.
1969	Child Protection and Toy Safety Act	Allows FDA to ban products so dangerous that adequate safety warnings cannot be given.
1969	Consumer Protection Credit Act	Banks, finance companies, and retailers must fully disclose true interest rates and all other charges to credit customers for loans, revolving charge accounts, and installment purchases.
1970	Public Health Smoking Act	Prohibits cigarette advertising on TV and radio, and revised the health hazard warning on cigarette packages. (Advertising ban extended to include "little cigars" in 1973).
1970	Poison Prevention Labeling Act	Requires safety packaging for products that may be harmful to children.
1972	Drug Listing Act	FDA is given access to wide information on drug manufacturers.
1972	Consumer Product Safety Act	Designed to (1) protect consumers from unreasonable risks of injury from products, (2) aid consumers in evaluating product safety, and (3) develop uniform product safety standards to minimize conflicting state and local regulations.
1975	Magnuson-Moss Warranty Bill	Requires that sellers make warranties available to buyers prior to purchase that are simply stated and fully describe the nature of the warranty along with the rights and obligations of the parties.
1975	F.T.C. Improvement Act	Expands interstate commerce authority; clarifies rule-making authority; provides for participation of consumer groups; provides new power for cease-and-desist orders; broadens power to order restitution.

ing practice that may be the subject of consumer concern for the purpose of shaping public policy."[15]

[15]Donald M. Kendall, "Industry and Consumer," *Dun's Review*, September 1969, pp. 111–112.

The Response By Individual Firms In addition to collective efforts to respond to consumerism, action has been taken at the company level. A study of 157 of the largest United States firms, 109 of which were consumer goods manufacturers, isolates some organizational changes.[16] Nearly 20% of the companies surveyed had created one or more organizational posts such as director of quality assurance or corporate director of consumer relations. The word "consumer" or "quality" in an organizational title fails to convey the extent of the corporate response. The significance of the organizational post likely varies from firm to firm.

Selected manufacturers and retailers have responded to consumer problems by instituting consumer "hot lines," complaint handling procedures, consumer education programs, labeling and packaging improvements, and more easily understood guarantees.[17] While significant steps have been taken by many firms, several barriers hinder such initiatives.[18] The source of a consumer problem is often difficult to identify. Superficial symptoms are frequently treated, while the core problem remains. Also, though the benefits of consumer response programs are often indirect and difficult to quantify, the costs are immediately apparent. Finally, the potential loss of a competitive edge deters corporate initiatives in this area. Costly efforts undertaken by a single firm to improve product safety may jeopardize the company's competitive position. Will the consumer respond to the safer, higher-priced brand? Many executives are reluctant to test this question in the marketplace.

These examples illustrate the kinds of industry reaction to the consumer protection movement. One could cite other cases of business' cooperation in this area. In toto, however, these efforts fall short of providing adequate consumer protection, although the potential of the industry-wide approach obviously has not been fully tapped.

The Government and Consumer Protection: Too Much or Too Little?

President Kennedy's general guidelines and Ralph Nader's specific suggestions for consumer protection, previously referred to, raise an important philosophical question. What should be the government's role in defending the consumer in the marketplace and redressing whatever imbalances exist in market transactions? Long ago we moved away from the laissez-faire, caveat emptor doctrine at one end of the spectrum. It is not clear what lies at the other end. A socialist state governed by central decision-making will not necessarily make the consumer's interests paramount.

Laissez-faire advocates argue that the force of competition protects the consumer's welfare. If a seller offers shoddy or unsafe merchandise, exaggerates

---

[16]Frederick E. Webster, Jr., "Does Business Misunderstand Consumerism?" *Harvard Business Review,* 50 (September–October 1973), pp. 89–97.

[17]David A. Aaker and George S. Day, "Corporate Responses to Consumerism Pressures," *Harvard Business Review,* 49 (November–December 1972), pp. 114–124; see also Esther Peterson, "Consumerism as a Retailer's Asset," *Harvard Business Review,* 51 (May–June 1974), pp. 91–101.

[18]Aaker and Day, ibid., pp. 114–124.

claims, or provides deceptive or extortionate credit terms, the consumer soon discovers it and transfers his or her patronage elsewhere. In many market situations, however, this buyer option has been an ineffective penalty. This is especially true in the sale of high-priced goods that an individual seldom purchases. Furthermore, many consumers, through ignorance or otherwise, may be incapable of detecting fraud or misrepresentation. This condition occurs in the ghetto, where uninformed or illiterate consumers buy goods whose terms of sale are unclear to them and whose purchase may put them into a tighter financial straightjacket. Finally, even the existence of vigorous competition does not ensure equitable treatment for the consumer. For example, intense price competition characterizes the retail sale of tires, yet the profusion of sizes and grades of tires thoroughly confuses the average buyer. The nature of the product makes their comparative evaluation difficult for most consumers. Casual inspection of a tire reveals little difference between a low-grade and premium product. And the product lasts long enough to make checking performance difficult.

The voices demanding completely unfettered competition grow weaker as time passes. Public policy in the United States has called for increasing government intervention on behalf of the consumer. Through our legislation we seem to be saying that the government's protection of the consumer from business should take several forms: the provision of safety from potentially harmful products and of information to improve buying decisions, protection against fraud and deceit, and the maintenance of competiton in the marketplace. Some legislation has been passed in the last nine decades to deal with these matters. Every year additional proposals are made to cope with one or more of these areas. In addition, there is an apparent trend toward proposals geared to protect consumers against themselves—to require motorcyclists to wear helmets when driving, to allow buyers of goods sold door-to-door a grace period for rescinding the sale with no penalty. Some measures of this variety have met consumer resistance— for example, the requirement that the driver fasten the seat belt before operating a car.

A Decision Point   Each reader probably has his or her own idea of the extent to which government ought to intervene in market affairs. Every government action in this area causes the diminution of someone's freedom to act in the (presumed) greater interests of others. Government intervention to protect the consumer usually restricts the sellers' freedom. The provision of safety standards for products or requirements for testing drugs before F.D.A. approval are cases in point. Some proposals for protecting individuals against themselves—for example, mandatory wearing of helmets by motorcyclists—may restrict the individual's freedom of choice without affecting the seller at all.[19] Many consumers may find themselves applauding moves that protect their interests in the market—where they recognize the need for protection—and denouncing those that "go too far." How far, one might ask, should the government go to protect people from their own mistakes? How does one weigh the net effect upon the

_____

[19]This argument ignores the possible adverse effect on motorcycle sales of requiring the supplemental purchase of helmets, which effectively raises the cost of motorcycle ownership and, possibly, reduces sales.

majority's freedom of action of a protective measure needed for the welfare of a minority? These are the kinds of questions that consumer-oriented legislation invokes.

CONSUMERISM AND THE FUTURE

Nearly two decades old, the current consumer movement shows no sign of diminishing in intensity. What accounts for its success and relative longevity? Several features of today's consumerism distinguish it from previous movements.[20] First are the quality and characteristics of current consumer advocates. They are pragmatists, not idealists. They seek to work through the system and change it rather than destroy it. Ralph Nader, for example, lacks Upton Sinclair's devotion to socialism and, while he is a vocal and articulate critic of present business practices, he appeals more to reason than to the emotion found in some earlier consumerism literature. Second, consumerism is a popular political issue. Even if the issue fails to help politicians, advocacy of consumerism doesn't seem to hurt them either. This condition permits politicians with strongly held proconsumer sentiments to advocate pet causes without fear of political harm. Finally, the present consumer movement is being institutionalized both at federal and state levels. Out of President Kennedy's Consumer Advisory Council has evolved the Office of the Special Assistant to the President for Consumer Affairs, which deals exclusively with consumer matters. Others advocate an even stronger voice at the federal level for those who use industry's products and services. Various states have also established consumer bureaus and committees to represent consumer interests.

While the issues, leaders, and tone of the consumer movement will change, consumerism will persist as a force in the marketplace. It is a force that requires the attention and reaction of the marketing manager.

Discussion Questions

1. What role should the government play in the protection of consumer interests?

2. If you worked as a salesperson for a company whose advertising misrepresented the products you sold, would you try to correct the misconceptions either by notifying your customers or by complaining about the policy to your boss? If not, why not?

3. Is a firm's concern for social responsibility consistent with a profit-maximizing policy? Explain.

4. What is the role of the business firm in society? Should it differ from what it now is? If so, in what way? Will society be better or worse off, on balance, given a changed role for business? What criteria of "goodness" do you use in formulating your answer?

5. Cite a company recently in the news that, in your opinion, is effectively fulfilling its social responsibility, and one that is not.

---

[20]See Bishop and Hubbard, *Let the Seller Beware,* for a discussion of these points.

6. Set up a checklist for the two companies cited in the previous problem showing whether the following parties' welfare is improved, worsened, or unaffected by the firms' posture on social responsibility:

   a. Each company's employees.
   b. Each company's stockholders.
   c. Each company's customers.
   d. The public-at-large.

7. If you were a large corporation's public relations manager, what policy would you recommend to the president of the company concerning the firm's reaction to the consumerism movement?

8. On balance, has Ralph Nader been a boon or a bane to the American society? To American business?

Suggested Exercises: Class or Small Group Assignments

1. In a letter to the *Wall Street Journal* (November 17, 1971), Fred P. Murphy, chairman to the Executive Committee of Grolier, Inc., wrote:

   > The fundamental question to be answered is this: Is it the proper role of government to take the consumer by the hand and lead him through every commercial transaction in which he may find himself involved? I submit that this type of governmental approach, which is really the basis for most of today's consumer activism, produces an unenlightened and dependent consumer, which is directly opposed to what I feel is the proper goal of creating an informed and independent consuming public.

   Do you agree with this statement?

2. Two manufacturers of desk-top mini-computers require output paper tape with slightly different widths. Users suspect that the differences may have been deliberately designed into the products to ensure the customers' purchase of their respective company's tapes. If their suppositions are correct, do you condemn the practice or praise the companies' managements for astute marketing? If you condemn the practice, are there feasible ways to curtail them? Should the government regulate such practices? If so, how might they accomplish the regulation?

NINE

Marketing's Role in Society: A Continuing Assessment

This chapter examines arguments that challenge marketing's role in society. The following questions guide the discussion:

- Can anyone except the consumer decide what product or service he or she should prefer?

- Does a high-level economy need demand-and-want creation to sustain economic growth?

- Does demand creation lead to the distortion of priorities—more material goods, less community goods?

- What are ethical marketing practices?

Let's consider these questions carefully.

NINE

Marketing's Role in Society: A Continuing Assessment

The evolving life styles, attitudes, and values of consumers require constant adaptations by the American marketing system. To meet myriad consumer wants and desires, the system delivers an expanding array of goods and services through a maze of distribution networks. Critics often charge that the marketing system saturates the public with the wrong bundle of goods—frivolous products that are of little value to their users, and to society. Fundamental questions arise. What is the correct bundle of goods? Who should make this decision?

Although our system relies primarily on the self-regulating mechanisms of the marketplace, government exerts a basic influence on business activity. The consumer choice process is affected in two ways. Antitrust regulation seeks to ensure the continuation of choice alternatives while consumer information legislation seeks to aid the consumer in making a rational choice among these alternatives. Government assumes a more dominant role in a command economy. This chapter examines contemporary challenges to marketing's role in society and assesses the present state of governmental influences on marketing.

FREEDOM TO CONSUME

Implicit in a command economic system is substitution of the state's judgment for the individual's concerning the goods to be produced. It is argued that "to justify the acceptance of a planned economy, it must be demonstrated that the three fundamental freedoms that consumers enjoy under the present economic system will be better protected under economic planning."[1] What are these "freedoms"? First is the "freedom, within the limits of his purchasing power of getting what he wants when he wants it, in the proper quality and quantity, at the place he wants it, and for a price he is willing to pay."[2] The second freedom flows from the first. It grants the consumer freedom to dictate what the system will produce. Buyers' "votes" in the marketplace spell success or failure for products. Producers receiving these signals schedule output and allocate resources accordingly. The third freedom gives the consumer the right to decide whether to spend or save his or her income.

Planning, as an alternate to free choice, raises several questions:

1. Can anyone but the individual consumer judge what product or service he should prefer?

2. Can anyone other than the individual consumer decide what he or she ought to prefer best in a product?

3. Can there ever be an "impartial" source of information about products, particularly those whose qualities are subjective?

4. Can there be any place for innovation under economic planning?

5. What deficiencies of human nature can economic planning overcome?

6. What standards of more socially desirable action can be set up under economic planning?[3]

---

[1]Edward A. Duddy and David A. Revzan, *Marketing* (New York: McGraw-Hill, 1947), p. 556. Used with permission of McGraw-Hill Book Company.
[2]Ibid., pp. 556–557.
[3]Ibid., p. 556.

Who Calls the Shots?

These questions imply answers which insist that the consumer, not economic planners, calls the shots. Defenders of a free market system see consumer sovereignty as a key feature of the system. Critics attack this position, arguing that sellers and advertisers manipulate consumers so that consumers dance to their tune rather than reign supreme over the marketplace. Jerome Rothenberg makes this argument:

> Consider . . . [an] extreme case. . . . There is only one firm. It uses part of its resources to produce some output without considering consumers' tastes. Then it uses the remaining part successfully to persuade the consumers that this output is exactly what they want. Are consumers sovereign here when their tastes change accommodatingly to output . . . ?
>
> Few would insist that the consumer in this case is sovereign in any useful sense.[4]

· Rothenberg realizes that life is not always this uncomplicated. First, persuasion does not always succeed. Ad campaigns fail; consumers reject certain products regardless of the pressures on them to buy. Furthermore, competing claims may drown out one another. Finally, one asks: What would happen if we multiplied the products available in Rothenberg's simplified world from one to many thousands? Now if a portion of total resources was set aside to induce people to buy them, would consumers' tastes still accommodate to available output? Even if the answer is "yes," one might then wonder which goods would consumers demand that they do not now consume, if persuasion disappeared? We can assume that they would continue to select from the vast array available to them. In a sense they would be no more sovereign than they were when persuasion (advertising) existed. But when the effect of persuasion had worn off, consumers would be free to make unfettered choices. The extent to which they ordered new wants would measure, roughly, the distorting influence of advertising pressure. One can only speculate what goods and services people would consume without advertising.

Marketing's critics may be surprised at the power of other factors in consumption such as social pressure and emulation. The international "demonstration effect," which accounts for the transnational spread of product preferences and consumption patterns, points up the power of emulation as a demand determinant. The same kind of want-generating influence undoubtedly works within an economic system. Advertising may reinforce the process, but it is hard to imagine that it would still not function in the absence of advertising. In any event, the issue of advertising's role in want-creation cannot be resolved without banning its use completely, an unlikely event.

AFFLUENT SOCIETY THESIS

The preceding discussion raises several important subissues that can be stated as questions. Does a high-level economy need demand- and want-creation to

---

[4]Jerome Rothenberg, "Consumers' Sovereignty Revisited and the Hospitality of Freedom of Choice," in *Social Issues in Marketing,* ed. Lee E. Preston (Glenview, Ill.: Scott, Foresman, 1968), p. 265.

sustain economic growth? Does demand-creation lead to the distortion of priorities, with the acquisition of more material things and gadgetry winning out over the consumption of community goods? If we restrict the freedom of consumers to decide their consumption priorities, what mechanism will replace them as decision-makers?

John K. Galbraith's *The Affluent Society* popularized the issues. Galbraith reminds us that the law of diminishing marginal utility should result in added output diminishing in importance since the marginal utility from its consumption declines. But he sees economists finding a way around this outcome. "While the marginal utility of the individual declines in accordance with the indubitable law, the utilization or satisfaction from new and different kinds of goods does not diminish appreciably."[5] Why should economists need to modify the law of diminishing marginal utility? They need to affirm the continuing importance of production as an economic activity. Production—and ways to increase it efficiently—lies at the heart of economics. So, Galbraith implies, economists extend marginal utility theory to provide a kind of occupational insurance.

The conventional wisdom holds that goods chosen yesterday are not necessarily more important (that is, do not have a higher marginal utility) than those consumed today. A person changes. Today he is different from the person he was yesterday. He has new wants and priorities. Galbraith finds it hard to imagine that later consumption is less urgent than earlier, and here he detects a flaw in the conventional position. "If the individual wants are to be urgent they must be original with himself. They cannot be urgent if they must be contrived for him."[6] This is the core of Galbraith's thesis. Also central to his argument is the assertion that "as a society becomes increasingly affluent wants are increasingly created by the process by which they are satisfied."[7] Furthermore, "it can no longer be assumed that welfare is greater at an all-round higher level of production than at a lower one. It may be the same. The higher level of production has, merely, a higher level of want creation necessitating a higher level of want satisfaction."[8] Advertising and emulation contribute to the want-creation. This phenomenon of wants depending on a "process by which they are satisfied," Galbraith labels the *dependence effect.*[9]

How Hard Are Consumers to Convince?

Let us analyze his thesis. First is the issue of the urgency of one's wants. Galbraith fails to demonstrate that wants, to be urgent, must originate with the individual. His evidence of wants' lack of urgency is that salesmanship and advertising must be used with intensity to convince people to buy. This argument overlooks the *possibility* that consumers do not require large doses of selling and advertising to persuade them to buy new products. Much advertising tries to convince people to buy a particular brand rather than the product itself. The failure of ad messages to penetrate the "noise" in the communications process

---

[5]John Kenneth Galbraith, *The Affluent Society* (Boston: Houghton Mifflin, 1968), p. 148.
[6]Ibid., p. 152.
[7]Ibid., p. 158.
[8]Ibid.
[9]Ibid.

also accounts for overkill in its use. Moreover, there is more advertising than there is time available to absorb it. This is bound to lead to enormous waste.

Wasted communication is not unique to advertising. Any teacher realizes that many of his "messages" fail to get through to his students. Barriers to communication are infinite. Students may be distracted by a pretty girl or handsome boy walking outside the classroom window, by a professor's annoying mannerisms, by the boredom of the subject which leads to switching off the listening mechanism. Recipients of ad messages may not "hear" for similar reasons. They may also require several exposures to a message to comprehend the value of a product. Also much advertising is wasted because those exposed to it—though they may understand the message and desire the product—may be financially unable to buy it immediately.

Advertising and Social Emulation

There is also the matter of the forces that stimulate want-creation. Galbraith dismisses those that arise out of advertising and social emulation. But can wants be written off because we acquire them this way? Should we treat them differently from those derived from education, from family associations and other personal relationships, and from the culture in general? Von Hayek claims that beyond innate wants of food, shelter, and sex, the others "we learn to desire because we see others enjoying various things. To say that a desire is not important because it is not innate is to say that the whole cultural achievement of man is not important."[10] He argues further that nearly everything we consume is influenced by our social environment. People do not intrinsically like literature or various art forms. Production of them creates their own demand. How does this differ from the affluent wants that Galbraith sees "created by the process by which they are satisfied?"

The Utility of a Stereo

Let us look in more detail at a fairly recent product development to determine how much utility it provides consumers. Stereo systems can bring quality music into an increasing number of homes. Growth in the product's demand stems from greater affluence, improved technology, increasing numbers of highly educated consumers, and a good deal of promotion. For many, this product development has had a culturally uplifting impact as it has encouraged the cultivation of "good" music. Here is a case of a contrived want, one that did not exist before product development and promotion created a mass market. Does the development provide consumers only marginal satisfaction—less than they derived from products that met earlier needs? In what other ways might buyers of stereo systems have spent their incomes? Would alternative expenditures have increased welfare? Whose? Who shall dictate the spending priorities? If funds were to be diverted to the public support of quality music, would the cultural level be greater than with the mass consumption of stereo music and classical records? These are the kinds of questions that Galbraith's argument immediately brings to mind.

---

[10]F. A. von Hayek, "The Non-Sequitur of the 'Dependence' Effect," in *Marketing in Progress,* ed. H. C. Barksdale (New York: Holt, Rinehart and Winston, 1964), p. 30.

Consumption and Satisfaction

If the diminishing returns that Galbraith refers to apply to wants beyond the elementary ones, the process must begin early in human development. People may relieve hunger pangs with a plate of beans, satisfy shelter needs with a cave or crude shack, and clothing requirements with a loincloth. Significantly, members of primitive tribes have been found to covet trinkets and various forms of personal embellishments without the perverting influence of Madison Avenue.

Does people's desire for more goods, which advertising has stimulated, create satisfaction? If the satisfaction from their consumption did not at least equal the prices paid for them, presumably consumers would refuse to buy them. Buying them must mean that the anticipated marginal utility from the goods' consumption must be greater than the marginal loss of the money spent on their purchase. Galbraith might reply that the gain in satisfaction is adequate only because advertising has led people to believe that the goods' purchase will satisfy their wants—wants, to be sure, that advertising has created. From a hedonistic point of view, the key question may be not how the demand was created, but whether the goods did or did not increase satisfaction. If one of humanity's goals is to pursue happiness, and the acquisition of goods helps achieve that goal, do we quibble over the way in which demand for the goods was created?

Perhaps people fail to achieve happiness by consuming goods, the need for which was obscure before a producer created it and an advertiser convinced them to buy it. In this case they might presumably refuse to cooperate with the "system." They could do so in one of two ways. They could remain within the ambit of the "persuasive" economy but refuse to bow to it. They could tune out the "hidden persuaders'" blandishments and let their free will reign. Alternatively, they could drop out of this world and into one that deemphasizes material possessions. A significant number of people have opted for the second alternative in recent years by living in rural communes rather than being integrated into an urban society.

Private versus Public Spending

Because our goals have stressed spending for private consumption expenditure, Galbraith finds us ignoring public sector spending. He argues that an affluent society, with most of its members' primal needs fulfilled, should reorder its priorities. Galbraith would achieve this reordering by deemphasizing private sector spending and transferring expenditures to the public sector. Presumably, this reordering would optimize society's welfare. Whether the failure of society to embrace Galbraith's solution is attributable to advertising's undue influence, a failure of our political process, public lethargy, or a flaw in the "affluent society" argument itself, remains for the reader to ponder.

SATIETY OF WANTS

Discussion of the dependence effect leads to a corollary issue. Can there exist a satiety of wants? This issue becomes important when we appreciate one of marketing's leading functions in a high-level economy. All of the traditional marketing functions, basic to any system, continue to be performed when an economy reaches a high level of development. As indicated, the relative emphasis of some may change over time. If demand-creation is seen as part of communications, this function takes on new dimensions and added importance as economies mature. A high-level, dynamic economic system requires large and growing markets to prevent stagnation. Much of the burden of sustaining growth, therefore, falls to marketers who conceive of unmet needs. This want-creating, want-fulfilling process, however, depends upon a continuing ability to create new wants. Hence the need to determine whether wants are subject to satiation.

Lack of Time
How may satiety arise? Several forces could lead to it. First is the scarcity of time.[11] People's desire for goods may be infinite but the time necessary to consume them is not. The argument continues: even if time were infinite, people eventually would choose leisure over the acquisition and consumption of more goods. There are two aspects to this consideration. First, people may choose leisure over work. This refusal to work will limit the income necessary to purchase further goods. Moreover, consuming goods requires time, so a choice of leisure also rules out additional consumption.

Saturation Theory
The second force leading to satiety is the belief that saturation levels exist in the acquisition of goods. This differs from the first factor, although they appear to be similar. The time limitation argument says, in effect, that time forces a saturation level for *all* goods beyond which one cannot feasibly consume. The second factor points to the existence of saturation levels for individual commodities and services. This condition is said to apply both to currently consumed goods and to durables whose consumption stretches over a long period of time. Analysts of the new-product development process see products exhibiting an S-shaped growth curve. They move from an introductory stage through market growth, into maturity as the product approaches a saturation level and, eventually, into decline.

The saturation theory ignores several things:

1. It ignores quality changes. People consume a finite, easily attained limit of food, for example, but food processors continually build convenience into their products, which shifts labor output from the family kitchen to the factory kitchen.

2. Saturation rates expand as consumers acquire additional versions of the same product. Second and third cars, homes, and television sets are cases in point. A corollary of this condition is the lower utilization rate of goods when more than one is purchased. This point ties in with the time limitation condition just discussed. This expansibility of saturation rates demonstrates that although time may limit *consumption,* it may have less impact on *acquisition,* which is the key factor in a discussion of satiable wants.

---

[11]For a discussion of the limiting effect of time, see Staffan Burenstam Linder, "Are We Approaching the Limit of Consumption?" in *Featuring Sweden,* No. 5, (1963).

3. People may elect to consume goods faster by discarding them before they wear out or by buying disposable products. Given the relatively faster increase in service costs than new durable goods costs, consumers may increasingly discard out-of-order appliances rather than repair them. Recent years have seen the introduction of a host of disposable products with no indication that the trend toward their use will lessen.

4. The saturation theory ignores the relative increase in services, whose growth potential is enormous. Growth curves tend to concentrate on material goods, yet the consumption of services grows relatively faster than that of goods in high-level economies. Obviously, even services must reach some point of satiety or we will observe, in fact, the Chinese proverbially taking in each other's laundry.

5. Despite Galbraith's hopeful title, a large percentage of the American people live outside of an affluent society. They might consume as much as the more affluent if they possessed the necessary income. So there is room for expansion of their consumption as there is for that of middle-income families who may aspire to high-income living standards.[12]

The time-constraint argument also has limitations. Leisure may, and usually does, involve the consumption of goods or services. Leisure and consumption are not mutually exclusive. One can even argue that increased leisure provides more opportunity for consumption than does a more work-oriented system. The time-constraint argument also ignores the time-saving element provided by many goods. These products, in effect, stretch the time available for consumption. Finally, the time-limiting argument fails to realize the nature of many consumption processes. It takes no more time to "consume" a $10 tie than it does a $5 one. There is no more consumption in driving a Cadillac than a Ford. One could multiply these examples manyfold. A Rockefeller has no more available time to consume than we do, yet he or she undoubtedly spends a good deal more money on consumption than we.

Important Questions Remain Unanswered

If wants are not satiable in the foreseeable future, there is still room for marketing to perform its function of visualizing unmet needs, creating products to meet them, and promoting their sale. But this leaves unanswered at least two more fundamental and philosophical questions. First is the question of whether the finite supply of the world's raw materials permits us the luxury of unlimited consumption. This used to be phrased in terms of the eventual need to face up to resource limitations. Recent ecological developments demand that we consider this problem sooner rather than later. The second question concerns the goals and purposes of humanity. Are people who are endowed with material possessions and work-saving devices more fulfilled and happier than those who lack modern comforts? Each reader can answer this question himself.

---

[12]Ulrich Herz, "Towards the Saturation Society," in *Theories for Marketing Systems Analyses: Selected Readings,* ed. George Fisk and Donald F. Dixon (New York: Harper & Row, 1967), pp. 181–183.

A final note: it is interesting that a discussion of satiety usually ignores the possibility of a limit on production capability. The limiting factor in continued growth is presumed to arise out of consumption. If one assumes zero population growth and no increase in the number of hours worked, higher output depends upon continual increases in productivity.[13] Can this process continue indefinitely? This question is no more easily answered than is the one concerning the satiety of wants. But as a growth-limiting factor, it looms as large in importance as does want-satiation. And certainly the limited ability of natural resources to sustain growth is a more probable candidate to put a ceiling on output than either consumption or productivity.

WHAT ARE ETHICAL MARKETING PRACTICES?

Ethics, as a branch of philosophy, has been concerned for centuries with standards for decision-making and proper conduct. Throughout the book we have examined a number of macro marketing issues that raise important ethical questions. For each issue, competing arguments were presented and objectively evaluated. Inevitably, the discussion pointed up the conflicting orientation of marketers, policy makers, and consumer representatives.

Frederick Sturdivant and Benton Cocanougher highlight the divergent views of business and its publics.[14] Corporate executives, business school students, blue-collar workers, and housewives were asked to evaluate the ethics of common marketing practices. Selected results are presented below:

1. "A distributor of bottled drinks recently developed a plastic, no-return bottle that is practically indestructible and will not deteriorate over time. Consumers appear to be very pleased with it, so the company plans to increase its use during the next year, even though it may create a littering problem."

   Decision termed "ethical" by 61% of executives, 27% of students, 34% of workers, and 24% of housewives.

2. "A manufacturer of a mouthwash utilizes a large-scale advertising campaign designed to make people feel that using the company's product will make them more popular socially."

   Termed "ethical" by 55% of executives, 44% of students, 28% of workers and 17% of housewives.

3. "A large auto manufacturer has developed a safety device that could reduce traffic injuries by as much as 50%. However, the device would increase the cost of each car by more than $300, which would

---

[13]Even if we do not postulate zero population growth, growth must cease eventually when the earth will sustain no more people. The assumptions here also call for a constant labor force size. Increasing the numbers of women employed outside the home, and expanding the working age limits, could help sustain higher output, but even with these changes, there is an eventual ceiling.

[14]Frederick D. Sturdivant and A. Benton Cocanougher, "What Are Ethical Marketing Practices?" *Harvard Business Review*, 51 (November–December 1973), pp. 10, 12, 176.

undoubtedly cause the company to lose sales to competitors. Therefore, the company decided not to use the safety device unless *all*
manufacturers are legally required to use it."

Termed "ethical" by 49% of executives, 27% of the students,
34% of the workers, and 24% of the housewives.[15]

Why the Gap?

What explains the gap between the views of business executives and other
publics? Stephen Greyser cites three factors.[16] First, critics and proponents of
marketing hold different views of the mechanism of the marketplace. Our discussion (in an earlier chapter) of advertising's role in society illustrates the
conflicting positions—the argument on the one hand that advertising is deceptive
and wasteful and, on the other, that it is entertaining and informative. Second,
". . . the consumer and the citizen within us, individually and communally,
are in frequent conflict regarding marketing and public policy."[17] As citizens we
are concerned about the depletion of energy, but as consumers we may desire
air conditioners. Market segmentation constitutes a third factor that widens the
gap between practitioner action and perceived community interest. For example, an advertising message geared to a specific market segment may be
inappropriate for nontarget community members such as children. While an
understanding of these conflicts may narrow the gap, disagreements will likely
remain.[18]

GOVERNMENTAL INFLUENCES ON MARKETING

Policy makers often argue that the gap between marketing practice and the
public interest should be bridged by legislation. Indeed, government agencies,
such as the Federal Trade Commission, and legislators at all levels are making
increasingly active attempts to establish and maintain a competitive environment
that serves the best interest of consumers. In recent years, each component
of the marketing mix has been affected by legislative or regulatory requirements.
Many of these requirements (discussed in earlier chapters) seek to provide the
consumer with more information—truth-in-lending, unit pricing, open dating,
nutrition labeling, truth-in-warranties, and so on. Have these disclosure requirements significantly influenced consumer or market behavior? George Day notes
that such proposals are often implemented "in the absence of relevant research
on actual or possible effects on consumer, producer, or retailer behavior."[19]
Many researchers argue that such legislative proposals should be "test marketed" before they are fully implemented.

---

[15]Ibid., pp. 10 and 12. Reprinted by permission.

[16]Stephen A. Greyser, "Public Policy and the Marketing Practitioner—Toward
Bridging the Gap," in *Public Policy and Marketing Practices,* ed. Fred C. Allvine
(Chicago: American Marketing Association, 1973), pp. 219–232.

[17]Ibid., pp. 221–222.

[18]Ibid., p. 231.

[19]George S. Day, "Assessing the Effects of Information Disclosure Requirements,"
Journal of Marketing, 40 (April 1976), p. 51.

William Wilkie and David Gardner cite common misconceptions among policy makers at the F.T.C. that provide insight into this research gap.[20] First, the policy maker assumes that consumers can always make better decisions if they are given more information. Only limited recognition is given to the actual needs of consumers or the environment in which the information is used. A second misconception results from the policy makers' "lack of concern with the quality or content of the message."[21] The assumption is made that a clearly stated message will be understood in the intended manner by all consumers. The third misconception is that ". . . information is processed in a uniform manner by all consumers."[22] Past experience with the product, the importance of the purchase and other factors that influence consumers' utilization of information are overlooked by the policy maker. Since the Federal Trade Commission and other government agencies will develop policy regarding consumer behavior with or without research, Wilkie and Gardner appeal for an expanded role of marketing research in public policy decision-making. Such research would significantly improve many public policy decisions.[23]

THE MOOD OF AMERICAN CONSUMERS

Let's close our discussion with an assessment of the mood of American consumers. How do they feel about the United States marketing system and current marketing practices? Figure 9.1 presents a composite picture of public attitudes toward marketing. Many of the questions posed to a national survey of nearly 700 consumers center on issues that were examined in earlier chapters.[24] Before looking at the survey results, consider for a moment how you would respond to each of the questions.

Note from figure 9 1 that consumers are somewhat skeptical about the adoption of the marketing concept by business. More than six out of every ten consumers either agreed or were uncertain that "let the buyer beware" is the guiding philosophy of most manufacturers. More positive attitudes were expressed about the operation of the United States marketing system. Few consumers disagreed with the position that the American marketing system operates more efficiently than thcse in other countries. The mood of consumers sours when attention turns to advertising, product quality, or middlemen. Interestingly, more than two-thirds of the consumers feel that concern for the environment does not influence the product choices of most buyers.[25] Again, the consumer-citizen conflict emerges.

---

[20]William L. Wilkie and David M. Gardner, "The Role of Marketing Research in Public Policy Decision Making," *Journal of Marketing,* 38 (January 1974), pp. 38–47.
[21]Ibid., p. 40.
[22]Ibid., p. 40.
[23]Ibid., p. 46.
[24]Hiram C. Barksdale, William R. Darden, and William D. Perreault, Jr., "Changes in Consumer Attitudes toward Marketing, Consumerism and Government Regulation: 1971–1975," *Journal of Consumer Affairs,* 10 (Winter 1976), pp. 121–135.
[25]Ibid.

FIGURE 9–1   THE MOOD OF THE AMERICAN CONSUMER

TOPICAL AREA/STATEMENT	PERCENT OF CONSUMERS				
	Strongly Agree	Agree	Uncertain	Disagree	Strongly Disagree
Marketing Concept: Despite what is frequently said, "let the buyer beware" is the guiding philosophy of most manufacturers.	7	31	29	30	3
Marketing Efficiency: The American marketing system operates more efficiently than those of other countries.	14	41	39	5	1
Advertising: Most product advertising is believable.	1	31	13	42	13
Manufacturers' advertisements are reliable sources of information about the quality and performance of products.	2	12	16	44	26
Product: Concern for the environment does not influence the product choices made by most consumers.	9	59	15	16	1
Over the past several years, the quality of most products has not improved.	12	43	11	31	3
Price: Higher prices of consumer goods are caused primarily by wholesale and retail middlemen taking excessive profits.	27	38	20	13	2

SOURCE: Adapted from Hiram C. Barksdale, William R. Darden, and William D. Perreault, Jr., "Changes in Consumer Attitudes toward Marketing, Consumerism and Government Regulation: 1971–1975." *Journal of Consumer Affairs,* 10 (Winter 1976), pp. 121–135.

A FINAL NOTE

Throughout the text, we have examined numerous issues falling within the domain of macro marketing. We have seen that several forces guide and direct the marketing system. Individual consumers, organized consumer groups, legislators, regulators, industry groups, competitors, and others make up our pluralistic system. The existence of pluralism means that business is influenced by all other groups (organized and unorganized) and it, in turn, influences them. Thus, the diffusion of power among the groups leads to a relationship often characterized by conflict, negotiation, and compromise. Each group has some power and, in turn, some responsibility. To the extent that marketers do not accept social responsibility obligations as they arise, other groups will eventually assume them.

Discussion Questions

1. What is consumer sovereignty?

2. Is society better or worse off when consumer sovereignty exists? Defend your position and indicate what criteria you use when answering this question.

3. "Resolved: Advertising forces people to consume goods and services that they do not need." Take a pro or con position and debate the issue with a friend or classmate.

4. Define the "dependence effect." Make and defend a case for or against its existence.

5. Galbraith says that "it can no longer be assumed that welfare is greater at an all-round higher level of production than at a lower one." Try to devise a research design to test whether, in a given society, a higher level of production results in more, less, or the same total welfare.

Suggested Exercises: Class or Small Group Assignments

1. The XYZ Company produces many lines of plastic film that are used in a number of different industries. One particular line of products, given 12 different names or codes, is in reality the same film from the same manufacturing process. The price of each of the 12 items is determined by analyzing the profitability of the industry that uses it.

    Is it ethical to sell the same product to different industries for different end uses at different prices, when in fact manufacturing costs are the same for the entire product line?

2. In April 1977, the AAA Company introduced a new cereal brand—HEALTHCO—into a test market. AAA provided a stock of the new brand to retailers and made them aware of the project strategy. An aggressive promotional campaign was initiated in the test market area. AAA planned to measure the success of HEALTHCO by using store shelf audits and advertising surveys. The firm had plans to introduce the new brand nationally in August 1978 if the test market proved favorable.

    The BBB Company had been working on a similar product, but as yet had made no plans to market it. Within one week of HEALTHCO's test market introduction, BBB became aware of it. BBB began auditing the HEALTHCO stock in the test stores carrying it. They also conducted telephone interviews to measure the effectiveness of AAA's advertising campaign.

    The BBB audits of the HEALTHCO test market showed it to be very promising. Thus, they introduced their new brand—VITAMIN PLUS—into the national market in July, one month ahead of the AAA product. VITAMIN

PLUS proved to be an overwhelming success and today commands the dominant share of the market. Meanwhile, HEALTHCO has been a disappointment for AAA.

Did BBB act unethically in its actions concerning the AAA test market?

Subject Index

Name Index

Firestone, O. J.   79n
Fisk, George   189n
French, Warren A.   83n
Friedman, Monroe   82
Fryburger, Vernon   102n
Fuchs, Victor R.   29, 30n, 31, 33n
Furuhashi, Y. Hugh   24

Galbraith, John K.   50, 102n, 172,
   185, 186, 187, 189, 194
Gallup, George   170
Gardner, David M.   101, 119, 192
Georgescu-Roegen, Nicholas   75
Goebel, John W.   89
Goldman, Marshall I.   36
Goodman, Charles S.   134
Gray, Robert T.   88n
Greyser, Stephen A.   66n, 106n,
   111n, 191

Hall, Margaret   36
Haller, Thomas F.   111n
Harrell, Gilbert D.   130n
Harwell,   32
Henderson, Hazel   76n
Henning, J. A.   59n
Herrmann, Robert O.   169n, 170n
Herz, Ulrich   189n
Heskett, James   32n
Howard, John A.   107n, 108n, 109n,
   110n, 114, 115n, 119
Hubbard, Henry W.   168n, 169n, 178n
Huegy, H. W.   26n
Hulbert, James   107n, 108n, 109n,
   110n, 114, 115n, 119
Hulswit, Frank T.   118n
Hunt, Shelby D.   18n
Hunt, Stan   76n
Hutt, Michael D.   130n

Isakson, Hans R.   130n

Jacoby, Jacob   81, 101n
Jeffereys, James B.   35n
Jensen, Walter, Jr.   86n
Johnson, William A.   158, 159n
Jolson, Marvin A.   117n

Kallet, Arthur   169
Kangum, Norman   174n

Kauffmann, H. C.   158n, 159n
Keats, John   104
Kelley, William T.   109n
Kendall, Donald M.   175n
Kendrick, John W.   31
Kennedy, John   125n, 170, 171,
   176, 178
Kettelle, John D.   118n
Kindleberger, Charles P.   12
Knapp, John   36
Knee, Derek   35n
Kohn, Carol A.   81n
Kotler, Philip   17, 18n, 126n, 157n,
   171, 172, 173
Kripke, Homer   128, 137n
Kuehl, Philip G.   112
Kunreuther, Howard   134

Lazer, William   17n
Leavitt, Harold J.   18n
Lee, Sheldon   92n
Lehmann, Donald R.   109n
Lehner, Urban C.   129n
Leighton, Robert A.   155n
Lenahan, R. J.   85n
Levitt, Theodore   79, 103, 104
Levy, Sidney J.   17
Linder, Staffan B.   188n
Little, Robert W.   145n
Loudenback, Lynn J.   89
Luck, David J.   18n
Lundy, Richard   147

Machlup, Fritz   100
Manischewitz, D. Beryl   82
Mann, H. M.   59n
Marcus, Burton   134, 135
Martin, H.   160n
Maurizl, Alex R.   130n
Mazze, Edward M.   86n
Mazis, Michael B.   112n
Mazur, Paul   5n
McCammon, Bert C.   145n, 157n
McCarthy, E. Jerome   24
McDermott, Dennis R.   155, 156
McNair, Malcolm P.   5n
Meadows, D. H.   75n
Mecham, J. W., Jr.   59n
Messick, Richard   158, 159n
Michaelangelo   104
Mindak, William A.   18n
Mitchell, R. V.   26n